'Julia Hope takes us beyond reviewing or cri
she sits amongst children who are reading,
some children's books that tackle one of the i
This is an important read for anyone interested in how children interpret
literature.'

**Michael Rosen, Writer, poet, performer, broadcaster and Professor of
Children's Literature, Goldsmiths, University of London**

'Carefully researched and eloquently written, Hope highlights the
importance of understanding the refugee experience. Through an in-
depth study, this book demonstrates how children's literature can enable
teachers to work through complex and contemporary issues in an
accessible manner. This book showcases both the importance of listening
to children's voices and the power of the primary teacher as a mediator of
text. Globally, as migration raises several human rights issues, this book
offers an invaluable contribution to primary education.'

**Dr Anne Dolan, Lecturer in Primary Geography, Mary Immaculate
College, University of Limerick**

Children's Literature about Refugees

This book is dedicated to my mother, Joyce Hope, who passed on to me her love of literature and sense of social justice, which forms the backbone of my work.

Children's Literature about Refugees

A catalyst in the classroom

Julia Hope

 is an imprint of  IOE Press

First published in 2017 by the UCL Institute of Education Press, University College London, 20 Bedford Way, London WC1H 0AL

www.ucl-ioe-press.com

British Library Cataloguing in Publication Data:
A catalogue record for this publication is available from the British Library

ISBNs
978-1-85856-696-2 (paperback)
978-1-85856-812-6 (PDF eBook)
978-1-85856-813-3 (ePub eBook)
978-1-85856-814-0 (Kindle eBook)

Typeset by Quadrant Infotech (India) Pvt Ltd
Printed by CPI Group (UK) Ltd, Croydon, CR0 4YY
Cover image is an illustration from *The Colour of Home* (2002) by Mary Hoffman, illustrated by Karin Littlewood. © Frances Lincoln Ltd.

Contents

Acknowledgements

I would like to acknowledge the tremendous help and assistance that I have received from various people during the course of this work, without whom it would not have come to fruition.

Firstly, thanks go to my PhD supervisors at Goldsmiths College: Dr Chris Kearney, who encouraged me to embark on the project originally; Dr Clare Kelly, who has guided me through the whole study, and whose constant faith in my abilities and my enterprise has maintained me at times when I would have given up; and Dr Charmian Kenner, who took over from Chris, and spurred me on, providing invaluable guidance, feedback and support. I would also like to acknowledge the different forms of backing and sustenance received from other colleagues in the Department of Educational Studies at Goldsmiths, particularly Dr Sarah Pearce who has stood by me through peaks and troughs.

Secondly, I owe a huge debt of gratitude to the two authors focussed on, Mary Hoffman and Beverley Naidoo, who gave generously of their time and experience, and Refugee Education experts, Jill Rutter and Bill Bolloten, who provided invaluable opinions, information and advice. My thanks also go to all the anonymous participants in this study: the teachers who were so open and helpful in allowing me to access their lesson plans, observe their sessions and interview them outside school hours; the children who enthusiastically offered their opinions, and showed me their drawings and written work with pride; and the school managers and administrators who gave me access to the field, and were so welcoming.

Thirdly, I want to acknowledge the patience and long suffering of my family. I cannot thank my husband, Dr Vincent Rich, enough for supporting and sustaining me through this long journey in many ways, and to whom I owe so much. I also would like to praise my three children, Rosie, Jessie and Caleb, who have shown interest and enthusiasm in my project, helping and encouraging me ever onwards.

About the author

Since childhood Julia has always been a voracious reader, enjoying the possibilities that literature offers to move across temporal and global boundaries.

Her first degree was in English Literature at Sussex University, and shortly afterwards she went to Zimbabwe to work as a Secondary School teacher in a township for two years, setting up a library in the school, and being deeply impressed by the power of literature to broaden human experience.

After taking a PGCE at Goldsmiths College, she taught in local primary schools in South East London for 16 years, mainly as a Refugee support teacher, and also working on Family Literacy with Refugee parents, gathering a wealth of insight into real-life refugee issues for children.

Following an MA in Education, she became a lecturer at Goldsmiths, teaching on the Primary PGCE programme, within which she runs a specialist course in children's literature. From there she researched and authored a PhD, which was to form the basis of this book – a study of engagement with children's books about the refugee experience in the primary classroom.

She is now very involved in the flourishing MA in Children's Literature at Goldsmiths, which she will be leading from September 2017, as well as writing and teaching her own course on 'Children's Literature and Controversy' for the undergraduate Education degree.

She lives with her husband in South East London, and occasionally her three children who move in and out at different times!

Introduction

Origins

From 1990 to beyond the millennium I worked as a teacher with special responsibility for refugee children in an area of London rich in cultural diversity, where 'new arrivals' from other countries were frequent, and where refugees made up a significant part of the school roll. One day I set a 7-year-old Angolan boy a task: to draw different modes of transport, starting with 'car' and 'bus', which he wrote at the top of the paper and supplied the appropriate picture. However, when I came back a while later I was horrified to find that the following images depicted aircraft dropping bombs, tanks and people firing ammunition, amputees with crutches, people sheltering in a church that was under attack and a lorry discharging soldiers (see Figure i). This was my first real encounter with the horrors of refugee experience and the images have stayed with me ever since.

Figure i: Pictures by a young refugee boy.

Later there were stories from Kosovan children of running from their burning houses, with no time to collect any belongings, and escaping with only the clothes on their backs. Afghan children also recounted experiences of fleeing with their families in the back of blacked-out vans, all the way from their mountainous country to the UK, keeping quiet and low as they crossed borders. These stories were indeed shocking and stirred in me a desire to share such knowledge, while a visit to the school by Jill Rutter, working for the Refugee Council, added breadth to my understanding of what refugee children and their families had to deal with once in the UK.

Welcoming and integrating refugee children and their parents was the focus of my work in school, and as my experience deepened, my confidence to tackle delicate subjects in a supportive way grew. I began to engage children in autobiographical activity, both oral and written, talking about their reasons for leaving their home country and the journeys they had undertaken to get to the UK. During Refugee Week some children would offer up their stories in front of an assembly, such was the climate of trust in the school. I realized that this was a particularly valuable way of getting to know them for the people they were, and validating their experience. Far from wanting to forget the past, the majority were keen to share their stories. I began to recognize the role literature could play here, providing a valuable insight into this growing and complex situation. As Coughlan (2012: n.p.) points out: 'books provide an answer, a bridge into the newness, and towards empathy and understanding and welcome'. As I started to investigate texts for children about refugees, I discovered that this was a relatively new but rapidly growing area, about which little has been written.

Overview of the genre and the study

Early investigations revealed that a considerable amount of children's literature that deals with the subject matter I have outlined exists. Identifying my field as covering post-war children's books written in English, published in the UK and dealing with the refugee experience, I initially found that in this emergent genre there were nearly 90 books. Most of them have been published in the last two decades and more are released yearly into bookshops. I limited the texts to those that portray the lives of children seeking sanctuary, which is the legal definition of a refugee, rather than other kinds of migrants. Since the 1950s, it is therefore possible to identify numerous books published in the UK that explore the refugee experience and include stories set in locations as far afield as Afghanistan, Bosnia, Iran,

Iraq, Nigeria, Somalia and Vietnam, targeted at an ever-younger readership (Hope, 2008).

As expected, these texts reflect the waves of migration into western countries in recent years, as conflicts escalate and globalization, as well as improved travel, lead a growing number of people to claim sanctuary in other countries. However, once I began to research further into the USA, Canadian, Australian and New Zealand markets, as producers and distributors of books for children written in English, as well as a few translated from other languages, I discovered that the list was endless, and have extended my search to over 250 texts (see Appendix). Those published in the USA dominate in terms of temporality, geographical spread and linguistic variety, but in recent years the other 'old settler colonies' have addressed the topic in new and innovative ways. Interestingly, books published outside the UK often depict other groups of refugees, such as the Hmong, from Cambodia, who generally settled in the USA, and those from Central and Latin America.

The last 60 years have also seen a change of attitude about exposing children to challenging subject matter through children's literature, including forced migration. When *The Silver Sword* (Serraillier, 1956), an early text about children in flight, was first published in the UK, it was not readily welcomed into the existing canon of children's literature. On being made into a television serial in 1957: 'many people wrote to the head of BBC children's television protesting that war was not a suitable subject for children' (Grossfeld, 1993: 192). We have come far since then, to the point where today the stories of children seeking asylum are an increasingly common preoccupation amongst authors, as they endeavour to reflect refugee experiences first hand or more often vicariously through encounters with those who have such histories. But what role do these books play in today's classrooms? Coughlan (2010: n.p.) asserts that: 'these inspiring books encourage empathy in their readers, which in turn has the potential to stir them to action. If children are to be empowered to change the world, they need to have access to these stories.'

To investigate further I chose two books by well-known authors in the UK, commonly used in English classrooms, with contrasting age groups. *The Colour of Home* by Mary Hoffman, illustrated by Karin Littlewood, and published by Frances Lincoln in 2002, is aimed at younger children – 6- to 9-year-olds – while *The Other Side of Truth* by Beverley Naidoo, published by Puffin in 2000, is suitable for a slightly older audience (10–13-year-olds). Taking a vertical trajectory, I interviewed the two authors and the illustrator of *The Colour of Home* and observed the books being shared in primary classrooms. I interviewed teachers and considered their planning and mediation and conducted discussion groups with children. I also analysed their written, drawn and dramatized responses to the text.

Summary of chapters

In Chapter 1, I introduce what is meant by 'the refugee experience'. I provide some basic definitions and statistics about current global and national positions and consider how these issues relate to young children. I look at initiatives to teach about refugee issues in school and suggest that children's literature offers a powerful medium through which to explore these challenging concepts.

In Chapter 2, I trace the development of children's literature about refugees historically from World War Two to the present day, discussing recent trends and how they relate to contemporary waves of migration. I raise the question of authorship and also consider the use of personal testimony and autobiography.

In Chapter 3, I consider the place of reader response theory in the primary classroom, used unconsciously by many teachers to allow space for multiple meanings and personal connections to develop. The role of the teacher as an 'enabling adult' (Chambers, 1991) fostering a 'community' of readers (Chambers, 1993), is crucial for employing a dialogic method, so that children can debate their opinions and move towards critical literacy.

In Chapter 4 I introduce the two books – *The Colour of Home* and *The Other Side of Truth* – and make some initial comparisons. I provide an overview of the study, outlining its rationale, design and scope, and explain the school data I drew on to provide a profile of the child participants. I set my study in context with others that aim to listen to children's responses to texts, and conclude that more of this work is needed.

Chapter 5 draws on my interviews with Mary Hoffman, Karin Littlewood and Beverley Naidoo, through which I consider their motivations and aims for writing and illustrating the books in question. I provide an insight into initial stimuli, contextual influences, prior and ongoing research and the editing process.

In Chapter 6 I explore the experience of *The Colour of Home* being shared in three lower primary classrooms. I look particularly at the role of the teacher in planning for reader response and critical literacy, while using the book to address the refugee experience via PSHE and Literacy lessons. The teacher is presented as mediator of the text, building a 'community' of readers via reading aloud and précising, questioning and discussion and relating to children's lived experience.

In Chapter 7 I examine how children made meaning from *The Colour of Home* when the book was shared in the classroom. Through words and pictures very young children demonstrated a 'beginning understanding' of the refugee experience. For many the book acted as a catalyst to make connections with their own lives, and all could identify strategies for welcoming newcomers. Slightly older children demonstrated a clear empathy, while those from refugee backgrounds provided poignant points in discussion.

In Chapter 8 I focus on exploring *The Other Side of Truth* in two upper primary classrooms. I details how teachers act as an 'enabling adult' through careful planning and discussion, and can encourage children to use the text to make connections with their lives, those in the nearby environment and others in the wider world. Teachers may also foster a sense of how to take 'social action', providing positive ways forward for older children.

Chapter 9 demonstrates, through children's voices, how older primary school students engaged with *The Other Side of Truth* in a sophisticated manner. In small discussion groups children offered their opinions, made connections with their own lives and backgrounds and debated with their peers, demonstrating how important it is for children to be heard and to listen to one another. They clearly understood the nuances of the term 'refugee', and demonstrated heightened empathy, as well as sensitivity, to potentially disturbing subject matter.

In the conclusion I offer ways forward for teachers through a seven-point framework for reference when sharing books about controversial and sensitive issues like the refugee experience. This includes inclusive dialogue, variety of response, addressing the 'constructedness' of the text and fostering a 'social action' ethos. I also consider ways in which the wider context of initial and ongoing support for teachers, as well as recent educational policy, can influence the fostering of good practice in developing critical literacy. Finally I make suggestions for further research in the field, creating a forum for real discussion that encourages children to make connections between the text, themselves and the wider world.

Teachers' concerns

Teaching about refugee issues can be seen as a controversial area, which can engender emotive discussion. Over the years, as a teacher educator at Goldsmiths, I have introduced a small selection of children's literature about asylum issues into seminars and workshops, through English, Citizenship and Diversity agendas. Some of my student teachers suggested that the subject matter was not appropriate for young children, while others maintained that children need opportunities to learn about the refugee experience. Several have voiced disquiet about reading some of the texts under discussion in the presence of refugee children – this may be upsetting for those who have gone through similar experiences – and this is an important matter worthy of consideration (Goodall, 2007).

Way back in 1979 Stinton reviewed children's literature that tackled racism and asserted that a basic consideration for omitting a book for recommendation was 'the pain it might give to even one black child' (p. 70). Perhaps the same could be said of the refugee child in the classroom, but Melzak and Warner (1992), interviewing Eritrean refugee children in Sweden, reveal a counter-perspective, showing that the young people in their survey wanted refugee children's experiences to be included in the curriculum. In a recent study Arizpe *et al.* (2014a: 318) asserted that when considering texts that focused on migration and refugeeness:

> teachers noted that newly arrived students began to participate more fully in the ongoing work of the class as they felt they had valuable contributions to make to the community of learning ... using strategies designed to take better account of their prior knowledge and experience. New arrival students were excited and engaged by the possibilities of storying their own journeys after encountering varied model texts, and unique stories emerged together with stronger voices.

Teachers can feel reluctant to broach such a controversial area for a variety of reasons, perhaps being wary of their own lack of contextual knowledge and ability to handle such a potentially divisive topic. A study by Oulton *et al.* (2004) of teachers' attitudes and practices in teaching controversial issues found that many feel under-prepared to tackle these in the classroom. Very few were able to recall any training they had received either pre-service or in-service, and were subsequently constrained in their ability to handle this aspect of their work. Cowan and Maitles (2012) also identify teacher anxiety over tackling controversial issues, particularly with young children, while Wooley (2010) argues for more support in this area in Initial Teacher Education (ITE) courses and Continuing Professional Development (CPD).

Reflections

This book is therefore intended as a resource for primary school teachers who are interested in engaging with children's literature about the controversial and emotive area of refugee experience. It is not a handbook of strategies to welcome and accommodate refugee children in the classroom, as amply provided for by the work of Jill Rutter and others. Its primary aim is to empower teachers to address refugee issues with *all* children in the primary classroom. Clearly there are many resources available that give factual content and statistics on the refugee situation. However, these need to be brought to life in the form of individual stories, which autobiography, personal testimony and sustained works of fiction are well placed to do. This book provides an in-depth study of children's literature about refugees and the impact it had in the classroom. It also offers a range of hands-on strategies for teachers working with *The Colour of Home* and *The Other Side of Truth*, which would transfer to other, similar texts. As such, the book contributes to a widening interest in texts for young readers about controversial issues, popular with teachers in school, Literacy coordinators and Education students at undergraduate and postgraduate level.

Chapter 1

The refugee experience

Introduction

Since the Iraqi invasion in 2003, ongoing conflicts in Gaza and the long drawn out civil war in Syria, mass movements of refugees are growing ever larger (European Council on Foreign Relations, 2015). Meanwhile refugees are commonly constructed socially and politically as 'other' (Ahmed, 2000), and misconceptions about their situation are firmly embedded in the national consciousness (Migration Observatory, 2011). A recent investigation into the reporting of refugees and asylum seekers in the media found that much was 'sensationalist and inaccurate' (ICAR, 2012), with negative discourses and scapegoating of 'bogus illegals' potentially inciting hostility, racism and even violence. Such perceptions percolate down to children in UK classrooms, through the family environment, newspapers and television reportage. Meanwhile teachers are expected to welcome new arrivals and safeguard the wellbeing of refugees and asylum seeker children. In this chapter, I aim to give teachers an overview of refugee theory and discourse, and point to avenues through which refugee issues can be introduced into the primary classroom.

Who are refugees?

According to the 1951 UN Convention Relating to the Status of Refugees, the technical definition of a 'refugee' is someone who has left his/her country and cannot return to it:

> owing to **well-founded fear** of being persecuted for reasons of race, religion, nationality, membership of a particular social group or political opinion, is outside the country of his nationality, and is unable to or, owing to such fear, is unwilling to avail himself of the protection of that country or return there because there is a fear of persecution.
>
> (UNHCR, 1951: 14)

An 'asylum seeker' is someone who has left their country of origin and formally applied for asylum in another country but whose application has not yet been concluded (Refugee Council, n.d.). A further term – 'internally displaced person' (IDP) – refers to uprooted people displaced within their own country (UNHCR, n.d.), who are thus not officially recognized as refugees.

Since the 1990s, the term 'forced migration' is increasingly used to avoid a refugee/non-refugee binary, and researchers such as Richmond (1993) have gone further to suggest that there is a blurred boundary between forced and voluntary migration, preferring a continuum between proactive and reactive migration. Richmond identified other variables in the process: 'push' and 'pull' factors, enabling circumstances – social networks, for example – and structural constraints – for example, immigration controls. More recently Castles and Loughna (2005) maintain that the category 'refugee' is being sidelined in favour of other terms such as asylum seeker, irregular migrant or undocumented migrant, or is subsumed under the asylum–migration nexus. However, the need for legal distinction is of vital importance in accessing entitlement and for this reason refugee agencies are understandably reluctant to accept any attempts to dilute commitments to refugees (Rutter, 2006; Morrice, 2011). Zetter (2007), meanwhile, argues for a continuing recognition of the relevance of the term 'refugee' in the contemporary climate of political turbulence.

Refugee statistics and policy

'Conflict and persecution caused global forced displacement to escalate sharply in 2015. Now at the highest level ever recorded, it represents immense human suffering around the world' (UNHCR, 2016a: n.p). By the end of 2015, there were 21.3 million refugees, 40.8 million IDPs and 3.2 million asylum seekers worldwide. This is 5.8 million more people than the year before. The year 2014 showed the highest annual increase in a single year, due mainly to the ongoing conflict in Syria. At the same time children under 18 constituted 51 per cent of the refugee population in 2015, up 41 per cent from 2009, with nearly 100,000 being unaccompanied or separated children (UNHCR, 2016b).

In Europe debate focuses on the increasing number of migrants trying to enter by various routes and means, with rescue and resettlement responsibilities becoming another political issue (Kingsley *et al.*, 2015). With constant exposure in the mass media, the plight of refugees is currently visible to children of all ages. Despite recent opposition from the British government to accepting refugees arriving through Europe from the Middle East, in 2015 the number of applications for asylum in the UK was 29 per cent higher than in 2014. The top producing countries were Eritrea, Iran, Sudan, Syria, Pakistan, Afghanistan, Iraq, Albania, Bangladesh and India

(Refugee Council, 2016: 1). Furthermore Parliament has hotly debated whether to accept some unaccompanied refugee children into the UK, and as yet we do not know the number of those who will be accepted and how they will be welcomed.

Calculating the number of children in the UK who have escaped conflict, or who are from refugee families and backgrounds, is problematic. But clearly teachers in UK schools – especially in urban centres – are likely to encounter refugee children. Awareness of global movements is therefore an asset. Furthermore, pupils themselves are helped by an appropriate understanding of what it means to flee to safety.

Theorizing the refugee situation

> Raising awareness of what it means to be a refugee ... is a vital step in understanding the needs of refugee children.
>
> (Bolloten and Spafford, 1998: 109)

If teachers aim to tackle refugee issues in the classroom, it is helpful if they have an overview of the main theoretical approaches and wider refugee agendas, so they can approach the topic well-informed and able to communicate the basic awareness needed to help children in their classes.

Ecological approaches

Family is the most important component in any child's life, and if stable and positive family relationships are maintained, children can prove very resilient. In fact children evacuated away from their families in the UK in World War Two, suffered more stress than those who stayed in heavily bombed areas with their families around them (Freud and Burlingham, 1943). A useful paradigm as a basis for refugee theory is Bronfenbrenner's ecological systems theory (1979), which sees the child as anchored at the centre of interconnecting layers – family, community and wider society, for example – that each play their role in the child's growth. Related to this, Baker (1983) – himself a refugee – formulated the concept of a 'relationship web' (see Figure 1.1) to highlight the challenges refugees face in reconstructing their lives and adapting to a new setting. The first diagram represents the series of relationships surrounding a person in a secure situation, whereas the second refers to a web that has been blown apart and needs reconstructing, as in the case of a refugee child.

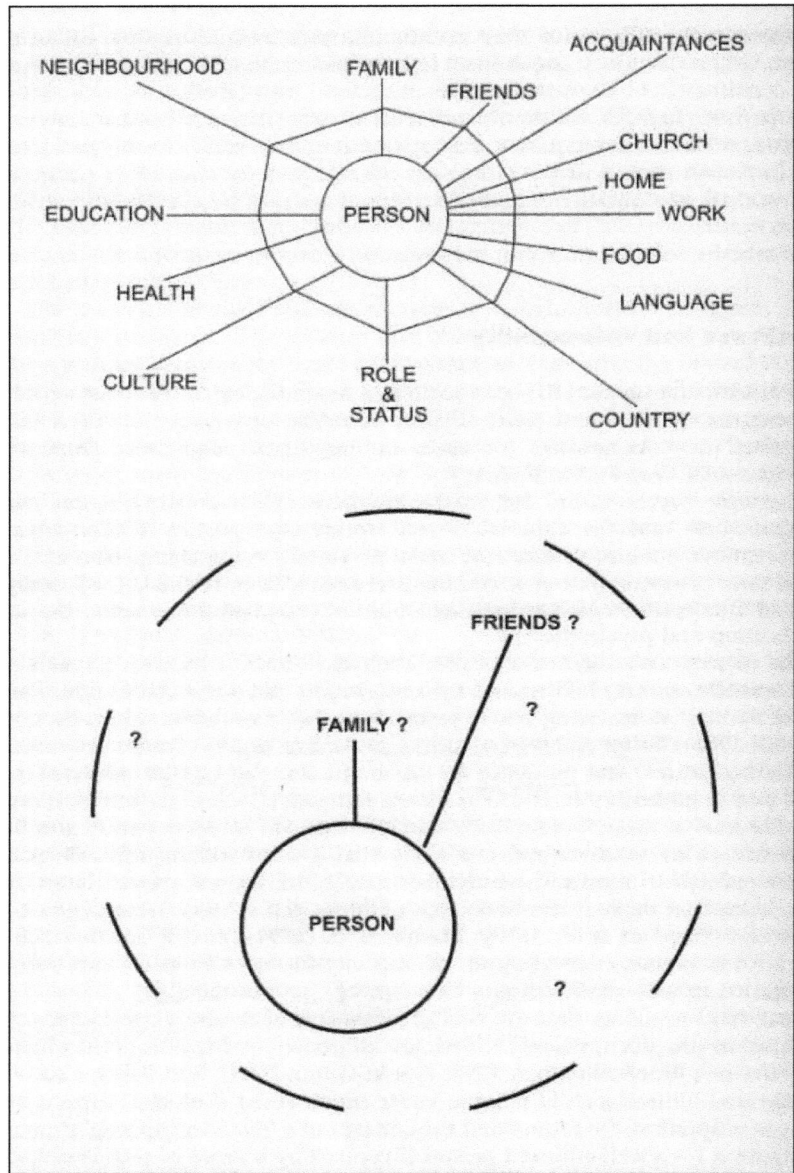

Figure 1.1: Relationship webs (Baker, 1983).

Teachers and classmates play an important role in helping a refugee build a life in a new country, and an awareness that a child may be cut adrift and in need of support is fundamental to understanding the refugee situation. However, Tolfree (1996) summarized protective factors in children's lives that could shield them from the worst exigencies: stable emotional relationships, social support, a positive educational climate and good role models.

Fazel and Stein (2002) detailed that refugee children could undergo 'three stages of traumatic experiences: while in their country of origin, during their flight to safety and when having to settle in a country of refuge' (p. 366). Hamilton and Moore (2004) also divide the refugee experience into three distinct contexts (see Figure 1.2): pre-migration, trans-migration and post-migration. They argue that combining these stages with an ecological model can provide snapshots of the different ecologies – family, school, community and the wider society, for example – that may surround refugees at each of the three stages, during which dramatic tensions can arise due to 'atypical' conditions (Hamilton and Moore, 2004: 8). This model is useful in demonstrating clearly that at all stages of the refugee situation, risk and protective factors will impact on the child. It also highlights that the experience is not concluded when they arrive in the host country – difficulties continue for many years afterwards.

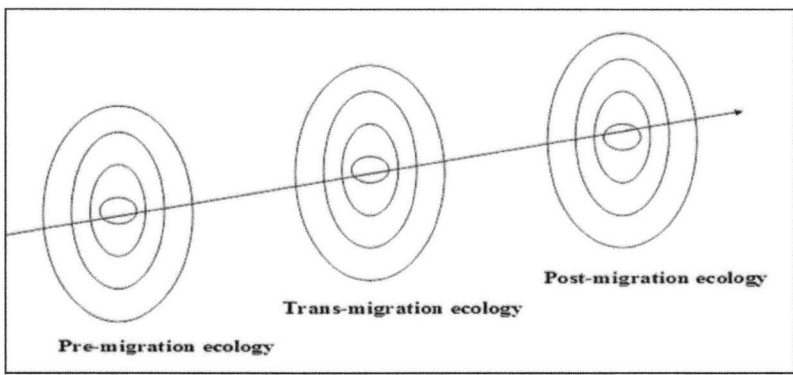

Post-migration ecology

Trans-migration ecology

Pre-migration ecology

Figure 1.2: Model of refugee adaptation and development (Hamilton and Moore, 2004). Reprinted with permission © RoutledgeFalmer.

However, using the same model extensively from a Canadian perspective to provide strategies for educators supporting refugee children, Stewart (2011) suggests that evidence provided by students' stories shows that the three ecologies are 'much less defined than originally assumed' (p. 52). In some cases there were still close connections to friends and family living in the country of origin. Others have contact with those suspended in the trans-migration phase, and memories of past violence that continue to haunt them, or are still struggling to cope with loss. Thus the distinct stages become blurred, and it takes time for school staff to piece together limited information about the pre- and trans-migration experiences, which shows how past experiences still affect refugees' lives. Watters (2008) argues that although past events are important, services should be aimed at the 'here and now' as a useful starting point, and that young people, while being caught up in adverse circumstances, are 'resourceful and capable in exercising agency' (p. 187).

Trauma vs resilience discourses

Trauma theory dates back to the late 19th century (Ringel and Brandell, 2011), trauma being seen as 'the results of having endured unbearable experiences' (van der Kolk *et al.,* 1996: 50). During World War Two, a still-ongoing dilemma was recognized: is it was best to bring traumatic memories to the fore or focus on stabilization (Kardiner, 1941). Some writers examine the trauma refugee children may have experienced, detailing the nature of Post-Traumatic Stress Disorder (PTSD) (Yule, 1998; Fazel and Stein, 2002), although it is fairly rare for children to suffer such symptoms and for an extended period of time. Woodcock (2002) sees that refugee children's particular vulnerability as stemming from legal, emotional and practical aspects, which can amplify one another. He suggests that an understanding of the 'triple jeopardy' that affects refugee children can help practitioners involved in their care. This includes children's own experiences, and their inability to articulate them, their parents' experiences combined with a lack of 'know-how', and the narrow remit of child and adolescent mental health services (CAMHS). Woodcock also points out that refugees have varying 'idioms of suffering' and that western psychological concepts might not be seen as relevant to them, as trauma is a social construction that not all people recognize. However, recent studies show that early childhood trauma can result in poor impulse control, aggression, difficulty with interpersonal relationships and poor academic performance (van der Kolk, 2005) and although refugee children commonly 'reach out in hope to the future' (Nial, 2005: 33), grieving and loss still need to be acknowledged.

Many refugee commentators contrast vulnerability with resilience and find plenty of the latter in most refugee children's approach to life (Richman, 1998). Rutter (2006) asserts that the 'traumatisation' of the refugee situation has dominated research to the extent that it has presumed homogeneity amongst refugee children, and leads to discourses of pity and non-action. Using discourse analysis Rutter (ibid) found that a humanitarian focus on trauma and pity is common among teachers, laying the blame for all refugee children's problems on pre-migration situations, and thus relieving themselves of responsibility for being advocates for better resources and higher quality educational experiences for those in their care. Pinson *et al.* (2010) contribute to the discussion by pointing to a compassionate professionalism amongst teachers, many of whom are not afraid to challenge the forcible removal and deportation of children and families. Throughout any analysis of the refugee experience, therefore, it is important to maintain a balanced view of the risk and protective factors present at stages in the process, and to move away from a 'trauma agenda' that blinds us to the positive aspects that may be part of the migrating child's life.

Tracking the refugee experience
Pre-migration ecologies
McDonald (1998) and Rutter (1998) point out that refugee children might have come from a wide range of countries, diverse class, ethnic and linguistic groups, families with different religious observances and sometimes conflicting political affiliations and a wide spectrum of educational backgrounds. The stereotypical view of a rural origin is very often inaccurate. Refugee children might well come from predominantly urban environments and might also have been wealthy prior to flight: 'those who have fled the world's poorest countries are primarily the urban middle class' (Rutter, 1998: 24).

Parents might have had high-powered jobs in the country of origin that made them a target for hostility. They might have been well-educated, and have often made the decision to flee with their children's welfare very much in mind. Refugee children might have been part of a large extended family or a small nuclear family, and their educational experiences can also vary significantly.

Children's understanding of the reasons for fleeing persecution and their experiences of the flight can also differ widely. Some will have fled from their homes at a minute's notice, possibly leaving behind everyday belongings, objects of sentimental value – photos, for example – and important documents like birth certificates. Some children may have been in hiding for long periods of time. Others will have been exposed to horrific acts of violence, both on themselves and on family members. Some will have experienced torture or genocide (Yule, 1998; Menter *et al.*, 2000).

Hyder (2005) points out that modern warfare has changed so much in character that in today's conflicts almost 85–90 per cent of casualties are civilians. This has huge implications for children's experience of war. Some refugee children may have even been involved in perpetrating atrocities themselves, as the use of child soldiers becomes more commonplace. The decision to leave may have been a long process, debated and discussed in secret, with the children not involved in the planning and execution. Or it may have been spur of the moment, without prior warning, arguably proving more difficult to cope with in the long term. Complicated, lengthy plans to obtain false passports or the decision to send sections of the family – the father, for example – off in an advance guard, might not have been shared with children, and as such they will have been spared some of the anxiety at the start of the experience.

Trans-migration ecologies

Children's experiences of journeys to safety may have been traumatic. Yule (1998) and Hyder (2005) observe that they may have travelled long distances lasting days or months, in cramped conditions, having to keep quiet for considerable stretches of time. They may also have been sedated to help them cope. Families might have travelled on forged passports that involve children in risky deception, or they might have been 'helped' by traffickers who are impatient of children's needs and even abusive in their behaviour, in return for large sums of money (Rutter, 2003). Asylum seekers might have spent long periods of time in refugee camps (Yule, 1998), which may be very cold or very hot, dirty, cramped and dangerous. In such places the risk of sexual violence towards women and children is very high, especially when gathering water or firewood.

One of the greatest stressors is the uncertainty and lack of information about how long will be spent in uncomfortable and unsuitable surroundings. This itself can cause physical and mental health problems, as waiting indefinitely takes its toll (Rutter, 2003). Children can often become the props adults unwittingly lean on, particularly older children, who are expected to look after younger siblings or support single parents, often women, to cope in such difficult circumstances. Conversely, children might not have been part of such dramatic events and might have simply boarded a plane to be met by a close family member at the other end of their journey.

Post-migration ecologies

On arrival, asylum seekers can face frightening situations, in which children are often active participants, and this can lead to further trauma after a potentially gruelling journey. The safety refugees envisage is not always immediately forthcoming. Some wait for long periods of time in inhospitable surroundings and are closely and sometimes threateningly interrogated when they are tired and confused.

> The process of making a claim for asylum, waiting for the Home
> Office decision and, if refused, making an appeal, often takes an

extremely long time, possibly several years, during which the refugees remain uncertain of their fate.

(Richman, 1998: 9)

If children are unaccompanied by their parents or carers, they will have to deal with these difficult situations by themselves, which can add greatly to their distress.

Once accepted into the country, the process is still not complete. Putting in a claim involves using lawyers, who are expensive and sometimes ineffectual. Compiling the evidence can be difficult without documentary proof. The onus is on the claimant to prove the case and in recent years 'a culture of disbelief' has prevailed and being deported back to a country where persecution is ongoing is an alarming prospect. Even when sanctuary is achieved, it may be only a temporary form of protection, contributing further to refugees' feelings of insecurity. Baker (1983) points out that refugees' initial settlement and adaption can take several years, but the residual effects of having had the experience may continue to affect them for the rest of their life, in the form of 'survivors' syndrome'.

Wider refugee agendas
Questions of identity

Refugees rarely have stability and security on arrival and if they left at short notice they can arrive feeling disorientated and bewildered (Menter *et al.*, 2000). In establishing a new life, they may well suffer from crises of identity and self-confidence. They are unable to interact satisfactorily with others because of language barriers and their previous biography is unknown or does not translate. Children may be unable to share their experiences with others for fear of negative reactions, and may possibly distrust all familiar adults: 'Becoming a refugee presents both adults and children with questions about who they are and where they belong, because they have lost the surety of their place in the world' (Richman, 1998: 31). Forced or sudden migration, in particular, interrupts an individual's developing biography, by abruptly cutting through all previous experience and characteristically causing confusion and dislocation. Sometimes children try to blank out their previous life as the memory of it is too painful, and parents may not choose to talk about the past for the same reason.

Also relevant are the theories of Hall (1992), who writes that ethnic and personal identity is shifting as a result of globalization. As the world grows increasingly interconnected, becoming more a single economic, social and cultural entity, concepts of personal and national identity are changing. With greater migration, new, 'hybrid' identities (Bhabha, 1994) are developing among people who have spent time in different countries. Refugees are a part of this phenomenon. Those in exile therefore have an altered identity that may combine influences from their past and present situations.

Culture and assimilation

What separates refugees from other migrants in official terms is that they have been forced to leave their country of origin, rather than choosing to do so – although the boundaries may well become blurred between the two. Whatever their bureaucratic status, refugees and migrants may suffer more grief over the loss of their home culture if rather than choosing to leave it behind they were forced to relocate due to overwhelming 'push' factors: 'The loss of the familiar culture with all its richness of customs, rituals, and relationships has been likened to cultural bereavement' (Richman, 1998: 34). However, Richman notes that children in exile often develop 'bicultural' identities, valuing aspects of both their past and present cultures. This may happen much more quickly for children than parents, causing strife in family relationships. It may also differ between one sibling and another, creating yet more tension.

Moreover, part of the refugee experience is the notion that those seeking asylum, remaining attached to their home country, might one day want to return to it and the many friends and family they have left behind (Hyder, 2005). This may cause refugee families to cling to their home culture more fervently than other migrants who move forward and embrace new mores with greater enthusiasm. The need to find others with similar viewpoints and lifestyles will be crucial in maintaining wellbeing, and children will often be expected to embrace new found communities with an enthusiasm they might not share with their parents. For other young people events and celebrations organized by their cultural community in exile will be their life-blood, and sustain them in their battle to readjust to their new circumstances.

Language barriers and racism

Children acquire a new language quite rapidly, especially when well-integrated into the school routines. However, the effect of initial communication problems on the long-term self-esteem of refugee children is undocumented. Vygotsky (1962) highlighted the importance of the interaction between language and identity by showing that individual consciousness is built from the outside through relations with others. He also showed that words play a central part not only in the development of thought but in the growth of consciousness as a whole. In terms of self-confidence and a sense of identity, acquiring the dominant language of the host country is essential for newcomers (Cameron, 2000). If interacting with those around them is not easy, their sense of identity and status are heavily affected.

Of the 33 refugee and asylum seeker children she interviewed, Richman (1998) reported that 19 had experienced racism and bullying and six of these had changed schools or were planning to do so. Similarly, in their study of young refugees from the Horn of Africa, Save the Children (1997) found that half the children had reported bullying and 25 per cent felt they had been the targets of racism. They were most commonly referred to as 'scroungers'. Rainey *et al.* (1997) found that young adults without any social contact with refugees displayed superficial sympathy but no identification with refugees' backgrounds and situations, seeing these as belonging to another world. This allows media stereotypes to take hold. Hyder (2005) notes that terms such as 'beggars', 'scroungers' and 'bogus' are frequently used by certain UK media when referring to asylum seekers in particular. She observes that some negative press coverage has an impact on children and families, with evidence of even very young children being abusive to refugee and asylum-seeking peers.

Education

Some refugee children and new arrivals might not have attended school at all, while others, again highlighting different pre-migration experiences, might have attended English medium schools in their home countries, or had a high level of education in another language and educational system (Rutter, 2003). Menter *et al.* (2000) observed, however, that children rapidly develop new expertise, including language and communication skills. As a result they obtain a tool that can shift the balance of power between them and their parents. Parents feel that they are no longer in control because they do not know the education system and do not speak the language. They therefore cannot liaise directly with school authorities. These authors stress, therefore that use of the home language should be preserved wherever possible, even in school, in order to communicate with parents and maintain identity.

Tolfree (1996) noted that, after family, attending school in the host country has the greatest capacity for supporting refugee children. Tolfree and Hyder (2005) both focus on the healing nature of 'play' for children affected by war and conflict, with Early Years provision in schooling well able to meet those needs. While giving structure and purpose, schools can

11

also provide psychosocial care on an informal basis, 'a situation in which young people can talk about shared experiences and integrate the meaning of events into their view of themselves and their world' (Tolfree, 1996: 58).

As Bolloten and Spafford (1998) note, schools have the potential to welcome and absorb asylum seekers and normalize the refugee situation. Fazel and Stein (2002) also argue that preventing refugee children's mental health from deteriorating is best undertaken in the school context. However, the situation is not always supported by adequate funding. Despite previous initiatives to ring-fence budgets specifically for refugee support, Arnot and Pinson (2005) found that recently there have been no specific funding arrangements targeted at asylum seeker and refugee children. Ofsted also argued that their needs were best addressed 'through mainstream approaches to inclusion and racial equality' (p. 5).

Teaching about refugee issues
Education policy
The Equality Act 2010 exhorts schools and other public bodies to 'foster good relations between persons who share a relevant protected characteristic and persons who do not share it' (HMSO, 2010: 96). Furthermore, under the Coalition Government, the new QTS 'Standards', effective from September 2012, include expectations for teachers to 'maintain high standards of ethics and behaviour ... by:

- having regard for the need to safeguard pupils' well-being
- showing tolerance of and respect for the rights of others ...
- ensuring that personal beliefs are not expressed in ways which exploit pupils' vulnerability.

(DfE, 2011: 14)

With the introduction of the new National Curriculum in England in 2014, under the Coalition Government, Citizenship as a discrete subject has been removed completely from KS1 and KS2, although there is an acknowledgement in the preamble that 'all schools should make provision for personal, social, health and economic education (PSHE), drawing on good practice. Schools are also free to include other subjects or topics of their choice in planning and designing their own programme of education' (DfE, 2013: 4). Although this sounds hopeful in theory, it is possible that from now on refugee issues will be left more to curriculum areas such as English, History, Geography and possibly Drama and Art to provide a platform, with the associated danger that without explicit inclusion in the curriculum, they may be ignored altogether. Furthermore, if children's literature about refugees is dealt with solely through 'literacy' teaching, which under the 2014 curriculum places much more weight on the teaching of spelling, punctuation and grammar, the subject matter of such texts may well be hijacked by an over-concentration on Literacy rather than literature objectives.

Identifying good practice

Schools play an important role in disseminating information about the refugee experience in order to foster greater understanding. To do so effectively children, and possibly teachers too, should be given access to alternative discourses on the refugee experience from the dominant media (Habib, 2008). These need to highlight elements such as the reasons for flight, the nature of the journey, the likely reception in the host country and the hostility and racism so frequently encountered when they are trying to establish a new life and integrate. An understanding that 'refugees are ordinary people, but had to go through extraordinary experiences' (Rutter, 1991: 4) is useful to encapsulate the notion that the conditions that caused their situation could happen to any of us at any time.

Some studies add further dimensions to the teaching of refugee issues in school. King (2003) reported on the potential for attitudinal change amongst primary school children when listening at first hand to the stories of a Rwandan refugee. Watts (2004) also demonstrates how drama workshops for young people could engender empathy towards refugees who had previously been dismissed as 'undeserving' (Sales, 2002). However, the methods by which refugee issues are introduced into the curriculum, particularly in secondary schools, are problematized by some researchers. Day (2002) highlights the use of 'Forum Theatre' – where students take on the role of a character – as a powerful learning experience when tackling refugee issues, but suggests that more factual information is necessary to supplement sessions. Furthermore, she asserts, it is empowering children with positive strategies to help refugees that will make learning meaningful.

Examples of good lessons that deal with refugee issues can be found in both the primary and secondary sectors. Learning about human rights, using the situation of refugees as a case study, and making cross-curricular links with History, Geography, Literacy, Art, Drama etc. is particularly effective. Claire (2004) showed how a combination of methods – such as discussion, high-quality literature (for example, reading *The Other Side of Truth* to the class) and factual research – can influence primary school children's perceptions. This in turn can affect whole-school approaches.

However, Rutter (2005) felt that isolated lessons that purported to tackle refugee issues, dismantle stereotypes and foster empathy were ineffectual, and criticized token, whole-school initiatives such as Refugee Week.

Using children's literature to teach about refugee issues

Studies show that the optimum way to give a rounded and reliable picture of the refugee experience is through a combination of hard data, personal testimony and discussion (King, 2003; Watts, 2004). Educators can provide data and facilitate debate, but organizing a visit by a refugee prepared to provide stories of their life and journey is not always easy. In the absence of such real-life speakers, 'literature is ... invaluable for enabling children to explore the affective as well as the factual aspects' (Menter *et al.,* 2000: 226).

Many of the factors that contribute to the refugee experience are represented in literature for children: 'In particular, the combination of imaginative identification with characters in novels, plus the psychological safety that fiction provides makes it a rich resource for dealing with controversial issues' (Myhill, 2007: 55). Myhill suggests a variety of drama and discussion activities as an excellent means of access. Drama provides opportunities for expressing ideas and opinions that can explore alternative perspectives, while discussion allows for a range of views. The latter need to be managed effectively, however, to give every child a voice. The role of the teacher is particularly important here in accommodating opposing views competently, knowing the topic well and not steering responses towards their own agenda. Guidance on using children's books to address topics such as war, terrorism, justice and freedom is given to teachers by Gopalakrishnan (2011), through basic principles such as showing that the story is 'real', setting the context, time period and situation, allowing students to react in any way, using a variety of discussion tools, and helping students make intertextual and narrative connections (pp.158–9).

Reflections

Awareness of the issues discussed in this chapter is important both for the teachers of refugee children and also their classmates, who are often called upon to perform a welcoming role, and whose friendship will be crucial to refugee children being accepted into the school and local community. Learning about what causes someone to become a refugee, the possible issues they might face and how to help them in developing a new identity in the host country is key to developing understanding and being proactive. Furthermore refugee children themselves – like all children – benefit from having their experiences reflected in the curriculum, to validate their life histories and empower them with a sense of belonging: 'What is clear is that schools have the potential to welcome, absorb and normalise the refugee situation' (Hope, 2008: 302).

Chapter 2

Children's literature about refugees

Introduction

If children's literature is a dynamic medium for presenting the refugee experience in the classroom, it is useful for teachers to have an overview of the range of texts available, so they can choose those that might fit their particular class's needs. A historical perspective would fit with the wider History curriculum, for instance, or a specific form such as diary writing might dovetail with the style of narrative being studied in Literacy. Perhaps teachers want to choose a text that relates to the profile of the class. They might want to build on community links to a specific area of the world, or reach out to a new arrival, although this has to be approached with caution. Sometimes a book is chosen that reflects the country-focus in Geography, or cross-curricular planning might begin with a title that generates multi-modal interpretations, involving the areas mentioned and incorporating Drama, Art and Music in the topic web.

In this chapter, I provide an overview of children's literature about refugees, from World War Two until the present day. I include commentators' views and consider the background of authors who write about the refugee experience. For ease of access, most of the texts I discuss are published in the UK, although some were published elsewhere and have become widely known and used. There is not sufficient space to consider in depth the wealth of titles published in the US, and also in Canada, Australia and New Zealand, as the focus of the book is primarily on the role of these texts in the UK primary classroom. However, I hope teachers can pick and choose texts from this broad sweep that they feel might have specific relevance to their class or curriculum, while using the insights gained from the present book to transfer to similar ones in the field. I begin the chapter by placing refugee texts in the wider genre of 'migration literature'.

The genre of migration literature

For more than a century the explicit study of human migration has been the preserve of social scientists: geographers, sociologists, anthropologists, social historians and economists (King *et al.,* 1995). Understanding came mainly from statistics or more recently some interpretive data – observation, particularly ethnographic – but such methods fail to capture what it really means and feels like to be a migrant (ibid.). Fiction can lead to powerful insights into the experience, being more personal and individual than statistics, and in this way provide a cross-over between social science and literature. However, migration literature was – and still is – regarded largely as autobiographical or documentary, with little attention paid to its literary value (Rösch, 2004), a point that also applies to refugee literature.

King *et al.* (1995) point out that migrant literature is slow to develop in a host country as it takes time to learn an unfamiliar language well enough to use it for literary purposes. The writing of children's literature seems to be a further step along this continuum, as some migrants – and refugees – do not come from countries where lots of children's literature is produced. According to Duffy (1995) much migrant writing is not by migrants but by writers who are of migrant ancestry or in some way the product of past migrations, or professional authors labelled or racialized by the society in which they were born – for example, Irish writers. Similarly, literature about refugees is rarely written by refugees, although several authors have migration stories in their pasts, as we see in this chapter.

As a genre, there are several easily recognizable themes in migration literature, dealing variously with the social contexts in migrants' country of origin that prompted them to leave, the experience of migration itself and their reception in the country of arrival, including experiences of racism and hostility. These closely mirror Hamilton and Moore's (2004) stages of refugee adaptation (see Chapter 1). However, refugee stories reflect *forced* migration, which, while sharing many aspects of migration literature, have other agendas. For that reason it seems that literature about the refugee experience is a 'sub-genre' of migration literature, although again the distinction is not always clear.

Tracing the development of children's literature about refugees
From World War Two and beyond
Arguably, the first post-war book written about and by a refugee child to be published in the UK is the widely known and chilling *Anne Frank: Diary of a Young Girl*. It was published by Anne's father in 1947 in the Netherlands (Anne Frank Museum, n.d.), and soon after in the US and the UK (Frank, 1952). However, although Anne is a refugee, being a German Jew who had fled with her family to Amsterdam before the diary begins, it can be argued

that the book is not a typical example of children's literature about the refugee experience. The fact that it centres on a long period of incarceration means it avoids dealing with the usual range of factors to which refugees are exposed.

I would therefore suggest that *The Silver Sword* (Serraillier, 1956) is the first widely known post-war children's book published in the UK that has the refugee experience as its central theme. Lathey (2005) asserts that this book marks 'a turning point from the popular, patriotic appeal of earlier war stories' (p. 62) to promote a didactic, even implicitly pacifist, message of the long-term consequences of war. It has lasted as a class reader in schools for over fifty years and has never gone out of print, testimony to the compelling nature of the subject matter. Children are still attracted to the idea of young people taking control of their destiny and depending on each other without adult support. Agnew and Fox (2001: 172) argue that as well as being full of dramatic tension and vivid images, the book does translate to present-day situations and makes 'the suffering of refugees accessible to readers when filtered through the literary restraints of the time'.

A Bear Called Paddington by Michael Bond was published in 1958. Hunt and Sands (2000) consider as dubious its depiction of a bear from 'Darkest Peru', who can only assimilate by forgetting his past life, amongst a display of fond images of empire in a post-imperial Britain. However, Smith (2006) sees the book as an early foray into the positive depiction of a refugee in children's literature, offering a departure from the past in that Paddington himself is 'an evacuee to London, not from it, thus framing London as a safe haven rather than a war-time place of danger' (p. 37).

The 1960s and 1970s saw the publication of two seminal books that addressed the refugee situation: *I am David* by Anne Holm (1965), originally published in Danish in 1963, and the first of a trilogy by Judith Kerr entitled *When Hitler Stole Pink Rabbit* (1971). Kerr was also the author of the *Mog* books (1970–2002) and the much-loved *The Tiger Who Came To Tea* (1968). Holm's book is an impressive piece of fiction that has been made into a feature film. It is deliberately mysterious and unfathomable. Its political and historical location is unique in that it is set in the Cold War and deals with a boy escaping from an Eastern European labour camp, under the then Communist regime (Marshall, n.d.). *When Hitler Stole Pink Rabbit*, however, deals with the author's lightly fictionalized story of escaping Nazi Germany, and fleeing to Switzerland, France and then England. Lathey (2005) cautions against accepting such accounts of wartime childhoods at face value, but although the time lapse may have led the author to view her journey through rose-coloured spectacles, she notes that: 'Kerr writes with feeling about the frustration of being unable to express herself in a new language' (1999: 51). Interestingly, family separation, rather than the refugee experience is presented as the greatest fear, and as such presents a valuable child's insight.

Again, the theme of Jewish refugees escaping Nazism during World War Two is the subject matter of Lois Lowry's *Number the Stars* (1989) and Michael Morpurgo's *Waiting for Anya* (1990). The support of the general population for those in flight – from Denmark to Sweden in the former and from France to Spain in the latter – makes for dramatic and compelling subject matter. Both are full of suspense, Lowry, in particular creating a celebratory story of the strength of the human spirit that 'delivers a distinctive lesson in ethical decision-making and behaviour' (Russell, 1997: 268) as a 10-year-old Danish girl helps her Jewish friend and family escape to Sweden. Morpurgo's classic also introduces the idea of the 'righteous Gentile'. It depicts the 'good German', helpful and friendly to the children 'beyond the call of duty' (Fox, 2001: 50), who turns a blind eye as they cross the Pyrenees into freedom. Nevertheless, the refugee experience is still presented as a wartime event, rather than a living reality for children in our classrooms today, and the focus is almost exclusively on the journey to safety.

However important these retrospectives are, there is nevertheless a danger that the refugee experience was presented to children only in terms of the past (MacSween and Laird, 2010). It is vital that we address the modern age, for our young people to understand that wars, persecution and flight are contemporary experiences as well. As Mary Hoffman writes to her young audience, in the introduction to *Lines in the Sand: New Writing on War and Peace,* an anthology of poems and short stories: 'You may be studying war at your school and learning about trenches and gas masks. But do you realise how many wars have been going on in the world since the last World War ended in 1945?' (2003: 4).

While many children's books about refugees have focused on the historical context, perhaps with the intention of employing a distancing technique, it is interesting to note that more recent literature on this topic now looks at current themes, growing out of present conflicts and modern life experiences. As Agnew and Fox (2001: 56) observe:

> Late twentieth-century children's novels present their protagonists
> not as heroic or saintly figures, but as ordinary people caught up
> in terrible events. Above all they demonstrate the inner strength,

resourcefulness and determination of ordinary people, rather than the glamorised heroics of earlier novels.

However, it was not until the 1990s that the stage widened to encompass contemporary conflicts. The growing number of refugees arriving in the UK at that time was paralleled by a gradual increase in related books, beginning with Elizabeth Laird's *Kiss the Dust* (1991), the story of an Iraqi Kurdish girl and her family who flee to Iran and thence to the UK. The book deals impressively with all aspects of forced migration. It marked a turning point in refugee stories by mirroring modern conflicts in children's literature. Interviewed at a conference in 2008, Laird (MacSween and Laird, 2010) disclosed that had she been writing the book 17 years later, she might have given the protagonist 'a bit more power' (p. 119), despite the powerlessness of her situation, to end on a more positive note. Pinsent (1997: 110) observes that:

> In recent years there have been a number of books which have represented the encounter between the expectations of the educational system and the experiences of children who have come into it speaking little or no English.

She argues that such books function to guide first-language English readers to understand the problems facing refugees. But they also help refugee children, as they become more competent in English, to come to terms with their situation.

Relating recent writing and geographical location

With the breakup of the former Yugoslavia in the 1990s, it was inevitable that several texts would focus on these events. Christobel Mattingley's *No Gun for Asmir* (1993) is based on the story of a Bosnian family fleeing to Austria, the author meeting the real life 'Asmir' in person and learning his story. *Zlata's Diary* by Zlata Filipović (1994) also makes compelling reading. Reporter Janine di Giovanni, who met Zlata in 1993 and wrote the introduction to the book, described her as 'the Anne Frank of Sarajevo', and her diary is unusual in being written between the ages of 10 and 13 as events unfolded around her. Seeing the privations of urban warfare in Sarajevo through the eyes of a young girl and the attempts to continue with normality while nightly shell bombardments gradually wreck the city's infrastructure and her family's lives, has a shocking immediacy, even more so as it is an autobiographical account. Gaye Hiçyilmaz's (1998) *Smiling for Strangers* is also set in war-torn Bosnia and follows a middle-class teen, fleeing from the violence that engulfed her family in Sarajevo aboard an aid convoy truck to England. Hiçyilmaz, a writer who is 'able to combine elements of two cultures and their meeting points into an artistic whole' (Lathey, 2001: 4), also highlights the unending plight of the Roma people of Eastern Europe, often compounded by fleeing to the UK, in two works that make an enduring contribution to refugee children's literature: *The Girl in Red* (2000) and *Pictures from the Fire* (2003).

Since it was invaded in 2001, Afghanistan has been the subject of several books, particularly about children surviving and fleeing from the Taliban. Deborah Ellis's trilogy – *The Breadwinner* (2001), *Parvana's Journey* (2002) and *Mud City* (2004) – traces a young girl who has to disguise herself as a boy to fend for her family, travelling to search for her father and subsequently escaping to Pakistan. It has won many awards. The first book in the series has been widely used in primary schools and Ellis has developed lesson plans, as have other teachers. Renowned Australian children's author Morris Gleitzman took a new departure in following Jamal and Bibi from Afghanistan to an Australian detention centre in *Boy Overboard* (2003) and *Girl Underground* (2004).

Two recent books also focus on the Middle East, but in highly contrasting styles. Michael Morpurgo has further addressed the refugee experience in *Shadow* (2010), also set in Afghanistan, depicting the friendship between a British soldier's dog and an Afghan boy, the bond between child and animal a familiar theme for Morpurgo. *Azzi in Between* by Sarah Garland (2012) is a graphic novel for younger children, about a young girl from a Persian family who escapes their home in an unnamed country, a deliberate choice on the part of the author. Now we also have a newly released book from the renown and aforementioned author, Elizabeth Laird, *Welcome to Nowhere* (2017), which finally tackles the situation in Syria and the fate of young refugees making the perilous journey from there, via a refugee camp in Jordan, to the UK. The author surrounds the text with plenty of contextual information and ideas of how readers can help in practical ways when responding to the book.

Another significant area of the world that contains a huge number of refugees and even more displaced people, is the vast continent of Africa, and although clearly not a homogenous whole, it is noticeable in its paucity of stories that reflect the experience of many of its inhabitants. Several books start in an African setting but then move swiftly to the UK – for example, Bernard Ashley's *Little Soldier* (1999), told in a series of flashbacks, about a child soldier's problems of integration from a fictional country in Central Africa to South East London. While the protagonist of Benjamin Zephaniah's *Refugee Boy* (2001) is half Ethiopian, half Eritrean, the book focuses almost entirely on his experiences in the UK and the campaign mounted by his classmates to fight his deportation. The two popular books that are the focus of this study also have partly African settings. Mary Hoffman's *The Colour of Home*, depicting a Somali boy's struggle to join a UK school, can be found in many London Key Stage 1 classrooms, while Beverley Naidoo's *The Other Side of Truth* and its sequel *Web of Lies* (2004b), follows two Nigerian children being smuggled into the UK and straddles Key Stages 2 and 3. Finally *Christophe's Story* by Nikki Cornwell (2006) and its sequel *Ahmel's Revenge* (2011) sensitively craft the tricky subject of the Rwandan genocide for young children.

Other perspectives

Some writers focus exclusively on what happens to refugee children when they come to this country. Zephaniah's *Refugee Boy* highlights campaigns to fight deportation, for example, as does *A Fight to Belong* by Alan Gibbons (1999), where the local population protests on behalf of the asylum seeker or migrant family and secures their future. Another angle taken is to view the plight of the refugee through a friendship between an English youth and a young asylum seeker, as in *The Dark Beneath*, also by Alan Gibbons (2003), *Ruby Tanya* by Robert Swindells (2004) and *Hidden* by Miriam Halahmy (2011). This approach is designed to foster empathy for the newcomer, filtered through the eyes of the narrator, with whom the reader is expected to identify. Recently, the UK publisher Frances Lincoln, well-known for commissioning children's books that deal with 'difference', has produced four *Refugee Diaries* by Anthony Robinson and Annemarie Young (Robinson and Young, 2008, 2009; Robinson, 2009, 2010). These depict the real lives of four young people from the Congo, Chechnya and Iraqi and Turkish Kurdistan. Using a combination of photographs, illustrations, maps, the children's stories and factual information, the books offer a useful mixture of resources. Modern perspectives are chillingly represented by Deborah Ellis in *No Safe Place* (2010), where young people meet from global locations in Calais, finally to be smuggled across the Channel to the UK.

Even more controversially, several picturebooks about the refugee experience have appeared since the millennium from a variety of western writers (Hope, 2007; Dolan, 2014b). *The Colour of Home* by Mary Hoffman (2002) was the first picturebook to appear in the UK on the topic, followed by *Petar's Song* by Pratima Mitchell (2004), which deliberately avoids geographical specificity. From Australia the bluntly named *Refugees* by David Miller (2003) examines the refugee dilemma in allegorical form, following ducks forced from their home and seeking a safe place to live, and

Ziba Came on a Boat by Liz Lofthouse (2007) is a contrastingly realistic and moving story of a young Afghan girl and her family fleeing to Perth in Australia on a crowded and leaky boat. From the US, *Playing War* by Kathy Beckwith (2005) tackles the effects of post-conflict trauma on a refugee child, and two books by Karen Lynn Williams and Khadra Mohammed – *Four Feet, Two Sandals* (2007) and *My Name is Sangoel* (2009) – reflect the lives of children from Afghanistan and Sudan respectively. The cunningly entitled *The Silence Seeker* by Ben Morley (2009) addresses the problems of a refugee adapting to a British urban landscape and touches on the issue of deportation. Other picturebooks are discussed in depth by Dolan (2014b), but recently *The Journey* by Francesca Sanna (2016), with both English and French editions, and *Stepping Stones* by Margiet Ruurs (2016), published as a dual-language book in English and Arabic, tackle the Syrian refugee crisis from the point of view of children through dramatic stories and creative artwork.

Personal testimony, autobiography and authenticity

The importance of personal testimony to distil experience has been continually reflected upon Primo Levi, no less, writer and survivor of Auschwitz:

> One single Anne Frank moves us more than the countless others who suffered just as she did but whose faces have remained in the shadows. Perhaps it is better that way; if we were capable of taking in all the suffering of all those people we would not be able to live.
>
> (1988: 56)

Some, but very few, of the books identified as dealing with the refugee experience are autobiographical, and those that are are generally not about modern conflicts. Possible reasons for this are discussed above, but those that do exist have a particular authenticity and resonance, over and above fiction by authors who have not experienced at first hand the stories they are telling. Such authors are immediately lent gravitas, guiding the reader to accept the content as 'truth'. Nevertheless, if we look at all the authors I have mentioned, it is interesting that many have a connection with the migrant experience, mainly by family association or through travel and work opportunities. Furthermore, as Rutter suggests, writers such as Ellis, Hiçyilmaz, Hoffman, Laird and Naidoo were all heavily influenced in their choice of subject matter by the strong work of the refugee charities sector in the UK and internationally (personal communication, 6 July 2015).

Gamble and Yates (2008: 155) note that there are 'some very good books written by writers who, although they do not live in the places they are writing about, have visited or conducted careful research'. Elizabeth Laird is an example of this. Born in New Zealand but growing up in South London, she has travelled far and wide, living and working in Malaysia, Ethiopia, India, Iraq and Lebanon (Laird, n.d.), and has written books about children from many of these countries. Questions are always asked about whether an outsider can legitimately tell the story of a group to which they do not belong, but Gamble and Yates ask how else these stories might be made available, and suggest that sometimes the outsider's objectivity can 'mediate to make the unfamiliar understandable' (2008: 155). Stewart (2008) points out that Deborah Ellis, herself from Canada, wrote *The Breadwinner* trilogy after travelling to Afghanistan and Pakistan, interviewing refugee women in camps there, which she later wrote up in reportage form (Ellis, 2000). Similarly Gaye Hiçyilmaz spent several years living in Turkey with her Turkish husband. Pinsent notes that a few children's books 'which seem to create a rather fuller picture of the situation of immigrants lacking the language of the countries they are forced to live in are by writers who have a close involvement with the culture they are depicting' (1997: 114).

Sometimes travel stimulates a departure from an author's usual oeuvre. For example, *Azzi in Between* (Garland, 2012) was written after a trip to New Zealand (Garland, n.d.), and is a far cry from Garland's former books that characterize a chaotic middle-class family enjoying a cosy Middle England family life. Nikki Cornwell's work as an interpreter for asylum seekers and refugees led her 'into the dark world of their stories and (she has) witnessed their suffering', about which she writes eloquently on her website (Cornwell, n.d.). Bernard Ashley, who already has a reputation as 'a 'gritty' writer in sympathy with the underdog' (Amazon, n.d.), went to Uganda as part of his research for *Little Soldier* (Ashley, 1999). As 'gatekeepers' of the refugee experience, these authors, if not using personal testimony or autobiography, arguably have a responsibility to their readers to present well-researched, sensitive writing that is as factually accurate as possible and does not 'other' their subjects. However, Mallan is concerned that by looking 'through Western eyes', books that aim to encourage empathy with those from different cultural, social and religious backgrounds might 'be used as a cultural tool for reinforcing existing dominant hierarchies and exclusions' (2013: 107). I return to this thought in Chapter 5 when I consider the background and writing process of Hoffman, Naidoo and Littlewood.

Reflections

If we are to share children's literature about refugees in contemporary primary classrooms we must be aware that books in this sub-genre of migration literature are written by authors who are not themselves refugees, but may well have a personal connection to the subject matter. Moreover, children's literature about refugees has been slow to emerge as an entity in itself, tending to focus back historically until the 1990s, rather than forwards to address contemporary conflicts. However, the 10 years before the millennium saw a rapid growth in publication to the extent that 'in the later 20th century the didactic novel for children began to confront political and social questions very directly' (Grenby, 2008: 83).

From 2000 onwards this has become a 'burgeoning genre' (Hope, 2008), with new books appearing constantly by both new and well-known children's authors. The surge also follows waves of migration into the UK. The books are rarely directly autobiographical, however, but are nonetheless vital for holding up 'windows and mirrors' to the refugee experience. Before we move on to consider my research I need to situate the analysis in a theoretical framework. In the next chapter, I discuss the development of thought and the pedagogical implications behind a growing attention to reader response, dialogic method and critical literacy.

Chapter 3

Reader response and critical pedagogy

Introduction

The development of reader response theory during the second half of the 20th century has had a major impact on the way we view books and their readers. At the same time pedagogical perspectives, such as the dialogic method, have grown out of literary theory. Students are encouraged to discuss their opinions as part of their learning. Educationalists, led by Freire, have developed a radical 'dialogic pedagogy', which has since evolved into a method of engaging with texts known as 'critical literacy'. The latter can be defined as a practice that 'melds social, political, and cultural debate and discussion with the analysis of how texts and discourses work, where, with what consequences, and in whose interests' (Luke, 2012: 5).

All these strands combine in the study of children's literature about the refugee experience, to give insight and direction to teachers wanting to tackle such texts and the accompanying controversial issues that might arise in the classroom. However, narrower national agendas in the UK for teaching Literacy and literature, within the confines of the given curriculum, add complexity and sometimes constraints upon teachers.

The development of reader response theory
Early influences

As early as 1938, Rosenblatt began to examine the reading process and elevate the role of the reader, focusing on responding to the literary text as a unique 'event', conditioned by multiple facets pertaining to the particular reader:

> The reader brings to the work personality traits, memories of past events, present needs and preoccupations, a particular mood of the moment, and a particular physical condition. These and many other elements in a never-to-be-duplicated combination determine his response to the peculiar contribution of the text.
>
> (Rosenblatt, 1938: 30–1)

However, it wasn't until poststructuralism emerged in the late 1960s, questioning the idea of any unified 'truth', that such theories were picked up and expanded on. Barthes' famous essay 'The Death of the Author' (Barthes, 1968) claimed that 'the birth of the reader is at the cost of the death of the author' (p. 148), and this remains one of the most controversial tenets of modern literary criticism. Barthes criticized the search for explanation in the person and history of the author, and stressed that the author does not have a single voice, but is only the originator of the text, subject to multiple linguistic influences. Thus 'the text is a tissue of quotations drawn from the innumerable centres of culture' (1968: 147). In reply, Foucault's essay 'What is an Author?' (1969) suggested that the abolition of the author is not possible, but no author owns the meanings or readings of his/her text, which needs to be considered as a historical construction, an ideological product.

By the 1960s and 1970s a school of thinking under the umbrella theory of reader response emerged, which has since expanded to all areas of the arts. Wolfgang Iser argued for a spectrum of possible readings (1972) between that of the 'implied reader' and the 'actual reader'. For example, the implied reader of a children's book about seeking asylum is often a non-refugee, while the actual reader might come from a refugee background or themselves have fled to safety. Iser also asserted that the reader brings to the work 'pre-understanding', a context of beliefs and expectations (Iser, 1976, first published in English in 1978), which is certainly true when approaching contentious issues around forced migration. The text produces 'blanks' or 'gaps' that the reader selects and organizes, excluding some and 'concretising' others – giving shape or meaning in the act of reading, according to their own context of beliefs. A literary work is incomplete until the reader has 'actualized' those elements that are left to the imagination, and teachers are often actively involved in enabling this process, perhaps challenging 'pre-understanding'.

At the same time Rosenblatt (1978) deepened her 'transactional' theory of literature, the idea of a two-way relationship with the text. She focused on the role of the reader, similar to that outlined by Iser. Rosenblatt likened the author/text/reader to an electrical circuit – all important to the production of meaning. A different reader will form a different circuit and therefore a different meaning. Relating this notion to my study raises the idea that a book about the refugee experience may create an entirely different circuit (or meaning) for a reader who has themselves become a refugee or has a refugee background, than one who has no understanding or familiarity with the migration experience.

Rosenblatt was highly critical of much teaching of literature where the interpretation of texts appeared mainly teacher-led. She chose to focus primarily on the student/reader. Rosenblatt developed a theory that reading could be divided into two contrasting ways of experiencing a text – the 'efferent' and the 'aesthetic', which are seen as a continuum along which the reader can shift backwards and forwards. The efferent – from the Latin *effere,* to carry away – involves a basic gathering of information and understanding of the content of the text. The aesthetic stance involves readers in an affective engagement with the text, through their own lived experience. The distinction between the two is relevant to my own work, in that refugee texts both provide background information and elicit an emotional response. However, more recently writers such as Fox (2007) suggest that both the 'efferent' and 'aesthetic' readings might simultaneously coexist. My study echoes this view.

Taking the transactional view a step further, Fish (1980) claimed that there is no objective work of literature, only interpretations. As readers, we are part of an 'interpretive community' in which we are trained, that gives us a particular way of reading a text. This is particularly pertinent in the primary classroom where strategies applied before to the act of reading therefore determine the shape of what is read rather than the other way round, as usually assumed. An individual's response is determined by the conventions of reading they have been educated into within a particular socio-historical context, using strategies that guide them to seek certain meanings. But critics such as Eagleton (1983) saw that Fish did not allow for individual or deviant interpretations, such as that of a refugee child in response to a book about seeking asylum.

In putting forward a theoretical evaluation of the role of the reader of children's literature, Harding (1977) suggested that the act of reading is like someone listening to gossip: 'a non-participant relation which yet includes an active evaluative attitude' (p. 59). Harding has problems with the term 'identification' and the idea that the act of reading is a form of vicarious experience. He feels this is too general a description of what happens when we read, preferring to consider a multiplicity of emotions from empathy, imitation, admiration or recognition of similarities – and I would add differences too. For Harding, the reader is similar to an onlooker, as they frequently know more about the situation than the individual characters do. They may also construct imagined events for the characters, beyond those that actually exist in the text. Harding maintained that, through reading, we are engaged in the discussion of life chances, the 'suppose ...' paradigm commonly found in children's talk. He claims that, 'we can release our imaginings from practical limitations and consider what might have been and what might be' (p. 61).

When considering children's response to text, Chambers (1995) looked closely at 'the reader in the book'. He looked explicitly at the mechanics by which the author forges an alliance with Iser's 'implied reader' to manipulate them towards the meanings he wishes to convey through such techniques as assuming the role of the god-like, all-seeing narrator or writing the character of the child in the first person. The author communicates to the reader, in both subtle and obvious ways, by their comments on the event in the story, or by the attitude they adopt towards the characters and their actions. Chambers asserts that authors achieve this through 'assumptions of commonality' (1995: 47), which may 'become so dominant in the text that people who do not ... make the same assumptions feel alienated by them as they read'. There is a link here with potentially different responses between refugee and non-refugee readers. I discuss this later.

Children's literature and ideology

How effective children's literature is as a transmitter of values and attitudes has been debated long and hard for centuries. Children are seen as important vessels of societal norms to take into the next generation, and writers may seek to perpetuate – or oppose – certain values, in an attempt to pass on their own worldview. The voices in children's books are also not of children speaking, but an image of what adults think children are like. As Rose (1984) pointed out, children's literature is a misnomer. It is commissioned, written and chosen for reading primarily by adults – be they publishers, writers, teachers or parents – to such an extent that Nodelman (1992) asserted that it has been 'colonized' by adults.

Many studies have concentrated on the reader's viewpoint when considering the effect literature has on children's belief systems. Hollindale (1988: 9) suggested caution with regards to this: 'ideology is not something which is transferred to children as if they were empty receptacles. It is something which they already possess, having drawn it from a mass of experiences far more powerful than literature.' For example, children may well have encountered refugee issues via the mass media before reading any of the books presented in Chapter 2. Thus children's books about refugees have relevance in the immediate present but sit within an underlying 'climate of belief' (Hollindale, 1988: 10) and attitudes about migration. Hollindale also maintained that an overly-didactic message can be counter-productive, merely reinforcing pre-existing prejudices.

Other writers have seen a variety of factors that determine how children's literature works in the transmission and reception of values and attitudes. Chambers (1991) highlighted the important part played by 'enabling adults' – teachers, librarians, parents, writers, publishers – who help children become literary readers. He pointed out that teachers always choose the text, without consulting or listening to children, thus putting them in a powerful position to develop children's attitudes and values. Wollman-Bonilla (1998: 298) listed three major reasons why trainee teachers reject children's literature as 'inappropriate for children':

- the text might 'frighten or corrupt'
- the text 'fails to represent dominant social values or myths'
- the text 'identifies racism or sexism as a social problem'.

With this in mind, there seems to be a discrepancy between acceptable classroom discourses and the wider world. Such fears, particularly of frightening children or presenting them with contentious issues, are frequently cited by teachers as reasons to hold back from reading refugee stories in the classroom.

Importantly, child readers, like adults, are subject to historical, social and cultural contexts. In the words of Cullingford (1998: 1): 'Not only the time in which the reader lives but the political outlook he holds will influence the interpretation.' In various ways, therefore, children's literature is part of, but may also challenge the prevailing ideology of the times. Stephens (1992: 2) maintained that 'the discourse of a narrative fiction yields up both a story and a significance. Ideology may be inscribed within both. Because this stance is often implicit, it renders fiction powerful in subliminally shaping attitudes, especially with a young, malleable audience. However, Sarland (2005) suggests that fatalistic views that see readers as victims of ideologically saturated fiction are simplistic, and that young readers have plenty of agency and are free to make choices about what they take from texts. This view usefully motivates the ongoing study of children's reader response, to promote a broad diet of literature and engage in discussion of controversial issues in the classroom through the medium of fiction.

'Windows and mirrors'

Using this evocative metaphor, Bishop (1990) argues that children have a right to books that reflect their own images and open different worlds to them:

Books are sometimes windows, offering views of worlds that may be real or imagined, familiar or strange. These windows are also sliding glass doors, and readers have only to walk through in imagination to become part of whatever world has been created or recreated by the author. When lighting conditions are just right, however, a window can also be a mirror. Literature transforms human experience and reflects it back to us, and in that reflection we can see our own lives and experiences as part of the larger human experience. Reading, then, becomes a means of self-affirmation, and readers often seek their mirrors in books.

(Bishop, 1990)

Bishop deplores the lack of children's texts that enable minority groups to see themselves reflected, but argues that those from the dominant group also need books that help them understand the multicultural 'salad bowl' that is American society. The extended metaphor works for children's refugee stories too: young refugees need to see themselves reflected in literature, and non-refugees need access to such experiences vicariously. Schwartz (1995), however, challenges this view as too simplistic, maintaining that: 'Mirrors and windows do not suffice. A critical postmodern pedagogy ... implies a much more global understanding of our place in social reality.' Schwartz maintains that an 'us and them', or 'we and The Other' duality is unhelpful. This concern may apply to differentiating between refugee and non-refugee readers, an issue I discuss more fully later. More useful, claims Schwartz, is to live '*sin fronteras,* to be a crossroads, to build bridges rather than walls' (n.p).

Many writers have addressed the dual role of literature in offering insights into our own and others' lives (Cullingford, 1998). Readers need to see themselves represented in books to affirm their place in the world (Bishop, 1992) but reading also helps children to develop their imaginations through story, thereby increasing their understanding of 'the common pool of humanity' (Britton, 1993: viii):

By providing children with opportunities to read about children in situations different from their own and children who live in other parts of the world living with life issues such as war, we can help children gain a greater understanding of the world they live in and the challenges children in other locations face.

(Smith-D'Arezzo and Thompson, 2006: 337)

Children can visit geographical and historical settings in books that are different from their own both spatially and temporally (Lathey, 2001). This can develop tolerance and understanding and clarify their own cultural identity. Such activities 'emphasise the part that children's literature plays in the development of children's understanding of both belonging (being one of us) and differentiation (being other)' (Meek, 2001: x).

However, I suggest that some narratives also play a powerful part in validating the experiences of those who feel *they* are 'othered' by mainstream discourses, such as refugee children. Gangi and Barowsky (2009: 9) assert that the 'windows' and 'mirrors' paradigm is particularly useful in helping children suffering the effects of war, terrorism or disaster, as:

> … having access to such books helps children know the world has not forgotten them and may help decrease their feelings of isolation by providing a bond with others when they learn of those who have experienced similar circumstances.

Bibliotherapy and cognitive literary criticism

The idea of a therapeutic 'bond' between book and reader reaches back to ancient Greek and Roman times (McCulliss, 2012). It has been formalized by the term 'bibliotherapy', coined originally by Crothers (1916). Lehr (1981: 76) defines it thus: 'Simply stated, bibliotherapy is the use of books to help people solve problems.' For the younger age group it 'involves a child reading about a character who successfully resolves a problem similar to the one the child is experiencing' (Sullivan and Strang, 2002: 75). This school of thought was further developed by Shrodes (1950), who added a framework through which the reader might pass, refined into three recognized stages: identification, catharsis and insight. Identification pertains to when a reader associates themselves with the character or situation in the literary work. Catharsis describes how the reader becomes emotionally involved with the thoughts and feelings of the characters and insight is achieved when the reader realizes that by relating to the character or situation they might learn to deal more effectively with their own personal issues. Such a process could potentially have huge implications for refugee children if they are able to use literature to help them come to terms with their experiences and new identity.

However, bibliotherapy is not without problems, and is certainly not a simple cure-all for refugee children. Yet the growth in 'problem novels', especially for adolescents, seems to suggest a pervasive sense of the healing potential of narrative. Some commentators, such as Clarke and Postle (1988), suggest there has to be a close degree of 'matching' between the book and the individual's personal circumstances for reading to directly stimulate therapeutic results. In contrast, Crago (1996) asserts that such matching is both impractical and potentially painful to the reader, a 'merging' of reader and text being much more likely if the correspondence is partly or wholly metaphorical, with the potential to 'slip past' the conscious mind. The introduction to this book flags up teachers' concerns with sharing books in the classroom that might mirror a refugee child's lived experience too closely. And it can be argued that bibliotherapy is outside a classroom teacher's remit and needs to be handled with extreme care. However, Doll and Doll (1997) and Lucas and Soares (2013) believe that school psychologists and counsellors should train educators and parents to work in partnership to apply bibliotherapy techniques.

Bibliotherapy has been credited with the potential to increase children's emotional intelligence (Goleman, 1995), and develop empathy. Sullivan and Strang (2002) believe that insight and understanding are strengthened by pairing literature with mediation between child and professional as sharing books is a familiar, child-friendly and non-invasive practice that most teachers include when they read in class. Lucas and Soares are more forthright approach, stating that 'books are essential to promote emotional, social, and cognitive development of children' (2013: 138). They claim that bibliotherapy helps increase the empathic understanding of others by promoting interpersonal skills and emotional maturity, as well as enhancing self-expression, problem-solving and coping skills. Lucas and Soares suggest that working with small homogeneous groups of children of similar chronological age and developmental level is the optimum model for sharing common experiences. In the I study describe in this book I demonstrate how the discussion groups I chaired provided a basis for shared reflection on the texts read in class. They also gave children an opportunity to offer opinions, hear the thoughts of others and 'enhance empathy, tolerance, respect and acceptance of others' (p. 145).

This approach links to an emerging school of thought: cognitive literary criticism or neuro-literary criticism. It has its roots in reader response but interacts with new trajectories in neuroscience, and looks at the relationship between fiction and the mind. Vermeule (2010) enquires 'Why do we care about literary characters?' and suggests that through 'mind reading' we develop the capacity to explain people's behaviour in terms of their mental states – their beliefs, intentions and desires. Vermeule argues that the tools used by literary authors to sharpen and focus reader interest tap into evolved neural mechanisms that trigger a caring response. Nikolajeva (2012) asserts that connections are made between the mediated experience of the text and emotional memories stored in the brain. These may be 'fragmentary and imprecise' (p. 276), however, as the discussion groups that I analyse later in the book bore out.

Writers in this developing area claim that Theory of Mind (ToM), or understanding the mental states of others, is a crucial skill for developing social relationships. Through a variety of neuro-scientific tests Kidd and Castano (2013) found that reading literary fiction – importantly of good quality – enhances affective and cognitive function. It also 'uniquely engages the psychological processes needed to gain access to characters' subjective experiences' (p. 378). As Nikolajeva points out, 'empathy is not a natural capacity' (2012: 289) and the skill of understanding other people's feelings needs to be fostered. Her contention is that picturebooks fulfil this function better than just text as 'visual stimuli play a stronger part in this process than verbal, since our visual skills are hard-wired in the brain, while linguistic skills are not' (p. 274). However, Mallan (2013) points to other research that questions such a direct correlation between children's literature and narrative empathy. She argues that 'fiction that engages a reader with the emotional plight of a character does not necessarily translate into actions in the real world towards people who are similarly suffering, marginalized, or victimized' (p. 106). Clearly the link between fiction, empathy and action is still up for debate. I return to it later when I present the data from my study.

The power of pictures and visual literacy

As *The Colour of Home* – one of the two books chosen for my case study – is a picturebook, some consideration of the genre is useful, as is a brief discussion of children's responses to books in which images are combined with narrative. Since the 1960s there has been an explosion in children's publishing of what we refer to loosely as picturebooks (Salisbury and Styles, 2012). But defining what they are and understanding how children 'read' them has been the subject of a vast array of writing and criticism. Classifying the picturebook genre, as distinct from other forms of literature, began in the US with the work of pioneering historian, Barbara Bader. In this now famous observation, she noted that:

A picturebook is ... foremost an experience for a child. As an art form, it hinges on the interdependence of pictures and words, on the simultaneous display of two facing pages, and on the drama of the turning page.

(Bader, 1976: 1)

Nodelman and Reimer (1992) suggest that the visual image evokes an emotional rather than intellectual response. This was made explicit in my interview with illustrator Karin Littlewood (see Chapter 5). Lewis (1996: 271) takes a more balanced approach and points out that picturebooks carry 'two different forms of signification: the verbal or textual and the pictorial or iconic. Meaning is always generated in at least two different ways.'

Writing in the field for several years, Nikolajeva argues that visual texts need their own scholarly metalanguage so that we can discuss their characteristics and reach (2006). She points out that it is important to distinguish picturebooks (deliberately one word) as books in which words and images constitute an indivisible whole, and argues that the overall impact of the work is achieved by the interaction of the two. Other texts can be designated illustrated books: where pre-existing text has been supplied with illustrations, such as in *The Colour of Home*, and pictures are subordinate to words – the story can be understood without the pictures. Nikolajeva and Scott (2001) differentiate between complementary picturebooks, where the images reflect and expand text or fill each other's gaps, and counterpoint picturebooks, where the words and pictures tell a different story, provide alternative information or contradict each other. I explore these different categories later in relation to *The Colour of Home*.

So how are researchers, teachers and indeed children to read, interpret and analyse the interrelated visual and verbal image? Kress and van Leeuwen's (1996) seminal work on 'reading images' looked at the relationship between structure and meaning, and were concerned with the uses to which images are put. They asserted that visual images are signs and symbols that have derived socially from a shared culture, encoding and communicating meaning. However, Sipe (1998) suggests that teachers often feel they lack the training in visual literacy to analyse and understand images in children's books and to help their pupils construct meaning for themselves from the pictures. Kress and van Leeuwen (2001) point out that written language has been the dominant system of meaning used in educational contexts, while visual image has often been seen as merely supporting the text rather than being a system of meaning in its own right.

Serafini has refined this view (2009), offering a 'visual grammar' that works to fuse together written language, visual image and graphic design to tell a story or offer information. He argues that if teachers are to guide children in constructing meaning from multimodal texts, they need to understand this interrelationship. The picturebook illustrator, meanwhile, uses prior knowledge, intertextuality, multiple perspectives, familiarity with language and story and play (Crawford and Hade, 2000).

> Picturebooks are invariably the first books that children in the developed world encounter. They shape aesthetic tastes, they introduce principles and conventions of narrative. They are part of artistic and literary culture but they are also entertaining, moving, thought-provoking and witty.
>
> (Graham, 2008: 106)

Arizpe and Styles (2003) found that children experience great pleasure and motivation when they read visual texts across a range of ages and abilities, and from different cultural and linguistic backgrounds. Such reading also afforded 'equality of access to narratives and ideas that would otherwise be denied to young readers' (p. 223). Nodelman (2005) goes so far as to argue that illustrations play a powerful role in conveying to children the overall story and 'meaning' far more directly than the words do, and can carry more allusions and connections than in the text. Children are good at analysing the visual features of texts. They make personal connections to actively engage with texts and draw on their own experience. And as Arizpe (2009) points out, for new arrivals with little knowledge of a host country's language and culture 'the visual image becomes a powerful source of information' (p. 134). Children's responses will be based on their home culture, personal experiences and previous encounters with text and pictures, and will help them to 'navigate' their new world. Dolan (2014a: 7) also endorses the significant role that visual literacy plays in contemporary classrooms:

> Recently published picturebooks are engaging, thought provoking and provide an excellent means of bringing the world into the classroom. Consequently, picturebooks have the potential to make abstract ideas and intercultural concepts more accessible for children.

Pedagogical perspectives
The dialogic method

Since the time of Socrates questioning, inquiry and discussion have been thought to stimulate critical thinking and illuminate ideas. Developed in the early twentieth century, Bakhtin's (1934) idea that the interaction of teacher and pupil, through dialogue, would lead to greater understanding on both sides, has fuelled much contemporary thinking on the nature of classroom discourse. Building on such early forays Brazilian educator Paolo Freire (Shor and Freire, 1987) defined his view of the 'dialogical method' as 'a moment where humans meet to reflect on their reality as they make and remake it' (ibid.: 98). Freire asserts that 'through dialogue ... we can then act critically to transform reality' (ibid.: 99).

This leads us to the theory of pedagogy, for if we are to discuss texts with children in exciting new ways, we must examine the mechanics of this 'talk about texts' (Wells, 1992; Maybin and Moss, 1993; Mercer *et al.*, 1999).

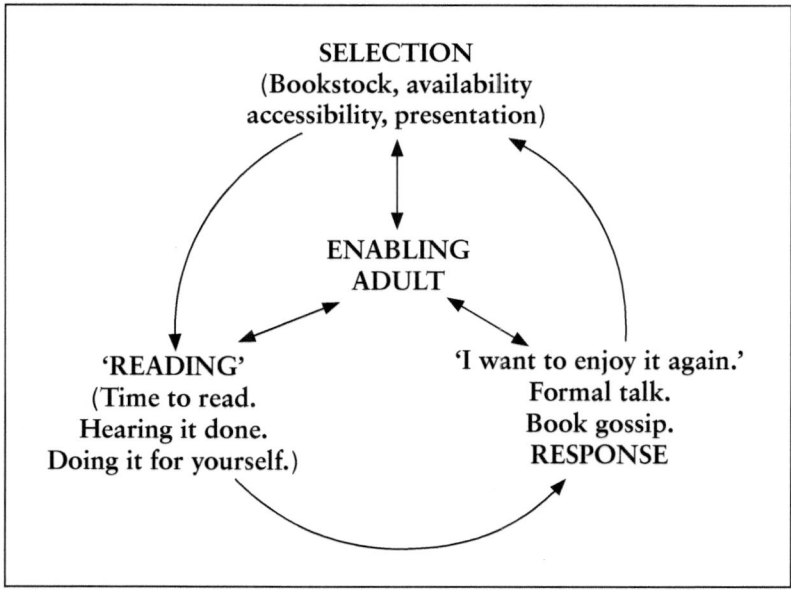

Figure 3.1: The Reading Circle (Chambers, 1991). Also appears in *Tell Me: Children, Reading & Talk with The Reading Environment* (Thimble Press 2011; www.thimblepress.co.uk).

Figure 3.1 shows Chambers' representation of 'The Reading Circle' (1991), which concerns the selection, reading and response to texts. He demonstrates how various adults impact on every part of the process. A vital part of the reading process is the opportunity to discuss what has been read with an adult or with other children, or both. Chambers asserts that through 'book talk' children arrive at a greater understanding of the meaning and significance of a book than they do as lone readers, and suggested ways in which teacher questioning could move from simple recall to more a critical engagement with the text. His Tell Me approach suggests that there is no single reading of a text but rather the creation of a 'community' of readers (Chambers, 1993), jointly discovering their own interpretation. Chambers asserted that all questions should start with 'Tell me ...' (rather than 'Why?') to add authenticity to the discussion and give the impression that the teacher is genuinely interested in the response, rather than 'testing' the pupil. His programme put forward a framework of questioning that should develop out of the following four starting points:

- was there anything that you liked about this book
- was there anything that you disliked?
- was there anything that puzzled you?
- were there any patterns – any connections – that you noticed?

(ibid.: 76)

Chambers's work is particularly pertinent to this study, as he highlights the position of the teacher in chairing group discussions with children about books after a common reading. He criticizes the usual system where the teacher chooses the topic, and through the kinds of questions asked, steers the class to a reading of the book that the teacher wants them to reconstruct. He observes that: 'The teacher raises awareness and is a contributor of specialized knowledge, a guide to further sources, and a synthesizer of disparate and often conflicting comment' (ibid.: 119) and carries enormous responsibility which is not always acknowledged.

Building on the work of Bakhtin, Skidmore (2000: 289) developed the contrasting concepts of 'pedagogical dialogue' and 'dialogical pedagogy'. In the former, 'someone who knows the truth instructs someone who is ignorant of it and in error'. Skidmore *et al.* (2003: 52) found that in this form the teacher 'rarely asks authentic questions; normally controls turn-taking by nominating the next speaker; keeps a tight grip on the topic of conversation; and does most of the talking'. By contrast, a teacher utilizing dialogical pedagogy is more 'light touch'. In this paradigm pupil utterances are 'chained' – one building on the other. Instead of asking pupils to recall events with a right or wrong answer, the teacher asks questions that have various possible answers, none of which is uniquely 'correct'. This opens pupils up to 'modification through considering other points of view, with the result that they attain a richer understanding of the story collectively than they would be likely to achieve individually' (Skidmore, 2000: 292).

Alexander (2008) built on and refined these ideas and observed how teachers as well as children talk in the classroom. He notes that the so-called 'recitation script' of what he calls a closed initiation-response-feedback (IRF) exchange, with closed teacher questions, brief recall answers and minimal feedback to 'report someone else's thinking' (p. 93), remains dominant. In his research comparing practices in primary classrooms in five countries, Alexander (2001) had found that in England, a veneer of geniality and openness masked a somewhat closed model, where the teacher, in looking for a specific answer, continually rephrased the question or even mouthed the answer in their quest for conformity, so that no conversation or dialogue took place. Alexander (2008: 112–13) identified five principles for good dialogic teaching. It should be:

- collective
- reciprocal
- supportive
- cumulative
- purposeful.

Following this John examined teacher–pupil interactions with text during three Key Stage 1 – 5 to 7-year-olds – shared reading sessions. She contrasted 'teacher-framed', 'pupil-framed' and 'collaborative' discourse in the classroom. In collaborative discourse, pupils jointly construct meaning with a teacher who facilitates them making their own views, knowledge and questions known. This creates an atmosphere in which children feel confident to contribute their own ideas, without the teacher 'acting as the arbiter of a predetermined agenda' (John, 2009: 130). Nonetheless the teacher still plays a strong role in the process.

Critical pedagogy and critical literacy

Freire saw that literacy can provide knowledge, and that an understanding of the world is crucial to empowerment. All children, whether or not they are refugees, come to school with prior experiences of life already shaping their attitudes, as education is not restricted to the school environment. They also bring these personal and worldly understandings to bear on their reading to make sense of the text. Learning to read enables them to comprehend and engage with the wider world, and a cyclical relationship is formed: 'Reading the world always precedes reading the word, and reading the word implies continually reading the world' (Freire and Macedo, 1987: 35).

For Freire, it is the role of the teacher to employ a critical pedagogy that should stimulate students to reflect and begin to comprehend the relationship between the many different worldviews. Instead of repressing students' creativity, teaching should encourage risk taking, stimulate students to doubt, to express themselves and to 'discourse about the world' (1987: 53). Reading should be emancipatory and transformative. Freire uses the Greek word 'praxis', which he defined as 'reflection and action upon the world in order to transform it' (1970: 33).

While Freire talked of critical pedagogy on the part of teachers, others were calling for 'critical literacy' – on the part of children. Scholes (1985), like Freire, saw that textual activity is a means by which to act within and upon the world. He identified three essential principles of textual study: reading (producing text within text), interpretation (text upon text) and criticism, (text against text), the last of which is the most significant. Scholes saw the role of the teacher as vital in helping students to engage with the multiple discourses of the text as human beings who have 'textual power'. Meek, too, identified that reading is more than just an immersive activity, and thus resolves the reader response/critical literacy conflict:

> Listening to a story and, later, reading one, involves both taking the story world as 'real' and knowing that it is not real. We encourage children to enter the world of the story ('getting into it') and yet we understand that they need to know that the story world exists only in the story.
>
> (1987: 110)

Recent writing in the UK, the US, and particularly the 'Australian school', focuses on modes of developing critical literacy in the classroom. Similarly to Scholes (1985), Freebody and Luke (1990) saw children as code breakers, meaning makers, text users, and finally text critics, where critical literacy occurs. Stephens argued in favour of a socio-political approach to texts, asserting that reader response theory is 'a dangerous ideological tool and pedagogically irresponsible' (1992: 68), as it creates the illusion that readers have a purely personal response and ignores the political and ideological currents – both explicit and implicit in the text – they are a part of. Teachers are commonly seduced by activities that promote individual interpretations of texts, reacting to the characters or the story, and might ignore the bigger picture or wider significance of the book within the socio-political world beyond the classroom.

In examining what I have chosen to call the 'constructedness' of the text (Fisher, 2008), readers need to ask such questions as:

> How do particular texts work? What effects do they have on the reader? Who has produced the text, under what circumstances, and for which readers? What is missing from this account? How could it be told differently?
>
> (Comber, 2001: 1)

In line with Freire, a vital part of critical literacy is in the linking of texts to children's own experience, highlighting their relevance to readers' lives (Comber, 2001; Hall, 2003). Characterizations, angles and debates on the meaning and use of critical literacy proliferate, so much so that Lewison *et al.* saw the need to synthesize the myriad differing definitions of it into four useful and interrelated dimensions:

- disrupting the commonplace
- interrogating multiple viewpoints
- focusing on socio-political issues
- taking action and promoting social justice.

> (2002: 382)

Similarly, Botelho and Rudman, in focusing on a 'critical multicultural analysis of children's literature', asked: 'who is represented, underrepresented, mis-represented, and/or invisible? How is power exercised?' (2009: xiv).

There is no neutral, context-free construction of meaning from texts, and readers are encouraged to consider the author's motivations for writing the text and their background. They should also think of the text as 'constructed' to serve a particular agenda or deliver a certain message that may need decoding. Aukerman defines critical literacy as recognizing that there are multiple possible responses to a text, that interpretations are contingent upon our histories and social locations, and that texts are not neutral, but by nature ideological. Aukerman petitions for 'dialogic engagement' (2012: 42). Students need opportunities to discuss the viewpoints of others and have their own views questioned and revised, understanding that multiple reading positions are 'socially constructed and ideologically charged' (ibid.: 47).

Government agendas

In 1998, the government introduced the National Literacy Strategy (NLS), intended as part of a major reform to improve standards of literacy in primary schools (Mroz *et al.,* 2000). This saw a 'shift away from a previous emphasis on 'one-to-one' learning experiences to a focus upon more communal forms of learning which place the teacher centre stage' (John, 2009: 123). While maintaining a focus on 'real books', the NLS signalled a radical change in approach, away from teachers reading individually with children, to whole-class and group reading sessions. Teachers and pupils read enlarged texts or 'big books' together, and in group or 'guided reading' sessions small, differentiated groups read multiple sets of the same book, under the guidance of the teacher.

Opportunities for the 'dialogic method' and 'critical literacy' would seem to open up in this joint sharing of texts and 'whole class interactive teaching' (Reynolds and Farrell, 1996; Beard, 1999), with ample chance to discuss, conject and construct meaning and response. However, many studies (Mroz *et al.,* 2000; English *et al.,* 2002; Burns and Myhill, 2004) noted that in fact the NLS model – with its rapid question and answer sessions and 'teacher-led discussion' (Reynolds, 1998) – led to a return to more traditional patterns of IRF (Initiation, Response, Feedback) exchanges that limit children's engagement with texts:

> Because of the teacher's claim to prior knowledge of the subject content, and right to control the pacing and sequencing of its transmission, pupils rarely managed to impose their own relevance outside the teachers' frame of reference.
>
> (Mroz *et al.,* 2000: 382)

Furthermore, time for teachers to read whole texts aloud to the class – the social act of 'giving of voice and breadth to a text' (Barrs and Cork, 2001: 216) – seemed to be compressed by squeezing the Literacy Hour into other times of the day (Collins, 2005) or replacing it with extracts from books. Ofsted (2002) bemoaned this position in its evaluation of the first four years of the NLS. As Collins (2005: 10) observed: 'The significance of reading aloud to children should not be underestimated', whether to pre-school, primary or secondary school pupils, in bringing the text alive and facilitating a 'social construction of meaning' (Yandell, 2013). By establishing a shared experience and a 'community' of readers, children are enabled to access texts beyond their own reading ability, and to build up listening and concentration stamina. It also encourages critical reading and allows for discussion and to explore and dispute the meaning of the text (McDonald, 2004).

The small group 'guided reading' sessions did not follow the more open model of 'literature circles' pioneered in the US by Harste *et al.* (1989), Daniels (1994) and Schlick Noe and Johnson (1999). These aimed to transfer informal talk about books into a more organized strategy. In this format children chose texts in small groups to discuss, and took up roles to direct and steer the proceedings. This kind of social interaction can prompt children 'to ask new questions, to wonder and to make connections with their own experiences and with the experiences of others in the groups' (King and Briggs, 2005). Instead 'guided reading' is a much more tightly controlled, teacher-led experience. Choice of text is pre-determined and compatible with ability, and the focus of the session set by objectives dictated by the NLS. Fisher (2008: 25) found in the guided reading sessions she observed that there was no opportunity for children to engage in collaborative discussion, create meaning or develop 'personal, analytical and critical response'. And King (2001: 35) warns that:

> Unless teachers are concerned with how readers actually respond experientially, emotionally and aesthetically to the texts they read, reading them may well be seen as a necessary chore rather than as a means of delight and exploration.

It appears that a highly constrained view of the value of literacy still holds sway, dominated by objectives and targets that influence how teachers encourage children to engage with literature. Reasons for reading have been neglected in recent years, not made explicit, and assumed rather than discussed.

Reflections

While the dialogic method and critical literacy are seen as dynamic and inspirational practices, and have many proponents, researchers often find that the reality in the classroom is somewhat different (Marshall, 2006; Cliff Hodges, 2010). Government agendas, curriculum constraints and formal, entrenched organization and methods impinge in many ways on eliciting reader response and facilitating any real discussion of children's analysis of texts, to the frustration of many in education. Furthermore, reading books that elicit creative and intellectually demanding responses and have 'transformative potential' and 'emotional power' (O'Sullivan and McGonigle, 2010) does not feature largely in the curriculum. While writers such as Roche (2015) continue to offer practical advice for teachers on

'Critical Thinking and Book Talk – CT and BT', discussion of children's responses to literature is often based unconsciously on tenets of reader response theory, the dialogic method and critical literacy. It is therefore useful for teachers to understand the origins of these ideas and to recognize such theoretical positions in practical day-to-day classroom work.

Chapter 4

A case study of two texts

Introduction

The two books I focus on are by well-known authors and are commonly used in English classrooms. *The Colour of Home* by Mary Hoffman, illustrated by Karin Littlewood and published by Frances Lincoln in 2002, is aimed at upper Key Stage 1 and lower Key Stage 2 – 6 to 9-year-olds – while *The Other Side of Truth* by Beverley Naidoo, published by Puffin in 2000, and also available on story-tape, is suitable for upper Key Stage 2 and lower Key Stage 3 (10 to 13-year-olds). In this chapter, I consider the books in depth, outline my study of them in the primary classroom and locate that study in the context of others that listen to children's responses to texts.

Two texts in detail
The Colour of Home

The Colour of Home is an illustrated, colourful picturebook set over 12 spreads. It has a traditional format, integrating text into the illustrations, with a clear interaction between the two. The text tells the story of Hassan, a Somali boy, who arrives in a school in the UK, feeling disorientated and homesick and speaking hardly any English. However, he paints a vivid picture of his home in Somalia, showing all his relations and attendant animals, including his cat, outside. But when the teacher praises his picture, he paints flames, blood, a gun being fired and smudges out his uncle from the illustration. When his mother comes to fetch him, he doesn't want to show her the picture: 'He didn't want his mother to be sad' (no page numbers). The teacher organizes for a Somali interpreter to come in, and Hassan explains his picture to them both. Soldiers had come and killed his uncle, among others, while he hid, terrified, under a bed (see Figure 4.1).

"When the soldiers came, I hid in my cousins' room," he said. "I didn't find out what happened to my uncle until later. My father came and fetched me out from under the bed and said we were leaving.

Figure 4.1: Detail of spread in *The Colour of Home* (Hoffman, 2002). © Frances Lincoln Ltd.

"We all went straight away, except my uncle. We had no luggage, only my father's prayer mat and *qu'ran*, hidden in Naima's bag of nappies. I wanted to take Musa, my cat, but my mother said we must save ourselves and not the animals. I cried then, not for my uncle, but for Musa.

The following pages show the family fleeing to safety, first on foot then by ship from Mogadishu to Mombasa, where they stayed in a refugee camp. After some time and following hardships, they continue by plane to the UK, where 'our new country seemed all cold and grey'. After relating these events, Hassan goes off to play football with a classmate. Later he paints another picture of his home in Somalia, this time with no people, only animals. This picture he shows proudly to his mother, and when they reached their new home in the UK, his father pins the picture up on the wall. Hassan begins to notice the colours in his new home, the sun comes out. In the final sentence he decides: 'Tomorrow he would ask Miss Kelly to tell him the word for home.'

The Colour of Home was published in 2002 by Frances Lincoln, a publishing company well known for its multicultural perspective. The book is unusual in that it seeks to represent the refugee experience for a younger age group, and is arguably the first picturebook on the topic to be published in the UK (Hope, 2007). I have introduced this book in many contexts, both in whole school assemblies during Refugee Week and in my work at Goldsmiths on the Initial Teacher Education course, in the context of English, Geography, Citizenship and Diversity sessions. Reading the book with children or student teachers has always engendered lively debate as to its use and appropriateness in a Key Stage 1 classroom.

The Other Side of Truth

The Other Side of Truth is a chapter book of 225 pages. It follows the story of siblings Sade, 12, and Femi, 10, the children of Folarin Solaja, a journalist in Lagos, Nigeria, under General Abacha's dictatorship. As Folarin leaves the house one Monday morning, having spent the weekend writing a controversial article, unknown assassins open fire and shoot the children's mother by mistake. The description of this event is deliberately oblique, and must stand as one of the most dramatic novel-openers of any children's book to date:

> Sade is slipping her English book into her schoolbag when Mama screams. Two sharp cracks splinter the air. She hears her father's fierce cry, rising, falling.
>
> 'No! No!'
>
> The revving of a car and skidding of tyres smother his voice.

Her bag topples from the bed, spilling books, pen and pencil onto the floor. She races to the verandah, pushing past Femi in the doorway. His body is wooden with fright.

'Mama mi?' she whispers.

Papa is kneeling in the driveway, Mama partly curled up against him. One bare leg stretches out in front of her. His strong hands grip her, trying to halt the growing scarlet monster. But it has already spread down her bright white nurse's uniform. It stains the earth around them.

A few seconds, that is all. Later, it will always seem much longer.

(Naidoo, 2000: 1)

This dramatic and violent opening led Pinsent (2005: 204) to describe the book as 'one of the most hard-hitting children's novels dealing with the plight of asylum seekers'. Giles (2009: 348) notes: 'Any expectations that readers might have that all Africans are impoverished are dispelled by the English book, which signals the fact that Sade and her family are members of Nigeria's professional middle class.' As the reality of the situation hits home, their uncle decides that for the children's own safety, they need to be swiftly smuggled out of the country and sent to their uncle in the UK, with Folarin to follow later.

Sade and Femi accompany Mrs Bankole on a flight to London, posing as her children, but she abandons them at Victoria station, where they find themselves virtually penniless, cold and afraid. They try to track down their uncle at 'The London College of Art' but he is away, so they are fostered, at first temporarily, and then for longer by a Jamaican couple. On attending school they come in contact with local children, some of whom bully and intimidate them. Sade also meets Mariam, a Somali girl in her class and hears Mariam's story of persecution at the hands of President Barre and his regime. Similar to Hassan in *The Colour of Home*, Mariam's family had fled on foot and by donkey to Mogadishu and from there by boat to Kenya, where they stayed in a refugee camp in Mombassa for six years, before making the journey to the UK. Meanwhile, Folarin enters the country illegally, but is arrested and detained. The children, desperate to help, manage to gain access to the BBC Newsroom where they are instrumental in publicizing their father's story. This leads to his release pending an asylum review. The story ends with the children reunited with their father for Christmas, but still facing an uncertain future.

As the author's note at the end explains (Naidoo, 2000: 225), the novel is set in 1995, immediately after the death of Ken Saro-Wiwa, a Nigerian writer, who was hanged for upholding the rights of the Ogoni people against the corrupt extraction of oil and consequent pollution of the area by foreign multinationals. The note gives the context to three political figures mentioned: Ken Saro-Wiwa, General Abacha, and President Barre of Somalia. In this way Beverley Naidoo deliberately uses 'intertextuality' – a term coined by Kristeva (1966) – as she interweaves fact with fiction and draws attention to this literary device. *The Other Side of Truth* received several awards, including the Carnegie Medal for 2000, the Nestlé Smarties Book Prize Silver Medal in 2000 and the Jane Addams Children's Book Award in 2002. It was also named Honour Book in an International Board on Books for Young People (IBBY) in 2002.

Initial comparisons

The first obvious difference when comparing the two books is that they address children of different age ranges. This is reflected in the ages of the protagonists and how the authors craft the refugee experience and related issues to suit the readership they envisage. As we can see, *The Colour of Home*, conveying Hassan's thoughts and feelings, encapsulates how a child comes to be a refugee and what might then ensue in their lives. *The Other Side of Truth* has a longer, more in-depth narrative, and deals also with all aspects of the experience, including a tale within a tale of another and more brutal story that illustrates the heterogeneity of forced migration stressed by Rutter (2006).

Another obvious difference is that *The Colour of Home* is a picturebook, giving us visual as well as verbal images in what Lewis describes as 'the bifurcated nature of the form' (1996: 207). The illustrations are as important as the narrative because of the interplay of words and images, and at times the pictures offer arguably greater depth than the text. In Nikolajeva and Scott's terms, *The Colour of Home* would be classified as a 'complementary' picture book, in that 'the words tell us exactly the same story as the one we can 'read' from the pictures' (2001: 14) and fill in the gaps left by each other. *The Other Side of Truth* contains no pictures, apart from on the cover, and leaves us to imagine the appearance of the characters, places, scenery and buildings that it describes. In a picturebook the illustrator's background knowledge and perspective are key parts in conveying the story and crystallizing the interpretation through the images presented.

Nikolajeva and Scott (2001: 29) reflect on 'whose book is it?', highlighting the difference between authors who are also illustrators, author–illustrator teams who work cooperatively and authors and illustrators who work separately, as in the case of *The Colour of Home*. Hoffman stated in my interview with her that she was happy with the work of the illustrator Karin Littlewood, because: 'She really understood what was wanted and she did a lot of research in local schools.'

Artist Karen Littlewood saw the illustrator's role as being equally important as the author's, in that the pictures operate in conjunction with the text and can be 'read' on their own, telling the story through visual means:

> I'm a storyteller with my images. That's the job of an illustrator. Because if there's a child who doesn't have English as a first language, he'll read the picture. So every single one of them is like that, they've got clues, they've got moments, so that if you take the writing away they know exactly what's happened. And it's as strong as that. The universal language is pictures.

The study
Rationale
Having identified a significant genre developing in its own right, I wanted to consider the use of children's literature for educating non-refugee children about the experience of others, and engage with the broader question of whether literature has the potential to change attitudes. I also intended to investigate how far children's literature about refugees could validate the lived experience of children who had links with forced migration. 'Validate' seemed the correct term to use, given its meaning to:

> demonstrate or support the truth or value of; make or declare legally valid; recognize or affirm the validity or worth of (a person or their feelings or opinions); cause (a person) to feel valued or worthwhile.
>
> (Oxford Dictionaries, n.d.)

As regards the refugee experience, 'validate' implies both the endorsement of a real situation and feelings emanating from this and a recognized official position. The latter is of less concern to children, but is nevertheless an important part of the right to claim sanctuary.

I chose these two books because they are so widely used in lower upper primary classrooms throughout the UK and beyond at present, and because they have high literary merit. Throughout the post-millennium explosion of texts about the refugee experience, these two titles have stood the test of time, demonstrating that they are intelligent and intelligible depictions of circumstances that can lead people to decide to flee, follow the refugee child protagonists on their journey to safety and deal with the problems of adaption and assimilation once they arrive. *Refugee Boy* by Benjamin Zephaniah, is the most often quoted book dealing with refugee issues, but it is more suited to lower secondary age readers.

The design of the research

Making a vertical case study of each book, through an author and illustrator/teacher/child trajectory, I traced the motivations and aims of the two authors and illustrator for creating the book, how the books were mediated by teachers in the primary classroom and how refugee and non-refugee children read, understood and responded to them. To focus on the dynamic between author/illustrator, text and reader, I carried out a series of semi-structured interviews with the authors and illustrator – Mary Hoffman, Beverley Naidoo and Karin Littlewood – an expert on refugee education, Jill Rutter, six teachers and a total of 27 children, two individually and 25 in discussion groups. Apart from the three creators and Rutter, who are well-known in the public domain, I've given the other participants pseudonyms to preserve their anonymity.

I also carried out classroom observations in five classes across two schools, took extensive field notes, considered lesson plans and schemes of work and analysed children's written and drawn responses to the books. Being able to gather a wide range of data lead to a useful oversight of the area. But as Hammersley and Atkinson (1983: 199) point out: 'One should not adopt a naively optimistic view that the aggregation of data from different sources will unproblematically add up to produce a more complete picture.'

The field of study

I undertook the research in two schools, referred to as Marlowe School and Creekside School, across three year groups: Year 1 (ages 5–6), Year 3 (ages 7–8) and Year 5 (ages 9–10). In Year 1 (Marlowe School), *The Colour of Home* was read in one lesson only, while in Creekside School the focus on the book straddled two lessons, allowing me to engage in lengthier discussions with the children. In Year 3 *The Colour of Home* was introduced over three weeks as part of the Literacy curriculum and similarly in Year 5 *The Other*

Side of Truth was studied over six weeks, which made more observations possible.

Both schools had around 450 children on roll and were chosen for their location in South East London, which serves a highly diverse community that includes several refugee families. This made it a particularly rich environment to research how children from diverse ethnic and cultural backgrounds – many of whom would be migrants, and possibly refugees – interpret texts. Both schools provided me with data from the official school database – about country of origin, languages spoken and the ethnicities of the children on roll but no official record is made of refugee status – so this could only be an estimated number. It is important that many children would not have experienced the flight to safety themselves, being second generation. However, the refugee experience can leave a long-term legacy (see Chapter 1). Families are deeply affected by sudden loss, dislocation, homelessness, unemployment and social isolation. This impacts on the child to a greater or lesser extent, possibly through news of ongoing conflict and the arrival of family and friends from the country of origin fleeing persecution.

Using school data

Statistically significant data from the two schools showed that around a quarter to one-third of pupils were identified by their parents on admissions forms as Other Black African. Some of these children may be refugees or from a refugee background – they come from such places as the Ivory Coast, the Congo or Rwanda, for example – however, many will not. Most of the children who come from Nigeria, for example, where there is little ethnic conflict, are in the UK while their parents study, or have had a family reunion. Also a significant number of children were identified as Somali or Vietnamese, all of whom are likely to be from a refugee background (usually second or third generation). In addition there were White European children such as Kosovars or pre-accession Roma from Bulgaria and Romania, from families who are also likely to have arrived here seeking asylum.

I uncovered more information by looking at the languages spoken by the children in the school. Potential refugee children, or children with a refugee background, include those who speak Albanian/Shqip (possibly of families from Kosovo), Pashto and Farsi (probably from Afghan families), Arabic (from Algeria, Yemen and elsewhere) and Kurdish. Furthermore, many of the French speakers were from Francophone Africa, most likely from countries generating refugees, and the Spanish speakers may well have been from countries in South America like Colombia, where rebels have recently made a peace deal with government forces ending 50 years of factional strife that has led many families to seek asylum in the UK. Adding all this data together, it is highly likely that roughly a quarter of the children on roll in each school are refugees or part of a family that has a refugee background.

Listening to children

Meek asserts that we need studies of children's literature that include the opinions of young readers today. Adults writing about the subject bring the sum total of their experience to the text, and can have a closed view of the impact of a book. 'We need to see children "performing" meaning under the influence of texts and learning to traffic in possibilities' (sic) (1987: 113). Hollindale (1988: 4) differentiates between 'book people' and 'child people' who engage in debate 'about differences of literary merit (book people) and about the influence on readers of a book's social and political values (child people)'.

To engage in 'childist' criticism (Hunt, 1991) children themselves must be consulted about the literature we choose for them, and their voices must be heard in critiquing it. As Barrs and Cork (2001: 14) put it: 'We are not very good at discovering what children think they are doing when they read, but if we ask them, they tell us things that we, as their teachers, might never have thought of.' Arizpe and Styles (2003: 248) found that when they 'listened intently to what they (children) had to say', teaching and learning became more effective. While recognizing that this is often difficult practically in a busy classroom, they felt strongly that sustained listening to children talking about texts needs to be included as a valued element of the National Literacy Strategy. We should extend the 'politics of voice' to child readers too. Yet as Gubar (2013) – who calls for a rise in the 'risky business' of including children in children's literature criticism – notes, few studies have included children's opinions of a book's content and subject matter, instead of simply assessing the pedagogical implications of textual discussion.

To investigate the possibilities of changing attitudes and challenging racism through literature, Naidoo (1992) spent a year with a class of young white people engaged in reading literature from perspectives that strongly indict racism. Although she observed instances when children had been opened up to 'difference', she reported no concrete evidence of fostering anti-racism but felt that the effects of the learning experience might not be apparent until some time later. On a more positive note, which is perhaps linked to the younger age of the participants, Lehr worked with a class of

US fourth-graders (approximately 9 years old) for two months, observing, teaching and talking with children and introducing them to stories about children 'living under oppression and fleeing oppression' (1995: 116). The stories included *Journey to Jo'Burg* by Beverley Naidoo (1985) and *Kiss the Dust* by Elizabeth Laird (1991). What emerged was that the books 'increased the children's knowledge about the world, expanded their personal views about freedom, and provided shocking glimpses of social injustice' (Lehr, 1995: 117).

Lehr's vision of the transformational power of literature is clear: 'It took them in at one level and left them at another' (ibid.: 119). However, she reports being shocked by one child's reaction, concluding that 'the literature is untamed, but so were their responses' (ibid.: 115). She also highlights an interesting perspective on why teachers might shy away from class discussions that link children's books with their own lives:

> The personal transaction that occurs is not prescribed; teachers cannot know what will happen when children begin reading and talking about real events, real problems, real episodes from history, spiritual journeys, and reflections.
>
> (ibid.: 116)

In one of the few studies of children's response to literature dealing with the Holocaust, Nicholson used *Rose Blanche* in a series of 'bookshare' sessions with pupils in Year 5 and Year 6 (9 to 11-year-olds). She pointed out that 'by glimpsing, from the safe distance of a book, a darker side of life' (1999: 59), children can extend their engagement with the human condition. In relation to writing about the Holocaust, Sokoloff describes herself as 'hungry for more evidence about how children react to the books they read' (Sokoloff, 2005: 185), and I agree. While adults review, ponder and discuss, the real subjects of the works – the children – sometimes get forgotten. An illuminating study by Habib (2008), which links closely with my own, interrogated reader response to sharing *Refugee Boy* as the set text in a South London secondary classroom. It concluded that the experience had a considerable social, emotional and political impact on Habib's class.

Reflections

Choosing two texts to focus on closely along a vertical trajectory proved worthwhile. By observing and talking to teachers and children in classrooms I explored whether author/illustrator motivations and aims were born out in practice. I also sought practical ideas of how to best engage children with the refugee situation, using the books as a catalyst and broadening out to promote discussion and response on a range of issues. I gained an insight into how individual children made meaning, based on their background and life experience. This was born out in written, drawn and dramatized production, but also by setting up opportunities whereby the children's voices could be heard.

Chapter 5
Two authors and an illustrator
Motivations and aims

For Suleiman, Josè, Naima, Dagma, Flavia, Brunilda, Hagar, Jo, Hasna and all the others who had to leave their first homes and were brave enough to find new ones – M.H.

(Dedication at the front of *The Colour of Home* by
Mary Hoffman (2002))

Introduction
Despite reader response focusing less on the author and more on the reader, 'critical literacy' holds that all texts are 'constructed' to furnish an agenda. To unravel what this might be, we need to find out who has produced the book, in what context and for whom. For this reason I followed a vertical trajectory in looking at the motivations and aims of the authors, Mary Hoffman and Beverley Naidoo respectively, in writing *The Colour of Home* and *The Other Side of Truth*. I wanted to see whether they had a clearly identifiable vision and, if so, to examine whether this was realized in practice with children in primary classrooms. Picturebooks generate meaning through both text and image, so I also sought the viewpoint of the illustrator of *The Colour of Home,* Karin Littlewood. The following chapter is based on interviews with the two authors and the illustrator and includes excerpts from an interview with Jill Rutter, a refugee education expert and prolific writer in the field.

Background to the authors and illustrator
Mary Hoffman
Mary Hoffman grew up in Hampshire, and read English Literature at Cambridge University (Hoffman, n.d). To date, she has had nearly 90 children's books published and focuses mainly on historical fiction, producing series of books in the same genre. She is also notable for writing picturebooks for younger children – such as *Amazing Grace* (1991), *Grace and Family* (1995) and *An Angel Just Like Me* (1997) – that deal with issues

of diversity. As she explained in the interview: 'my children are of mixed race in that my husband is half Indian ... they would talk about this sort of thing and I thought, "you never see this in books"'. This realization led Hoffman to tackle more broadly the position of those who are not from white, middle-class, two-parent families.

Duffy (1995) suggests that it is the descendants of migrants, rather than migrants themselves, who write about the theme of exile, and in my initial research into the authors of the books for children about the refugee experience, I suggested that many have a connection with migration that is not immediately obvious (see Chapter 2). Hoffman, for example, explained to me that the theme of migration has reverberations both for her husband's and her own family, her great grandfather having moved from Germany, perhaps because he was Jewish, and experiencing racism on arrival in the UK. So Hoffman is not a migrant herself, but her wider family has experienced migration and persecution.

Karin Littlewood

Karin Littlewood is originally from Yorkshire and studied graphic design at Northumbria University, followed by an MA at Manchester Metropolitan University, where she specialized in illustration (Littlewood's website). She has collaborated on over 40 children's books published in the UK and worldwide, and now writes and illustrates her own work. She has often been asked to work on texts that deal with what she describes as 'tricky subject matter ... subjects that a lot of people don't really want to discuss, but they need discussing'. Littlewood feels it was this focus that led to her being approached to illustrate *The Colour of Home*.

Littlewood also has migration in her family background. Her German mother came to England as a translator in the early 1950s and married her British father, a leading light in the Twin Towns initiative. This was intended to foster friendship and understanding across countries. As a child she experienced anti-German prejudice at school: 'people called me a Nazi and said my grandad was Hitler. I knew that wasn't true. It didn't bother me.' Although she has never been to Somalia, Karen travelled around Kenya for several months in the early 1980s with her college friend who was from a Gujarati Jain family. This gave her some insight to draw on when illustrating *The Colour of Home*.

The images Karin Littlewood created have had a strong impact on the children's 'reading' and interpretation of the book (see Chapter 7). However, her position as an outsider to the world she depicts pictorially is contentious, as is Hoffman's role of authoring the experiences of 'the other'

– discussed in Chapter 2. Noll (2003) maintains that because authors and illustrators play a part in children's developing knowledge and attitudes, it is crucial that they be responsible to their young audiences for portraying cultures accurately. She argues that, though challenging, being an outsider does not necessarily preclude one from authentically depicting a culture, but writing and illustrating a book that is culturally authentic is difficult without some kind of relevant experience.

Beverley Naidoo

Beverley Naidoo has written significantly fewer books than Hoffman (Naidoo, n.d.) – six novels to date and ten picturebooks and collections of short stories. Her first three novels for children and a collection of short stories were set in South Africa, with *Journey to Jo'burg* (1985) banned there until 1991. She has also published her PhD, which looked at the transformatory potential of children's literature that tackles racism when shared with a Secondary class of all-white adolescents, and found very little evidence of changing attitudes in the short term (Naidoo, 1992 – see Chapter 4). After elections in South Africa became more democratic in 1994, Naidoo turned to writing about children from other African countries. *The Other Side of Truth* and its sequel *Web of Lies* (2004b), for example, deal with children coming to the UK as refugees from Nigeria.

Naidoo was born into a white, middle-class family in Johannesburg, and grew up under the repressive apartheid regime. She graduated from the University of Witwatersrand in 1963, but at the age of 21, was detained without trial for eight weeks in solitary confinement for her activities in the anti-apartheid movement. After this she fled to the UK in 1965, becoming a refugee herself, and was unable to return to her homeland until 1993. Although she acknowledged that this pre-migration experience was in common with her characters:

> … it was only later when I came to look back … and thought that indeed I had come from South Africa as a refugee, but being white, as having this colour skin I was not regarded as a refugee … I didn't experience the hostility that I would have experienced as a black South African coming in … and I wasn't experiencing racism, but nevertheless there was the element of disconnection anyway.

In this way Naidoo had a direct connection with Sade, the protagonist in the book, having experienced the same dislocation from the past and disconnection from the present.

I didn't actually realize it at the time that I was writing Sade's flashbacks, I just knew that she was going to have flashbacks. And it was only, you know, rationalizing it later, and then realizing, hold on, isn't that what I myself did, you know, when your head is somewhere different from where your body is?

This direct experience is unusual amongst those who write about the refugee experience for children, as we saw in Chapter 2.

Pinsent (2005: 204) points out that Naidoo's fiction: 'is more strongly politicized than that of many children's writers, perhaps because her identity as a white South African did not allow her to shirk the issue of inequality'. This may be a factor, but it is worth observing that being a white South African does not automatically politicize a person. However, Naidoo's family had yet more migration in their history during the nineteenth and early twentieth centuries (Naidoo, 2009), her father moving from Cornwall where tin mines were closing, to South Africa where gold was being discovered. Her mother's family also fled the pogroms against Jews in Russia and thus experienced persecution themselves. Furthermore, Naidoo's husband, whose name she has taken, was also a South African exile, of Indian origin. This has interesting parallels with Hoffman, as both women have chosen to embrace diversity in their marriages.

Debates and dilemmas
Giving voice to the voiceless and author authenticity
In writing about the refugee journey, a situation she has no direct experience of, Hoffman could be said to be 'speaking for the subaltern' (adapted from Spivak, 1988) a position she was clearly conscious of. However, Spivak's case is that if no one were to 'speak for the subaltern', their voices would not be heard. This is Hoffman's position too when she talked about being commissioned to write the book: 'I was the person who was asked. What should I say? 'Oh no, I don't think I should do that. I think you should wait until a refugee is ready to do it'? It's a question of, 'Do we need the book, or not?' Hoffman said it takes time for refugees to contemplate or be in a position to author a book, particularly in a second language to their own, and especially a children's book, which may be outside their cultural domain (King *et al.*, 1995).

Naidoo felt strongly that it was important to encourage people who had had the refugee experience to write: 'that's an important political issue, and we should be looking to see ways in which that could be … because we could all benefit. We would all gain from hearing those voices.' When

I asked her whether she saw her outsider viewpoint as a problem, Naidoo fiercely defended the writer's responsibility and integrity, pointing out that without this, much literature would not exist: 'I mean, can we never write a novel about the 16th century because we haven't lived then? Can men never write about women, and women about men, you know, adults about children?' However, Naidoo did recognize her own limitations when she conceded that she hadn't felt able to base the whole novel in Nigeria, having only visited the country for one weekend. 'I wouldn't have dared to attempt that.'

Nevertheless both authors could be seen as mouthpieces of the refugee experience for children, drawing on their imagination, their research, and their credentials as writers to explore and distil a situation for others. Both felt strongly that the writer's lived experience is irrelevant, and that it is the quality of the writing that is the issue in any literary effort. Littlewood felt the same, defending her position with passion:

> Does it matter when you're drawing pictures, what colour you are? It doesn't matter what colour, what race, whatever, as long as you've got the empathy, as long as you've done your homework and you do it in the right way, nobody's bothered. ... If you get the right author and the right illustrator, it's magic and it doesn't matter.

In seeming contradiction to this remark, however, Littlewood was thrilled to recount what she saw as one of her greatest accolades, which outlines one of the enduring debates about author authenticity:

> I do have a friend who works with *Medecins Sans Frontieres* and he worked in Somalia in incredibly dangerous situations. He took (the book) over and gave it to all the doctors and they said 'oh! Does she know Somalia? Has she been to Somalia? Is she Somali? Is her husband Somali?' And you know, that was great, fantastic. And I thought ... I've done my job.

Furthermore, Hoffman, Naidoo and Rutter all acknowledged in their interviews that someone who had been through the refugee experience, though able to claim more authenticity, would not necessarily write a better book than an experienced writer describing the events. They also felt that the book should be judged on its literary merits and potential to engage the reader (see Chapter 2).

Issues-based literature and 'heavy' themes

When asked if her book had a message or purpose, Hoffman was clear:

> Well the message really is to encourage tolerance and
> understanding and acceptance because, um, and to be welcoming
> to anyone to whom we give a home in this country, because most
> of us, thankfully, will never know what it's like to have gone
> through what these people have gone through.

However, when I asked Beverley Naidoo whether she considered her work
to be 'issues-based', she became very animated:

> Absolutely not. Would you say to Nadine Gordimer, what issue
> have you got in this book? No, we don't do this with adult
> writers. It's something very peculiar when it comes to children's
> literature. And I don't know why it is. Maybe it's because of the
> world of education and in some way we've got to categorize it.

Naidoo preferred the term 'witness literature' (Naidoo, 2004a), following the
definition of celebrated South African writer Nadine Gordimer, as 'a genre
of circumstance or time and place' (Gordimer, 2002: 6) where the writer,
although not necessarily part of the culture about which they are writing,
bears witness to the experiences of those caught up in a specific time of
historical significance. It could be said that Gordimer's work is the collective
story of a 'significant life experience' through a mediator who testifies or
bears witness, as a 'testimonial novel' (Bickford, 2008: 133). Naidoo echoes
this by explaining that the stories and characters in witness literature 'are
umbilically connected to their wider society' (Naidoo, 2004a: 4). Writers
like Naidoo attempt to stimulate 'critical literacy' among their readership,
challenging them to ask questions, 'showing not telling', and hoping that
her books will 'disrupt assumptions and beliefs that are otherwise taken for
granted without reflection' (Giles, 2009: 344).

Another area of criticism levelled at books about the refugee
experience for children – sometimes by my own students – is that they
deal with 'heavy' themes that are too old for the age-group, and could be
distressing for children to read about. Reynolds suggests that there are
tensions inherent in 'socially committed' (2005: 191) children's literature
between preserving innocence, naivety and optimism about the future, and
developing social understanding. However, Rutter felt in her interview that
much writing for young children contains violent and frightening elements,
and she argued that this was not a reason for 'shying away' from certain

books. Littlewood echoed this when discussing *The Colour of Home*, in which she chose to portray the violent events in the story using symbolism (Lewis, 2001):

> The reason why it's so popular … you know every school has got it … is because it does tell the truth. It says they had to leave home for a very good reason. I put a big pair of boots in there, you know for the soldier and I didn't draw the whole soldier … I put the boots, and it's up to the children to think then 'What does that mean?' … and the butt of a gun, so I feed them little bits of information.

Littlewood explained how she had also introduced the book to very young children and built on their empathy and desire to help classmates. This links to the social action or 'praxis' advocated as part of critical pedagogy (Freire and Macedo, 1987 – see Chapter 3):

> I have actually even worked with Nursery on that one. I just do it in a different way. We draw pictures of boats and aeroplanes, and I say 'he had to leave his home, but you'd be alright. You'd look after him.' … and they say 'Yes, we'd look after him.'

Naidoo held that children are exposed to violence on television and in video games, but do not actually confront the reality of blood and gore in armed combat, and its consequences for human beings' lives. She felt that out of a better understanding came positive action for change, led by young people to influence their future:

> If we don't open out to young people, to keep them sheltered from it, how do we ever help them to think 'what do we do about it?' Yes, I can understand when that young person says, well I'm going to go and I'm going to boycott this or I'm going to do that, to feel a release and that actually coming together we can deal with it.

Trauma discourses and the concept of resilience

Both authors were very aware of the concepts of trauma and resilience, and spoke about them in their interviews. When Hoffman summarized the story in her initial synopsis to the publisher, she wrote: 'It is about the adaptability of human beings and their resilience and willingness to start again when life has dealt them an appalling hand.'

Although she mentioned trauma at one point in the interview, it was only a fleeting reference, and she quickly reverted to the theme of resilience: 'I thought it was just right to do it this way, to show just how awful an experience could be, and how traumatizing, and yet how you could recover from it.' Hoffman was also aware of the potential refugee reader at this point and felt the book had a positive message for them too. She had wanted to find a way of saying: 'You can have an experience like this and come through it, and survive and life doesn't end.'

Naidoo had researched the work of psychologists writing about how children deal with trauma, and in her interview, she spoke constantly about the power of imagination, taking her readers on a journey, entering into the lived experience of others, echoing the notion of Bishop's 'windows and mirrors': 'You know, these children have gone through traumatizing experiences, and I think we have to be sensitive to their trauma. But what we can draw on is the strength of character in these young people.' On one hand, she strives to portray resilience, as she said in her own words: 'I think I've always felt a big responsibility in that I have to bring my characters through, my main characters through, so that at the end of the novel, they have to survive.' On the other hand she also is careful to show that refugee children's problems are not all over once they reach the host country, and that their struggles continue in the post-migration ecology on many levels – see Hamilton and Moore's three stages of the refugee experience (2004).

The writing and illustrating process
Motivation, purpose and aims

Because of the perspective of 'difference' in her writing, Hoffman related how publisher Frances Lincoln, had approached her with a very simple brief, to write a picturebook about the refugee experience. Hoffman explained that she and the publisher had not discussed the message or purpose of the book any further, and she was left to her own devices to find her way of meeting the requirement. Hoffman was clear in her own head about the dual purpose of her enterprise, which again had a 'windows and mirrors' paradigm:

> I think it seemed obvious to me that the purpose was to write about the asylum seeker experience for two reasons, so that asylum seekers could see themselves reflected in a book, which they weren't at the moment, and that those who were not asylum seekers, could understand what the asylum seeker experience was … I thought the most important thing really is for people

who are not in that situation, to put themselves imaginatively in that situation, and see what it would take to uproot you from everything you knew.

Frances Lincoln approached Littlewood to illustrate the book after it was written, based on her previous work:

> I think it was because they knew that I could handle ... all the things that that book throws at you. I was sent the text and I looked at it and I thought 'Wow! This is going to be a really strong book, and it's going to be very difficult, but I'm really keen on doing it.'

Naidoo's motivation was more nuanced. Having already written three books from the point of view of Black South African children, she was influenced by major political events that made her change tack in her work. In 1990 Nelson Mandela was released from jail and the country began slowly to move toward universal suffrage, with the first democratic elections in 1994. Having written so graphically about the effects of apartheid on children's lives, Naidoo felt, as that brutal system came to an end, that she would look elsewhere for stories that would challenge injustice. Her aim was more subtle: 'I'm always interested in what's hidden and what isn't immediately obvious and so I knew there would be interesting stories to tell from the refugee perspective, because they are the people who are invisible.' When asked if she intended the book to have a message or purpose, Naidoo became almost angry, probably because this is a question to which she has had to respond continually: 'No, I never write for a message or a purpose, because otherwise wouldn't I rather be a journalist, wouldn't I rather be a propagandist, wouldn't I rather get up on my soap box in Hyde Park corner?' Naidoo constantly used the metaphor of the writer taking the reader on a journey, engaging them in asking questions and exploring what it is to be human at a certain point in history, or contemporary society.

Influences on the writers
After being approached by Frances Lincoln, Hoffman thought back to two autobiographical pieces that were written for her when she was Writer in Residence in 1997, as part of the European Year Against Racism. About the first one she said:

> There was a little boy from Zaire whose major preoccupation had been that he had to leave his dog behind. He was a refugee or an asylum seeker ... But he, all his emotions about what had

happened to him had been focused on being separated from this dog, and he was looking forward to getting another dog here.

The story about the dog became the basis for Hassan's cat Musa in the book, who he misses desperately. The other piece of writing was by a Somali boy, a copy of whose work Hoffman gave me at the time of the interview:

> When I was little I lived in Somalia with my mum, dad, two brothers, two sisters and three cousins in a big house in a big village. The village had one main road. We had 3 cars. My uncle killed a fox with his car. One very hot day the soldiers came to fight. They came in trucks. Came guns. It was noisy. I hid in my brother's room. They stopped fighting. My family got in they [sic] cars and went to another country. The first time we tae [sic] to England they wouldn't let us ... and the second time ... us stay. I felt shy because I didn't speak English. I went to school then I learned [some parts illegible].

It is interesting that this extended family lived in a big house and owned three cars, which they used for their escape, whereas Hassan's family travel for miles on foot. As discussed in Chapter 1, many refugees come from urban environments, where they have lived wealthy lives by comparison to the rural population, and only experience poverty and overcrowding following migration: 'I'd not settled on which African country he comes from, and I said I wanted it to be an actual named country, not just a vague amalgam of African countries', Hoffman told me. Researching statistics on asylum seekers and refugees showed her that after Hispanics, the largest non-white asylum-seeking groups in the UK and the US were Somalis. She therefore decided to make the protagonist Somali.

Similarly, *The Other Side of Truth* is set in an identified African country, its action located in Lagos, Nigeria, the name of its first chapter. Naidoo (2009) describes in detail the process and influences that informed her choice of subject matter for the book. As a keen follower of African politics, she was moved by the execution of Ken Saro-Wiwa. The book opens on the Monday after his execution. Naidoo researched newspaper articles at the time, one example of the 'intertextuality' (Kristeva, 1966) that makes the novel so rich and real. In fact she classes herself as a special kind of writer, who is influenced directly by historical events: 'This is living history in a way. Writers like myself, who write out of real life, we're writing about those real situations. Yes, we are drawing on a very rich fabric of reality.' Shortly after arriving in the UK, Naidoo met a PhD student who was one of the first lecturers at the University of Ife, in the North of Nigeria. She befriended him and his wife and has maintained a lifelong, family friendship with them. This friend was elected a senator in Nigeria, but after surviving an assassination attempt and becoming disillusioned by the deep corruption in Nigerian politics, fled to the UK as a refugee. I asked her if this man was the prototype for Sade and Femi's father in the novel, and although she felt that basing a character on one person was 'just too constricting', she acknowledged that the family had given her a sense of:

> a family at a certain class level in Nigeria, and a certain cultural background, highly educated, tremendously valuing education, valuing traditional culture, which had a very strong moral framework, which believed ... that we should tell the truth.

Moreover, this middle-class, educated and politicized family acted informally as advisers and editors when Naidoo was writing her book.

Background research for writing and illustrating

Hoffman undertook extensive research when writing the book, 'far more than you would expect to do for a picturebook'. To deepen her understanding of the circumstances of forced migration, she attended a weekly drop-in centre and lunchtime club for refugees and asylum seekers at a Homeless Action unit, befriending and mixing with the refugee women she met there. In this way she had been privy to many details of the refugee experience, and had gathered a wealth of stories, which served to add clarity and incident to her book. One Somali woman's story in particular formed the basis of the journey taken by the family in *The Colour of Home*. They had left their home and gone to Mogadishu, taking a boat to Mombasa, where they stayed in a refugee camp for some time, long enough for the mother to conceive and bear her third child. Sparked by this, Hoffman's original intention had been to depict Hassan's life in the Kenyan transit refugee camp in greater detail, using details she had learnt of at the drop-in centre.

Hoffman also stressed how it had taken time to build up the trust of the women in the group and for these stories to emerge, the research engaging her emotionally and requiring greater personal commitment than she had intended. Nevertheless such interaction had made her acutely aware that asylum seekers were often wealthy people in their home country and that the contrast with their present situation was often hard to deal with: 'When you are an asylum seeker or refugee, your life gets stripped down to the basics ... They were women who had homes of their own, houses of their own, you know and it strips you of your pride.' Although she did not visit Somalia as part of her research, Hoffman also sought out a Somali women's group, and talked to four women to find out further details of Somali culture and family life. She gave the roughs of the book to the Somali women to look over, clearly sharing the enterprise in this respect.

Littlewood, too, looked close to home to verify her illustrations, finding a local school in which she met a young Somali mother and her son, who was a pupil there:

> I just took a few photos of the mother and the boy, and the little daughter ... But that came after I'd done all my sketches ... I just wanted to make sure it was accurate, and I wanted to know how her hijab was folded and things like that.

For the image of the house in Somali, which features prominently in the book, Littlewood accessed pictures from the University of London's School of Oriental and African Studies (SOAS), a leading institution for the study of Asia, Africa and the Middle East:

> You didn't have access to Google images then so I would have gone to SOAS ... and just saw something really simple that looked like it was homemade ... I needed it to stand out because it was very important. It was a small house where everybody lived inside.

In contrast, Naidoo's own South African background might have helped her understand Nigerian life. When researching the book, she visited Nigeria for a weekend, but also had many Nigerian friends to draw on for inspiration and advice. During her time in the country Naidoo was shown around by Nigerian friends, taking pictures, literally and mentally. She also felt that an author's attitude to their research was important in compounding authenticity: 'It depends how open you are to something, you can spend twenty, fifty years in a place and not actually really live it at all. You could spend a weekend in a place and thoroughly live it.'

Furthermore, Naidoo went to visit Rutter, then working as Education Officer at the Refugee Council, having already thought that she would write about two children arriving as refugees from Nigeria. She also went behind the scenes of the UK Border Agency at Heathrow Airport, to a detention centre in Oxfordshire and to Lunar House in Croydon, where the Immigration and Nationality Department orchestrate the asylum process. She asserted: 'it was vital to me not to be accused of fabrication' (Naidoo, 2009: 338). Naidoo also continued visiting many schools in her capacity as children's author, and talked to refugee children where she could, demonstrating an active interest in addressing the refugee perspective. In a final twist of 'life acting upon literature' (Naidoo, 2009: 340), as she went to accept the Smarties Silver Award for the book, Naidoo heard the shocking news of Damilola Taylor's death, an Angolan refugee boy murdered on his way home from Peckham Library. As a result she asked that the book to be dedicated to him, and organized an ongoing donation of 10p to the Refugee Council from every book sold.

Author/Illustrator perspectives on reader response

How to garner response is a challenge for any writer or illustrator, particularly if the book is targeted at young children, but it is still possible to uncover their reactions to the story, instead of relying on teachers and other interested parties. Visits to schools by my three interviewees were drawn on as evidence of reader response, as were communications from teachers and children, which were generally received by email.

Refugee children as readers

When I asked Hoffman how she thought refugee children would react to the book, particularly if they had been through a similar experience to Hassan, she stressed the potential catharsis such literature might provide:

> I hope that it would enable them to talk about their experience to somebody, as Hassan did in the story. Because he had all these nightmarish images in his head, and he was very blocked, and very unable to take part in what was going on in the school because of that.

The links with bibliotherapy – discussed in Chapter 3 – are clear. However, many teachers and student teachers question whether publicly introducing children's literature about refugees during lesson time is the best forum. This is a point worth considering. Littlewood also offered an intriguing insight into a different, perhaps more resilient approach, possibly drawing on her German mother's experience of the UK in the early 1950s:

> I also feel like they've left that world behind, it's the same post-war as well, you don't want to dwell on the past and I totally understand that as well, you don't want to talk about it because you're looking that way now, and it happened, but let it go and just look forward.

Naidoo had some evidence of reader response in the form of correspondences she had had with child readers. This of course is mainly due to the fact that her book targets an older age group, who are more likely and better able to express their reactions to a text:

> I had an extraordinary letter from a little boy on *Web of Lies*, (the sequel to *The Other Side of Truth*) an 11-year-old child in Islington, who said 'how do you know, how do you know me? How can someone like you write, you know … ? This is me.'

In common with Hoffman, Naidoo felt that her book would not be disturbing for refugee children if read in the classroom:

> My experience tells me, shows me that refugee children themselves will see a story as being about another refugee, as being distant and different from them, but will be kind of affirmed by somebody who's perhaps had similar experiences. There's an aesthetic distance.

Rutter affirmed this perspective when interviewed, stressing that sensitivity is key as is a good knowledge of the children in the class and their likely backgrounds. She echoed Naidoo's idea of distancing:

> I think for most children they can put an aesthetic distance between themselves and the child in the story, but be affirmed by that child having to survive new in Peckham in a kind of rough tough school … I think they won't relive the experience. Other things will trigger and make people re-live the experience, like news items, loud bangs.

Littlewood also stressed the positive opportunities for connection *The Colour of Home* offered newly arrived refugee children. She felt that the illustrations could communicate the story for those who had only an elementary grasp of English. Her mantra was that 'illustration is a universal language', which chimes with research by Arizpe *et al.* (2014b) into the use of a wordless picturebook that could reach across linguistic barriers:

> One of the schools that I went into, there was a little boy that had arrived from Afghanistan three days before in the classroom and we did this project … and I just remember this little boy with bright green eyes looking at me, hadn't a clue what had happened … and he did the most amazing drawings. He did the entire project that we were doing as well, if not better than a lot of the children there. I think it just meant that the children could understand.

One question I was particularly interested in asking was how the authors thought children might feel about the negative portrayal of their country in the books. As before, Hoffman had no evidence on which to base her assertions, a position she was honest about:

> I can only guess about that. Somalia *is* a violent, war-torn country and ... I think it would be wrong to show it in any other way and you do see that rather peaceful picture in the first image that you get, that he has in his mind when he's trying to paint his home, so it's not always like that, but in a way, that's the kind of idyll which is shattered by the experience that leads to their having to flee and that must be common to anyone who has lived in Somalia, surely?

Hoffman's stance was that the more storybooks there are about asylum seekers, the better, and Somalis in particular are little represented in the literature (see Chapter 2).

Although many years after its publication, Littlewood still carries out numerous visits to schools to engage children with *The Colour of Home*. She recounted that she has received constant positive feedback from Somali children on encountering the book, although many of them are now second-generation migrants:

> I was in a school last week and a little girl said 'My mum looks like that!' Its quite often the parents that have had that experience these days with the Somali community ... so they'll sort of say 'my grandma still lives over there', but they don't live in a little house like that ... so I think the fact that there's a lady with a hijab on there and the kids just love it.

However, Naidoo told me that when she went into schools and talked about *The Other Side of Truth*, she was at pains to stress that the time she was writing about was a specific point in the political development of Nigeria, not always the norm:

> I always point out that this is Nigeria at the time when the soldiers had stolen the government, and I point out if I'm talking with children that now Nigeria has a democratically elected government. I have to say that there are all kinds of problems.

This is an easier standpoint to take with regards to Nigeria than Somalia, which has had political instability and civil war – and consequently negative press – for far longer.

Non-refugee readers

From her frequent visits to schools Littlewood was well placed to assess how *The Colour of Home* might enable very young children from a non-refugee background to understand the situation more fully. She approached this by relating it to their own ubiquitous lived experience of starting school, and especially those who moved schools later on:

> We'll talk about what it feels like for them to come into a new school and some children go ... 'I came into the classroom and I didn't start off in this school and I was 10 when I came to this school' and to them it was as traumatic as, you know, coming from a different country, so they all know, even on that level.

Littlewood also reported that children made direct links between the book and their newly arrived classmates, demonstrating welcoming strategies and a 'social action' approach at a basic level that involved them both indirectly and directly in the experience:

> It helps them because quite often they will say 'Hassan! We've got a Hassan in the class! He's from Somalia,' or they'll say 'so-and-so, she's just come from ... She doesn't understand but we'll help her. It's alright, it's ok because she'll understand the pictures.' That's quite a normal thing that they'll actually tell me about their friends in the class.

Hoffman saw the purpose of *The Colour of Home* as two-fold for non-refugee readers. First, it aimed to give children a clear idea of why refugees had come to the host country. This 'suppose' paradigm (Harding, 1977) is vital to communicate a useful understanding of the totality of the refugee experience:

> There was so much ignorance about why asylum seekers were here.... 'People have come just to make a better life' or something. No, it's to *have* a life as opposed to being murdered or tortured or raped, or whatever.

Second, literature provides a vicarious experience, one that can engender empathy and understanding:

> I think by telling the story of one child, but personalizing it, it makes it easier to identify with ... To see the refugee experience from the inside, from inside somebody's head.

However, Hoffman was well aware that her books could be contentious, and perhaps challenge prejudice and cause controversy:

> These are dangerous waters, but you can't write any book without a risk of upsetting somebody or … I think the risk is worth taking for the benefits that could accrue in this case.

Hoffman's point was to give children ideas of what they might do to help a refugee arriving in their classrooms, reflecting the 'social action' approaches noted by Littlewood that are empowering for non-refugees.

Naidoo's idea was that shifts in perception are not necessarily immediate, that questioning and opening up possibilities can take place but over long spaces of time, if at all (Naidoo, 1992). Her approach is one of planting seeds that may or may not germinate, depending on the character and life experiences of the reader. In reference to her books set in South Africa she told me: 'I've had letters from young people who then went on to join the anti-apartheid movement as a result of that, because this happens.' As discussed, Mallan (2013) questions whether such a direct correlation can be made between children's literature and narrative empathy, but Smith-D'Arezzo and Thompson suggest, that providing opportunities for children to read about others living in war zones and other stressful situations, 'hopefully, will help them to become better global citizens in an increasingly challenging world' (2006: 337).

Reflections

The Colour of Home and *The Other Side of Truth* are widely used in primary classrooms across London, popular because they tackle a controversial issue – the treatment of asylum seekers in the UK in the 21st century – in a form that is accessible to children. Yet their role in understanding and validating the refugee experience – the stated aim of both authors – has never been researched. Although the initial motivation for the two books differed, one commissioned, the other organic, the backgrounds of the two authors – in terms of age, class, intellectualism and family links to migration themes – are startling in their similarity. Littlewood also had migration and prejudice in her background, endorsing suggestions that prior experience in some form motivates authors and illustrators to produce such texts. From my interviews with all three it is clear that both books aim to reach out to children with a powerful message and strong images, and thorough background research is an important component of the writing and illustrating process.

Chapter 6

Teachers as mediators

Introduction

During my interview with Mary Hoffman she commented on the feedback she had received about *The Colour of Home*:

> I've had very, very favourable reader response, and the number of people ... who have written to me ... would indicate to me that it is finding the kind of audience I hoped it would. That is to say that it is being used in schools, that it is popular, that people are taking it seriously.

I now examine whether Hoffman's aims, as discussed in Chapter 5, are borne out in practice when reading *The Colour of Home* in a primary classroom. In this chapter, I look at the role of the teacher as a key 'enabling adult' (Chambers, 1991) in introducing a text that deals with refugee issues. The chapter is built on observations of children reading and responding to *The Colour of Home* in what I have called Marlowe School and Creekside School. I made these in two Year 1 classes and one Year 3 class. I also interviewed four teachers – April and Nerys from Year 1 and Charlie and Simon from Year 3 (pseudonyms are used throughout) – and looked at their planning.

Planning for reader response and critical literacy
Teaching The Colour of Home through PSHCE in Year 1
Jill Rutter told me that:

> I think the discussions around the book have been far too constrained by the remnants of the literacy hour, and teachers' creativity has been constrained, and using things like Circle Time to explore some of the issues in the book is very rarely done.

Although not explicitly mentioned in the National Curriculum in England 2000 (DfEE/QCA, 1999), the two areas, as Rutter highlights, that have tended to address refugee issues are Literacy and Personal, Social, Health and Citizenship Education (PSHCE). The latter was a non-statutory subject in primary schools, but has now become something of a preamble

– called only Personal and Social Education (PSE) – in the new National Curriculum in England 2014 (DfE, 2013). As I collected the data for my study before the new curriculum came into force, both of the Year 1 teachers in Marlowe School and Creekside School were reading *The Colour of Home* with their class as part of PSHCE and related the lesson to the National Curriculum in England 2000 (DfEE/QCA, 1999). The 'learning objective' of April's lesson was 'learning about and empathizing with others' while Nerys's focus was 'Communication: Feelings/Emotions: Understanding of other cultures'.

Both teachers mentioned the scattered nature of PSHCE, which, unlike Literacy, tends to consist of isolated lessons where a topic is not sustained over several weeks and thereby lacks depth and follow-up. Rutter (2005) has highlighted problems with token lessons about the refugee experience, as raising more questions than teachers can effectively deal with. She reiterated this in her interview, saying: 'I think a … one off lesson on refugees and migration really does "other" refugee children.'

April also voiced frustrations about the lack of time to relate her reading to the children's own experience of starting school: 'If I'd spent more time on it we would have maybe talked more about their feelings of coming into school. I could have milked, you know, I could have got a lot more work out of it … and in more depth talk about these things …' However, with the removal of PSHCE as a discrete subject area from the National Curriculum in England, these opportunities to engage with the refugee experience through children's literature have been narrowed.

Differentiation in Year 1

As Year 1 approached *The Colour of Home* in one or two discrete lessons, it was interesting to consider how teachers planned to differentiate the children. Both asked for a written response from those they thought had a 'higher ability' in Literacy and a drawn response from the rest. The work that April set the class demonstrates this clearly. Nine 'lower ability' children were asked to 'Draw a picture of your favourite part of the story.' The rest of the class were asked: 'What do you think about this book?' These two tasks ask for different levels of engagement with the text, the first requiring a simple response to a potentially disturbing book, the second much more complex in its demands, asking children to consider the text as 'constructed' and to give their opinion about it.

Excerpts from Nerys's plan show the work set for three groups following the reading and questioning:

> Group 1, teacher led (High Ability): How do you think Hassan was feeling at different points in the book? … Why? Children to write down their thoughts/opinions of this book. What do they think the message of the book is?

> Group 2, teaching assistant led (Average/High): Tell the children that like Hassan they are going to use pictures to tell his story … Discuss six main events in the story which they are going to put into pictures.

> Independent (Low Ability) and (Average/Low): Art: Paintings of own home.

Again, Nerys asks the 'higher ability' group to give their thoughts/opinions on the book and what they think the 'message' is, whereas the middle and lower groups either retold the story or responded to the images. Nerys had more support in the classroom in the form of a teaching assistant, so two groups had the input of an adult steering the discussion before the children were asked to record their thinking on paper. I observed in my field notes that the use of small discussion groups in Nerys's class worked well when the children were expected to offer their opinions, and generated better written work as a result.

Literacy objectives and appreciation of the text in Year 3
Where *The Colour of Home* was studied as part of the Literacy curriculum in Year 3, the learning objectives were by necessity more focused on developing children's skills, particularly in writing, as the quote from Charlie's interview demonstrates:

> I suppose it's just one of those texts that, it encourages and inspires them … to improve their writing and to talk more about the text, particularly in the classes that we have, particularly at this school … and *The Colour of Home* provides a lot of opportunity … for pair work and talking about it, and that enables them to talk through, and then it will reflect in their writing.

The Year 3 teachers had adapted a scheme of work provided by a Local Authority (LA) advisor who had been brought in to work with Simon, the previous Year 3 teacher, using *The Colour of Home* in the classroom. The scheme was divided into five parts:

- introduction and being new
- home

- moving
- objects
- feeling settled/belonging.

The scheme focused far more than most on the delivery of information (see Rosenblatt's 'efferent') – about the author, the illustrator, Somalia, the war, reasons for leaving a place – and also engaged with feelings and emotions, developing vocabulary and definitions of terms. In this way children's attention was drawn directly to the subject matter of the book. Functional literacy skills were developed through responses to the text, addressed as a by-product rather than dominating the focus. The scheme did engage with critical literacy – through an early discussion about the author and the illustrator, it considered the 'constructedness' of the text (Comber, 2001), for example – and there was some possibility for generating 'social action' (Lewison *et al.,* 2002) in terms of children welcoming newcomers into the class.

Charlie based his planning on the LA advisor's scheme of work with the previous Year 3. The text-level objectives for the three weeks were:

Week 1: I can express my opinion clearly, listen to others, evaluate and recall facts, write in role, and adapt my writing in response to a text.

Week 2: I can retell a story verbally, sequence events of a story, act in role, empathize with characters and create an image based on text.

Week 3: I can obtain specific information, use language that is appropriate to the reader, adapt my writing to suit a purpose.

Tackling a book such as *The Colour of Home* through the National Literacy Strategy (NLS) rather than PSHCE guidance has the advantage that more time can be spent on it. Working with the text over three weeks affords greater opportunity to discuss the issues that arise in greater depth, which has to be preferable when dealing with such complex subject matter. Moreover, in Charlie's class the children were asked to engage in several stimulating tasks: writing a diary entry about Hassan's first day in school, making a story board about his journey from Somalia, writing Hassan's feelings throughout the story, preparing and asking questions of 'Hassan' and writing a book review. Finally, my field notes record Charlie telling the class that they will:

write their own version of *The Colour of Home*. Their story will be about a boy who joins a new school and misses his old home. Teacher discusses that although it will be using *The Colour of Home* as inspiration, it won't be a direct copy.

Without the prerequisite that the protagonist has had to flee, when reworking the story children can choose a place they like on the migration/refugee continuum, and thus access their own entry point.

Addressing the refugee experience in Year 3

In Year 3 there was also more time to develop a specific understanding of the nature of the refugee experience in its different phases, as depicted by Hamilton and Moore (2004).

CONCEPTS OF HOME AND REASONS FOR LEAVING

The scheme from the previous year, which formed the basis of Charlie's plans, introduced the pre-migration situation by asking the children to look at Hassan's pictures of home in the book and discuss similarities and differences with their own homes. By contrasting the words 'home', 'house' and 'to feel at home', it asks teachers to bring out the different meanings of the words. Identifying the non-physical aspects of sanctuary – for example, feelings of isolation or belonging – is useful for understanding the refugee situation. The scheme looked at Hassan's reasons for leaving in the general context of why people have to move:

- establish that Hassan had to leave because of the war in his home, but that there are lots of reasons why people have to move;
- in talk partners brainstorm reasons for people moving. Collect children's suggestions onto strips of paper and display;
- in pairs/threes sort cards with reasons on into categories, e.g. forced/chosen, happy/sad.

This session brings to the fore the triggers that motivate people to leave their home country, and the emotions generated by migration. It also meets the Literacy objectives of speaking, listening and writing, and gives the children some 'real' issues to communicate about.

In his plans Charlie tackled Hassan's concept of home and reasons for leaving in pictorial form. He directs the children to focus on feelings about this:

Children given copy of paragraph describing Hassan's drawing. They draw their own version and down one side write words/

phrases describing image ... They then alter their drawing and list new words/phrases down other side.

When Charlie asked the children to scribble out the picture as Hassan did, my field notes record:

All class draw over and smudge out original picture using black and red pencils. The room suddenly becomes really noisy! The atmosphere in the classroom is electric! All very animated.

In this way Charlie shapes the class's response by encouraging the children to empathize with Hassan, confront the refugee experience in a kinaesthetic manner and address the cause of flight – see Sullivan and Strang (2002), discussed in Chapter 3. The chosen task sets the children's imaginations on fire and the excitement in the room showed that Charlie had skilfully mediated an emotional reaction from the children towards the text, the 'aesthetic' side of reader response (Rosenblatt, 1978).

TAKING FLIGHT

The LA advisor's scheme of work asks children to discuss which objects they would take if they had to leave their home in a hurry. Ten special objects are passed around in a suitcase and they have to choose two and explain why, along the lines of the activities Rutter saw as vital to accompany a text. In his interview, Simon, who had taught the book the year before, appreciated that good ideas that actively engage children in empathizing with the refugee experience, had been introduced by the LA advisor:

I think his cat was left behind so we had some discussion about 'If you had to leave, what precious possessions would you take with you? What would you leave behind?' ... She had a bag, and in her bag she had a few items which meant something to her, so she would pull out an item and ask them what it was and then she'd give the story behind that artefact, so I did the same as well.

As noted, discussion is an important part of sharing a text in class, as are spin-off activities that might be generated by considering the 'significance' (Stephens, 1992) of the story. The teachers' role in activating the empathy that can be incited by the text (Sullivan and Strang, 2002) is clear, and the fact that both teachers took part in the exercise showed that adults as well as children may have to make difficult choices under pressure, and that this could happen to any one of us at any time.

ARRIVAL IN THE NEW COUNTRY

The first session in the LA advisor's scheme of work focused on the feelings of being new in a class and welcoming new children, playing on the common ground many children might have with a refugee child arriving in this country, and activating 'emotional memories' (see Nikolajeva, 2012). Charlie's plans included role play between the newcomer, a welcoming child and the teacher, which helped immerse the children in the lived experience of the refugee child (Vermeule, 2010). This active learning strategy develops speaking and listening through the use of drama, which is encouraged throughout the Literacy curriculum. It also encourages the 'social action' children could take in helping an outsider adjust to their new situation. Furthermore, children are able to make links with their own experience (see Rosenblatt, 1938; Freire and Macedo, 1987), and fill in the 'gaps' left in the text (Iser, 1976). Doing so can activate their imagination. The final session focuses on feeling settled and belonging, comparing how Hassan feels at the end of the book to the beginning. The plan asks teachers to highlight signs of this from the text: 'play football, make friends, paint another picture, show his mum, look after sister, smile, notice the colours, begin to learn English'.

This links with Baker's relationship web (1983) – discussed in Chapter 1 – which is destroyed or fractured during the flight to sanctuary and needs rebuilding in a new place. Teachers are often key people in this process, as the text shows when the teacher enables Hassan to reach a resolution. This also brings *The Colour of Home* to a 'happy ending', despite not being the fate for refugees generally. It is, however, regarded as an important part of children's literature, especially for the very young. What the scheme does say is: 'stress positives and resilience e.g. bravery, new life, being at school, friendly teacher and children, learning new language and skills'. Viewing refugees as resilient and proactive (Rutter, 1985; Masten *et al.*, 1990) rather than as vulnerable victims is useful, but if encouraging empathy is also a target, negative feelings and events must also be addressed.

Teachers mediating the text
Précising the script
As I sat and watched April read *The Colour of Home* to her Year 1 class, the role of the teacher 'stand(ing) in for the author by giving the text a 'voice' when reading to the child' (Meek, 1988: 10) played out clearly before my eyes. I realized that the children were not accessing the actual text but a version of it that April wanted them to receive, according to her professional vision of what would engage them most. The text was

interlaced with points of information and questioning, and remade through this 'running metatextual commentary' (Luke *et al.*, 1983: 118). April not only changed the wording of the book, she also dramatized it, giving voices to the characters and stressing parts she felt were important or frightening. Barrs and Cork (2001) noted that teachers 'perform' the book as they read aloud, bringing the page to life. An excerpt from my field notes, taken during my visit, demonstrates this process well:

> The T. (teacher) departs from the script and explains everything clearly. She relates rather than reads it. 'That's what Somalia looks like' says the T. ...
>
> All are horrified with the change of picture (when Hassan paints over it). No one could explain why he might do this. T. gathers speed, having got their attention.
>
> She makes Hassan's voice very frightened, dramatizing the script.

April draws the children's attention to the pictures, endorsing Littlewood's point that they are a 'universal language' (see Chapter 5), commenting on them and providing her own interpretation. Luke and Luke (1989: 252) note that: 'tacitly and intentionally, teachers will emphasize and de-emphasize, select and exclude', and through this process a subject position is covertly constructed (Baker, 1991). In her interview April felt that she could have précised the book more and explained her motivations for doing so: 'I think it's quite wordy for my age children, the Year 1s actually, and if I had had time I would have cut it down a lot.'

Nerys also saw a need to précis *The Colour of Home* because of time constraints and the need to maintaining the children's concentration:

> I think the text is accessible and again the illustrations do help the children to understand. I feel the story itself can be a little bit long ... but you can shorten that ... and make that easier for the children ... You might be able to use it in a different way, perhaps just looking at the pictures and talking around the pictures rather than going through the whole story.

Nerys similarly highlights the role of the illustrations, echoing Littlewood's idea that they provide a 'universal language'. She saw no problem in using the pictures as a stimulus rather than engaging with the language used by the author and pertaining to the text. In doing so she endorses another of Littlewood's points – that the book can be 'read' visually as well as verbally. The teacher, as an 'enabling adult', is thus an active participant in the 'transactional' nature of the reading experience, as envisaged by Rosenblatt (1978) and can mediate powerfully in the construction of the circuit of meaning. Arizpe and Styles (2003) point to a strong correlation between the quality of children's drawings in response to texts and the input from their teaching during the study of the book – see Chapter 7.

Questioning and discussion

Using her professional practice, developed over many years, April questioned the children while the book was being shared. This demonstrated 'dialogic engagement' (Aukerman, 2012) and showed how teachers as 'enabling adults' shape meaning during the reading process. My field notes recorded the proceedings, here interspersed with my commentary:

> T. says 'it starts in a school, just like this one.' (Teacher relates to the children's own experience)

> T. asks 'Who is Mrs King?' 'The teacher' they respond. T. says 'She wants to make him feel at home, welcome.' (Teacher frames targeted questions and makes suggestions about the text.)

> T. points to Hassan's face. 'He looks a bit sad. There are some happy things and sad things in this book.' (Drawing attention to an illustration and overview of contents.)

> 'How do you think he's feeling under the bed?' 'Scared.' (An open question encouraging empathy.) 'Who's this soldier?' (A closed question – hoping to address the 'significance' of the text.) One child points at gun. Another notices the cat. Somali girl says 'That's my country'.

> 'What's happened to the uncle?' 'He's dead.' 'Soldiers killed him.' 'They're in danger.' (An open question leading to a variety of answers.)

Using the illustrations as a stimulus, April builds the situation up through her 'booktalk' (Chambers, 1995). She focuses the children's attention on the story and in the spirit of 'collaborative discourse' (John, 2009), asks them to offer their interpretations, all while maintaining control of the discussion.

When Nerys reads the book, she pauses over the pages where Hassan and his family are driven from their home by violent events, to direct the children's attention to this particular aspect:

> T: What's happening? Ch (child): He's hiding. T: Why? Ch: Soldiers are there. (Open interpretive questions.)

T: Do you think they might kill him? (Asks the children's opinion.)

T: What's happening in this country? (Open question.) Children suggest 'War'. T: Yes.

This extract shows that Nerys does not hold back from addressing the violence in the text. She also uses the 'suppose paradigm (Harding, 1977) and asks open-ended questions, eliciting the children's opinion. Nerys appreciates the children's contributions but firmly approves one particular answer, and thereby subtly moulds the response towards one accepted meaning.

After the reading, Nerys's questioning continues, to entice the children into a whole class discussion of the book. Pearson, an educational website that provided inspiration, suggests the following when planning for an appreciation of *The Colour of Home*: 'Discuss with children what it means and feels like to be homesick. Ask them to share stories of their own experiences with homesickness. Ask children what they know or have heard about wars past and present.' Comber (2001) and Hall (2003) consider linking texts to children's own experience to be good practice in Literacy teaching. Below we can see that Nerys is working with ideas from the Pearson plan, demonstrating that in practice interpretations may come from a third level of mediated meaning, one that is not immediately obvious.

T: Why is he sad? Ch: Because he doesn't know English. Ch: He misses his cat. Other children offer ideas: New school. New country. T: Homesick is when you miss something. (Teacher directly introduces vocabulary from Pearson.)

Similarly, it is helpful to encourage teachers to address the topic of war directly and may embolden reticent practitioners to engage in discussion they might think is too controversial for Year 1 (see Wollman-Bonilla, 1998). We have already seen the concept of war raised, and here Nerys tackles it in depth, in line with the Pearson plan:

T: Why did he have to leave? Ch: Because there was a war. T: What's that? Children offer ideas: When they have a battle. Fight another country. A big massive fight.

Again Nerys takes a variety of suggestions and encourages the children to contribute their ideas. Finally we reach a big question, not detailed anywhere in the plan, that is crucial to a critical engagement with a text:

T: The message? What does this book tell us about? Any ideas?

Ch: He misses his country.

We can see how difficult class 'discussion' is in Year 1. Rather than engaging in a free-ranging conversation about the 'significance' of the text, the children responded better to questions that targeted specific parts of the text or were related to their own life experiences.

When a substitute teacher, Sam, comes to teach the lesson to Year 3, the following extracts from my field notes record how he mediates the text. Sam starts by talking about Hassan's painting, which he says he found quite disturbing, giving his own reaction from the outset and thus showing the children what kind of response he expects from them. Here we see them complying with that view:

Ch: He put a man with a gun and bullet coming out shooting his uncle.

T: What did he do to one person?

Ch: He smudged out his uncle.

T: What really happened?

Ch: The uncle died.

T: Did he die a natural death?

Ch: No. He was killed.

T: Do you think Hassan saw this?

Ch: Yes.

T: Do you think it's a good thing for a child to see?

Here we see that Sam elicits the response by engaging in 'pedagogical dialogue' (Skidmore, 2000). He builds up a picture he has in his mind and transfers it to the children's, not through telling but by questioning. Interestingly, he erroneously leads the children to believe that Hassan witnessed the killing of his uncle, although the text makes clear that he does not – 'I didn't find out what happened to my uncle until later' – and asks them to make a judgement about it. This echoes Fish's (1980) famous title *Is There a Text in this Class?* where actual content is superseded by the 'suppose' paradigm, as suggested by Harding (1977).

Finally, in Year 3, having read the book slowly over five lessons and engaged in various activities to respond to the characters and plot, the children are asked to sum up their thoughts about the text in its entirety. The beginning of this session was based on Chambers's *Tell Me* (1993) approach of identifying likes, dislikes, puzzles and patterns in a book (see Chapter 3). This has been adopted by the Power of Reading project, run by the Centre for Literacy in Primary Education (CLPE), and was doubtless taken on board by Charlie because the school participated in it. This reveals another source of inspiration in the planning cycle and also suggests that good Literacy pedagogies can lead children to be critical and exploratory.

Relating to children's lived experience

April and Nerys both tried hard in their meta-textual commentary to relate the story to children's own experience of having newcomers in their class, possibly lacking sufficient English skills to communicate fully. Simon described in his interview how his class had made the connection between the book and the lived experience of a boy in their class, demonstrating a 'merging' rather than 'matching between a reader and the text' (Crago, 1996; Clarke and Postle, 1988).

> At the time there was a boy who'd come from Slovakia, so ... and he had no English and he'd just arrived in the class ... He wasn't an asylum seeker. He just came for an economic ... reason, and he took a long time to pick up English words, so at the time there was that sort of thing about 'Oh, Stefan can't say this', and 'Oh look, Stefan said this', and so children were feeding back to me about things he's started to say.

Charlie also endeavoured to relate the initial part of *The Colour of Home* to the children's lived experience, asking 'Hands up who was born in another country?' He uses his questioning to encourage empathy from the children towards Hassan:

> T: Imagine you are Hassan standing at the doorway. How will you feel? ...
>
> T: What is he thinking about?
>
> Ch: Thinking about what his house used to be like. He misses his family ...
>
> T: Why is he feeling lonely?
>
> Kadiye: Suddenly realizing how far away he is from his family. ...
>
> T: How is he feeling now?
>
> Ch: Unhappy. Memories of the war.

Here Charlie employs a consistently open style of questioning, asking the children to put themselves in Hassan's place and imagine his thoughts and feelings – see Theory of Mind, discussed in Chapter 3. Interestingly, one of the respondents is Kadiye, one of only two Somali children in the class and usually very quiet. Although he had never been to Somalia, he might have been motivated by the refugee legacy to some deeper understanding of the issues of family separation than other children had. For him, this may have been a transformative moment.

Teachers' own experiences

Charlie's class also benefited because the session about Hassan's journey to safety was taught by Sam, a substitute teacher. Sam relates Hassan's experience to his own of arriving in the UK as a South African Asian, without friends, family or accommodation, and his feelings of loneliness and fear. This lesson demonstrated what a key figure the teacher is as an 'enabling adult' in filtering the text. My field notes record:

> T has been talking to the class about his experience of arriving in England for the first time. He is talking to the children and explaining that both he and Hassan come from Africa. T. draws a quick map to show Somalia and South Africa, where the T comes from.

Earlier I mentioned personal testimony as a particularly beneficial way to teach about refugee issues, and although Sam's story is not of a refugee, there are enough similarities to bring the situation alive to the class, demonstrating how migration/forced migration is in fact a continuum (Rutter, 2006). However, Sam was careful to point out the differences as well – he already spoke English, he had chosen to come – but he still felt very lonely and fearful when he arrived, as Baker's 'relationship web' (1983) suggests – see Chapter 1.

> T: Do you think they were absolutely happy now, or do you think they still longed for home? When I came, I wanted to go home every day.

Sam gave the children some information about the location of the book and related it to his own country of origin in a hand-drawn map. That Sam was so open as a teacher about his status as a migrant to the UK, and ready to share his own feelings of insecurity with the class, gave Hassan's position as a refugee to Britain a positive value and also deepened the possibility for empathy. Sam's input thus enhanced both the 'efferent' and 'aesthetic' responses to a text that Rosenblatt (1978) identifies.

Teachers' perceptions
The impact of school ethos

As our school populations grow more culturally and ethnically diverse and reflect myriad different student experiences such as seeking asylum, there have been calls to work on 'pursuing a whole-school approach toward building a culturally responsive ethos in which all students are valued' (Johnson, 2003: 17). Three of the teachers who participated in the study – April, Nerys and Simon – commented that the ethos of their schools was vital in setting the tone for children's attitudes to newcomers in general and refugees specifically. They thought this was reflected in the children's responses to the *The Colour of Home,* as the children were familiar with the issues. As April put it, 'We encourage our children to welcome new children, so I think it's very good for that, because we get children all the time who just come in, who are new.'

Nerys observed that she had never heard any negative comments about refugees and asylum seekers in school: 'You might get it in Key Stage 2, but certainly not ... I didn't ever hear it with the young children. Not at all. I don't know if their understanding is deep enough to really be able to make those, those comments.' Simon corroborated this, stating that the welcoming ethos of Marlowe School was a very important feature. In my own visits I certainly did not observe any anti-refugee feeling:

> It doesn't show itself in the school ... Whether it shows itself in the community is another matter, but I don't think it does. I think this is such a varied community, like it's a varied school. It's extremely rare because of the mixture of children, for one thing and because ... the ethos that's been built up over the years, without doubt.

Knowles and Ridley (2005) make the point that this whole school antiracist ethos needs to be embedded in regular classroom work, not just a tokenistic celebrating of diverse cultures that ignores 'hard' issues of attitudes and racism. They also stress that the process is never complete. Unlike the others, Charlie mentioned that when he had taught *The Colour of Home* the previous year:

> ... some of them used insults kind of loosely based around ... I think it was FOB or 'F' 'O' 'B' for Fresh Off the Boat, or something

... and they'd heard that saying from some of the Year 6 kids and they kind of used it for when you're not quite together, and you haven't quite, you know, got a lot of money, or you don't know what you're doing, 'oh look at you, you're fresh' ...

This was the first time that anti-migrant feeling, counter to the school's welcoming ethos, was acknowledged as a possible part of the pupils' repertoire. Charlie's observations revealed that there may have been anti-migrant images at play, but these had lost their precise meaning and were used as more random insults.

Using and understanding the term 'refugee'

My field notes detail that when April started reading *The Colour of Home*, she introduced the protagonist, Hassan, and the location of the book as Somalia. I recorded that thereafter she employs the term 'refugee' directly:

T. tells the class that Hassan is a refugee. Does anyone know what that means? Two put their hands up ...

They have to come to their country and have to go to a different country if something happens. (This appears to be a very good definition from a 6 or 7-year-old.)

People are friendly and say come to our country and are friendly.

In this way April immediately brings the refugee experience to the fore and the children's answers display a rudimentary understanding of the issues at stake. In the following extracts from her interview, April sets out her ideas of what the children in her Year 1 class might understand of refugee issues after reading the book in class:

They understand that some people need caring for more, or some people are sad or ... but the concept of being a refugee and homeless, I don't think we've gone into it in great detail ... I don't think they've got a definition of a refugee ... But it's a good start for them ... It's a beginning understanding ...

April felt that the children's understanding was largely aided by the pictures, echoing Littlewood's stance (see Chapter 5), but at their age the concept of forced migration was beyond them. In terms of the wider message of *The Colour of Home*, she felt that her children grasped the more superficial elements of welcoming newcomers to the classroom:

They could relate to that problem of being new in a school. ... it probably makes them more aware of how other children feel, and of course every year they're new to a class, so I think that helps too.

As we have seen, Nerys is much more direct than the other teachers about confronting the issue of war, although in her interview she states that it has arisen before, when children talk about the personal migrations of those in the class:

At the beginning of the year when we look at the cultural heritage of the class, we do talk around why people move from other countries and sometimes they will say 'fighting', so they are aware of things like that.

Although she did not use the word 'refugee' during either of the teaching sessions I observed, Nerys felt the children understood the position of new arrivals in the classroom, or had maybe experienced this themselves, as the school had a highly mobile population. The specific nature of the refugee situation, however, was something she felt did not need to be spelled out.

Simon believed that *The Colour of Home* had managed to change perceptions, but mainly about what it is like to have a language barrier and about welcoming new arrivals. He observed that the word 'refugee' was only used when it came to Hassan's journey, and suggested that the children were possibly too young to embrace the concept:

We did use the word refugee because of the fact they had to ... flee during the hours of darkness, and why they had to go ... The time it came up was obviously when he had the story of why he had to leave, so then it did definitely come up. The soldiers ... the picture of the boots and him climbing under the bed.

When asked whether he thought his Year 3 class were aware of the word 'refugee', Charlie was equivocal:

No, I'm not 100 per cent sure, to be honest. It did come up in one of our discussions and yet again it was only really one or two of the higher literacy and more able children that would put their hand up ... and they would have an idea ...

Violent themes
Wollman-Bonilla (1998) noted that teachers frequently rejected texts because they might frighten or corrupt children, implying that school

should be kept separate from society. In contrast, April was not put off by the book's seemingly heavy subject matter:

> I am prepared to show children things like that ... because it's in context and it's not celebrating guns or doing anything like that ... so it's clear that it's the bad people have the guns, so I don't think it's a problem at all really ... and they can cope with those things.

Interestingly, in a review of Deborah Ellis's (2005) *Three Wishes: Palestinian and Israeli Children Speak*, in the *Toronto Star*, a 10-year-old girl, Evie, defended the use of violence in Ellis's books, asserting: 'If children are tough enough to be bombed and starved, they're tough enough to read about it' (fishpond.co.uk, n.d.). When asked about the violent image of the soldiers coming in while Hassan hides under the bed, Nerys replied:

> Most of the kids see so many things like that anyway. It might have been that many, many years ago we might have thought that was too shocking for them to see ... I actually don't think it really shocks them now.

Simon suggested that despite the violence of the subject matter, the book demonstrates the resilience of children who have had experiences of these kinds, as long as they have the right support:

> They see films with guns and people being forced to move and all this sort of stuff, so the subject matter was something they could understand, and ... that the boy was able to paint pictures of how he felt and he had someone to talk to as well, didn't he?

In Key Stage 1 generally, teachers tended to engage with the themes of newness and welcoming rather than the 'heavier' themes that develop an understanding of the refugee experience. If they did focus on the more difficult areas, they did not explain this through the concept of war, and in fact *The Colour of Home* itself does not use the word 'refugee' at any point. However, the next chapter relates how when children in Year 1 were asked to précis the story, many referred to war, bullets and guns. Furthermore several of the books made by children in Year 3 depicted situations where the protagonist was fleeing from a violent situation, although this was not given as a necessary part of their narrative. Teachers also tended to focus on possibilities for 'social action', thereby building on children's capacity for agency in the process (see Sarland, 2005).

Awareness of refugee children's lives

During her interview April commented: 'No one was directly refugee in that class ... so they couldn't relate to the fleeing aspect.' This was probably true, and April's knowledge of the class was such that she was sure no particular child had fled to escape persecution, it being clear that the two Somali children were born in the UK. One of these children identified herself at once, as my field notes show:

> T. introduces Hassan and Somalia. Anyone know anything about it? There are two children in the class from Somalia. One says 'that's my country'. T. asks 'Can you speak the language?' The girl replies 'I say to my aunt that I want to go and visit'.

Nerys also began her reading of the text by highlighting Somalia, but in contrast to April, she named the two Somali children in the class. When asked if she had any refugees in the class, Nerys included these children, as we had just been talking about them in depth.

The following comments from Charlie's interview shed further light on the matter:

> When you start in a new class, ... Your file of children's data ... you'll have main language or whatever, and there'll be a large chunk of children that'll have a separate language as their main language but their country of origin won't necessarily mean they were born in that country ... It's not something you bring up in parent/teacher conversation ... there's nothing else in any of our data files.

Charlie's comments demonstrate the need to train teachers better in how to identify children from a refugee background, and the possible special awareness needed when working in a cosmopolitan context. I suggest that this is an important area to be covered, both on ITE courses and again when teachers have their own class, via INSET and CPD.

When tackling refugee issues through literature in the classroom, it is vital to consider whether such texts can be potentially disturbing for refugee children who have had a similar experience. Charlie makes the point that this is entirely possible: 'I think there's a potential, perhaps, if it mirrored ... if there's quite a close similarity between the reasons why they left, how apparent it was to them when they left, which we don't necessarily know.'

Nerys stated that she would still read the book if a child was uncomfortable with subject matter but:

> Perhaps if somebody had just come from another country where
> ... something might have just happened to them, then that might
> be too distressing in a whole class situation ... So it might be at
> a later point, it might be a discussion in a smaller group, it might
> even be on a one-to-one or a partner basis.

However, in practice it is difficult to organize such provision. Usually teachers
have to rely on their professionalism to consider the potential effect a text
can have when used in the classroom. Knowledge of individual children and
their backgrounds, however, is crucial if practitioners are entrusted with
such delicate decisions.

Reflections

> In any classroom, the teacher is the interpretative authority on
> the text for the students. The narrative is filtered throughout the
> teacher's talk about the text, that is, the teacher mediates the text
> to the students.
>
> (McDonald, 2004: 18)

Responding to a book as complex as *The Colour of Home* is not easy, and
tackling such a controversial area in only one or two lessons is not conducive
to productive reading and response. As this chapter shows, teachers play a
key role in filtering the text, through reading, questioning and discussion,
overlaying the story with their own preconceptions, personal life histories,
knowledge of key concepts and socio-political perspectives. As Galda *et al.*
(2001) note: 'How discussions are structured reflects the beliefs and practices
of the classroom teacher.' In terms of planning for engagement, McDonald
(2004) points out that reader response, bringing children's life experiences to
the text, remains the dominant way of working for most teachers, whereas
critical reading practices ask that the text is brought forward for judgement.
The first position demands some departure from the reading, the second
needs more time to teach the text effectively. Finally, teachers' awareness of
the children's backgrounds is part of their professional responsibility, and is
especially relevant when reading sensitive texts about the refugee experience
in the classroom. In the next chapter, I explore how far teachers' mediation
affected the children's responses to *The Colour of Home*.

Chapter 7

Children making meaning

Introduction

> To be critically literate, children have to be helped to question
> how they make sense of the world and interpret it, and to draw
> on their own experiences.
>
> (Fisher, 2008: 26)

In this chapter, I consider how children in Year 1 and Year 3 responded
to *The Colour of Home* through the discussion and activities planned by
their teachers. Year 1 were read the book and invited to respond over one
or two lessons only, but what they produced still provides rich material for
analysis. Year 3 studied the text over three weeks and, as Arizpe and Styles
(2003) found, the highest levels of response came from children who had
time, space and opportunities to produce their own visual texts.

   Madura (1998) categorized children's responses to visual texts as
descriptive – involving retelling and plot summaries – *interpretive* – making
comments about the story, and relating it to personal experiences – and
thematic – showing an appreciation of the themes, styles and techniques an
author and artist displays. In my study the children's responses came mainly
under the first two levels of this simple model, although there was an extent
to which they engaged with overall themes raised by *The Colour of Home*.

Multimodal response in Year 1

> Young children switch with great ease between the different
> modes of word and image ... They move from talking to making
> and to drawing, according to the different purposes of their
> activity.
>
> (Styles and Nobel, 2009: 118)

As interest in picturebooks and multimodality has grown, looking at
children's response has shifted from a focus simply on writing to include
oral and pictorial responses. Leland *et al.* (2013) suggest that multimodal
responses to literature build on every child's communication potential in
making meaning from text. This echoes Arizpe and Styles's (2003) study,

which included open-ended discussion, individual interviews and drawing in response to picturebooks. In Year 1 producing their own visual texts was often key to the children's process of interpretation.

The interaction of words and pictures

The following section looks at some of the children's written and drawn responses to *The Colour of Home*, which illustrate their ability to respond to the refugee experience through the interaction of words and pictures. How to analyse children's multimodal expressions has been debated for a while. Early on Moebius (1986) identified certain graphic 'codes' that operate within the elements of design and expression in picturebooks. These include: positioning on the page, perspective, framing, use of line and use of colour. Lewis includes line and colour in his 'key features of the visual image' (2001: 103), but adds action and movement, size and location and symbolism. I find Rabey's (2003: 118) expanded model the most useful, with its suggestion that pictorial responses can be analysed in terms of:

- *literal responses* – whereby the child draws people or events from the text to communicate story and content
- *overall effect* – considering qualities such as the aesthetics of the image and a discussion of colour, tone, form and line
- *internal structure* – examining the composition for balance and the relationship between objects or characters and their relative scale.

Figure 7.1: 'The soldiers came to the house'.

Rabey also asserts that 'a visual experience demands a visual response true to its original form' (ibid.). Several children wrote their own title for their picture, or the teacher scribed a caption for their image, and in many instances the interaction between the words and pictures is worthy of comment.

In Figure 7.1 the picture does not seem to depict the scene the scribed caption suggests, as the people drawn look like family members rather than soldiers. It is also not clear whether the figures are standing outside the house or running away – either is possible. This is a contradiction that was repeated continually. Furthermore, many of the houses drawn by the children are not of a rural African dwelling, as in the book, but of a stereotypical British house. This image is not therefore a literal response to the text but is filtered through the frame of the child's own experience. However, the use of colour relates well to one of the dominant themes in *The Colour of Home,* and thus reflects a consideration of the overall effect of the picture in response to the book. So too does the internal structure, which highlights the importance of home and family in the story.

Figure 7.2: 'the soisu kidoll the grudad' (*The soldiers killed the granddad*).

In Figure 7.2 we have a good example of attention to internal structure, as the piece contains a 'picture within a picture', the actual scene to the left, and Hassan's depiction of his house and cat to the right, complete with blazing sun. The attention to detail in line and form are exceptional here, and the overall effect is therefore one of care and reproduction, although again the house diverges from the image in the book. Here the writing that goes with the picture does not fit with this idyllic scene at all, and disrupts the idea of a literal response.

Figure 7.3: 'Miss Kate was sad Bcos he Made a new Picher was smler that was nise and clen and not red'.

Similarly, in Figure 7.3, there is a contrast between the artistry of the image and the child's ability to sum up the moment in words. (Miss Kate was sad because (so?) he made a new picture was smaller that was nice and clean and not red.) The picture evokes in colour Hassan explaining the events behind his picture to the interpreter, a key moment in the story. The image pays careful attention to overall effect and internal structure via colour, form, line, balance and scale, with the interesting detail of the character's legs seen as if through the table. Such a depiction shows an intimate engagement with the subject matter, and a highly literal response.

Figure 7.4 is an intricate depiction of the whole story in a series of finely drawn images, demonstrating again an engagement both with overall effect – in terms of colour, form and line – and with internal structure, through balance and relationships. At the top a stick person fires a gun at another, who is wounded, if not killed, and subsequently the family leave their house. At the bottom, Hassan's school picture is shown on an easel, in three stages: painted, painted over and repainted in colour, with a yellow sun shining brightly in the corner. This child, although again unable to respond to the book adequately in writing, has assimilated all the aspects of the story and is able to reproduce it in pictorial form. This literal response shows they have completely understood the narrative and the conventions of visual representation, and embraced all aspects of the refugee experience Hamilton and Moore's (2004) three stages outline.

Figure 7.4: 'I O uncle The new picture'.

Where the children's responses contain both writing and drawing in conjunction, meaning is inscribed within each mode, as with picturebooks themselves (Lewis, 1996). The contrast in many cases between the clarity of the picture and the confusion of the words endorses the need to provide children with opportunities to respond in a variety of ways that suit their preferred mode of expression. 'In the case of younger children, their drawing often showed understanding they were unable to articulate' (Arizpe and Styles, 2003: 225). The conflict between visual and verbal response shown in my data is intriguing, and although reasons can only be a matter for conjecture, it is possible that Sipe's idea of 'personal resistance' (2008: 166) is in play here, with children finding the subject matter too disturbing to depict in images, despite being able to engage with it in words. Whatever the case, we can see from various reader responses that the overall theme of the refugee experience has been depicted by the children in different ways, and with dramatic expression. They have clearly understood the story in great detail and demonstrated a dynamic relationship with the text. Their drawings show great care, for example, and are vivid in terms of colour, form and line.

Responding to the refugee experience at different levels

As we saw, written and drawn response to the text in April's Year 1 class was set at two levels, according to ability. While a small group were asked to 'Draw a picture of your favourite part of the story' (samples of which I have already discussed), April asked the rest of class: 'What do you think about this book?' The question links with critical literacy, where children are asked their opinion on something and to comment on the book as a 'construction'. However, this group preferred to descriptively retell a significant aspect of the story, which suggests that critical literacy is a practice that needs to be fostered over time. For example:

> he DiD lick The School he DiD Fil lick home We hav a new boy Joining us at Shcool today HassA Didt wont to son his pichc to his mum and sister.

> (He did like the school. He did feel like home. We have a new boy joining us at school today. Hassan didn't want to show his picture to his mum and sister.)

Across April's class the children's writing focused most frequently on the picture and Hassan's mum, but also on having to leave the cat behind and some violent aspects of the story. The new school and the welcoming teacher featured highly, and the children remembered the name of Hassan's country of origin, perhaps because there were two Somali children in their class, one of whom was vocal in declaring 'that's my country'.

Nerys discussed the book with the 'higher ability' group and asked them to write their opinions of it and explain what they thought its 'message' might be, again attempting critical literacy. However, despite constant encouragement, the children seemed challenged by the concept and again their response was merely to retell the story (see Figure 7.5). Their response does, however, refer to the main elements of the refugee experience: war, flight, leaving pets behind and language barriers.

> When Hassan lived in Somalia a war happened so he had to go to a different country. He felt very sad because he had to leave his cat. Hassan had problems to learn English and Miss Kelly introduced a Somali person to help him learn English.

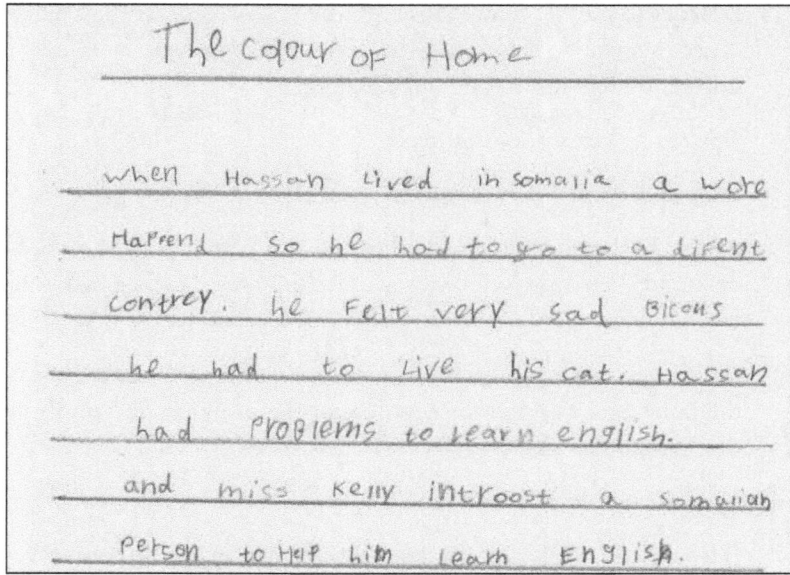

The colour of Home

when Hassan lived in somalia a wore
Harrend so he had to go to a difent
contrey. he Felt very sad Bicous
he had to Live his cat. Hassan
had problems to learn english.
and miss Kelly introost a somaiiah
person to Hep him Learn English.

Figure 7.5: Précis of *The Colour of Home.*

In Nerys's 'higher ability' group the painting was again generally high profile, but many more children identified the sad feelings associated with one of the learning objectives, 'Feelings/Emotions', demonstrating a degree of interpretation. In contrast to April's class, all of Nerys's group refer to bullets, guns or war in their writing, reflecting her focus explicitly on the theme of war. Some children wrote about Hassan having to leave Somalia, fewer about leaving his cat. Finally, an important element for this group was Hassan's experiences of a language barrier in his new school, and given that another of Nerys's learning objectives for the session was 'Communication', this clearly struck a chord with the children's personal interpretations. Such comparisons between the two Year 1 classes point clearly to the role of the teacher in directing the children's attention to aspects of the story they planned to highlight. As Arizpe and Styles assert, with reference to children interpreting visual texts, 'teachers *do* make a difference' (2003: 245; emphasis in original).

Empathizing with newness

The discussion group in Nerys's Year 1 class talked about Hassan's arrival in his new class. As David was of a Caribbean origin, Elbasana was from Albania, Anca from Romania and Habib from Pakistan, there was clear empathy with 'newness', whether first hand or by association.

David: He's in the new school, but he talks a different language, cause he can't understand because other people will talk a different language and he talks Somali.

JH: Yes ... How does that feel?

Elbasana: I know! Sad, sad.

Anca: At the end though, happy ... I think at the end he might be happy because one (sic) was telling the teacher what he was saying.

JH: Can you imagine going to a country where you didn't speak the language? Going to a new school there? What do you think that would feel like?

Habib: I would be worried.

JH: How do you think it would feel coming to a new country?

Elbasana: Scary and sad.

Anca: I would try to make friends.

Here the children show they have directly understood the problems Hassan faces: the language barrier and the loneliness. However, they also tackled issues of resilience (Rutter, 1985; Masten *et al.*, 1990), finding someone to communicate with and the need to make friends, which links with Baker's (1983) relationship web.

One dimension favoured in critical literacy is a 'social action' approach (Thibault, 2004) where students make decisions on important social issues. Nerys's Year 1 class were very good at identifying strategies to welcome new arrivals, arguably because their teacher encouraged such dialogue in response to *The Colour of Home*. Their responses show this:

Try to speak his language.
Make him feel happy.
Teach him their language.
We help them make friends.

Again the importance of rebuilding a 'relationship web' for newcomers resonates. Maria suggested using a same-language buddy to help a newcomer acquire English:

Maria: I had a person that was my friend, Stephen, I helped him cause he speaked Spanish.

JH: Ah! So they chose you specially to help because you spoke Spanish.

Maria: Yes. I was helping him.

Talking about own lives

Daniel, from China, and Maria, from Colombia, were both born in the UK but still had strong links with their country of heritage and had visited several times. I asked them if they had to leave suddenly, how they would feel:

Maria: Bit sad ... Because I would miss everything.

JH: What would you miss particularly?

Maria: Friends and family.

JH: Right. And would you miss any *things* at all? You said you'd miss friends. What about *things?*

Daniel: I would miss my toys, if I just left all my toys, and I would just stay without.

Maria: I always bring some toys.

JH: Do you?

Daniel: When I went to a different country, I just bring my favourite toy.

Later in the discussion both children made the important point that toys and friends can be acquired elsewhere, whereas family members can't. Their answers were clearly based on experiences of moving from one country to another for holidays or family reunions. Moreover, they both demonstrated an understanding of what it is like not to speak the host language:

JH: What do you think it would feel like if you arrived in a classroom not being able to speak the language that all the children could speak?

Maria: Lonely.

Daniel: Every time I go to China, everyone can talk in Chinese to me, and I don't really know what he's talking about.

Both children were used to moving between two worlds and encountering language barriers. They both engaged with their countries of origin enthusiastically, the positives and negatives were clear in their minds, and they were keen to share their knowledge with me.

The depth of reader response in Year 3

In Year 3 the children had the opportunity to respond to *The Colour of Home* in more depth as it was studied over three weeks as part of the Literacy curriculum. Using Hamilton and Moore's (2004) model of the refugee experience as a three-staged process, encompassing pre-, trans- and post-migration aspects, I analyse their writing, drawing and discussion for their overall understanding. Other considerations emerged, however, such as how the children reacted to the potentially disturbing violence depicted in the text, how they identified themes such as isolation, belonging and welcome, and how they related the text to their own lived experience, including the specific reaction of Somali pupils.

Hall (1998) argues that readers need to be made aware of the fact that the text is a crafted object that has ways of presenting 'reality', and that both could be otherwise. This understanding needs to be fostered in children, and teachers should encourage them to be 'actively, and collaboratively, involved in reading beyond the lines and making personal judgments about the extent to which a text has achieved its purpose' (Fisher, 2008: 26). I discuss the extent to which this was possible with Year 3 below.

The three weeks of study culminated in the children producing a 'counter-text' from different viewpoints. Behrman notes that this is an important part of critical literacy, as it 'can serve to validate the thoughts, observations, and feelings of students' (2006: 494). Behrman feels this offers students from underrepresented groups in particular, occasions to speak from the point of view of those who are often silenced or marginalized, and thereby empowers them.

Understanding the refugee experience

Three samples of Izzy's work in Year 3 show an in-depth understanding of the refugee experience one girl has built up over the three weeks spent studying *The Colour of Home*.

In Figure 7.6 Izzy skilfully reduces Hassan's story into six main points. She focuses mainly on Hamilton and Moore's (2004) first and second stages of the refugee experience, although briefly demonstrates an understanding of the final, post-migration stage too. She clearly relates to Hassan's fear and deprivation, using highly evocative words – 'terrified', 'speechless', 'cramped', 'frightened' and 'famished' – that suggest a deep level of empathy, but ends on a positive note with 'over the moon'.

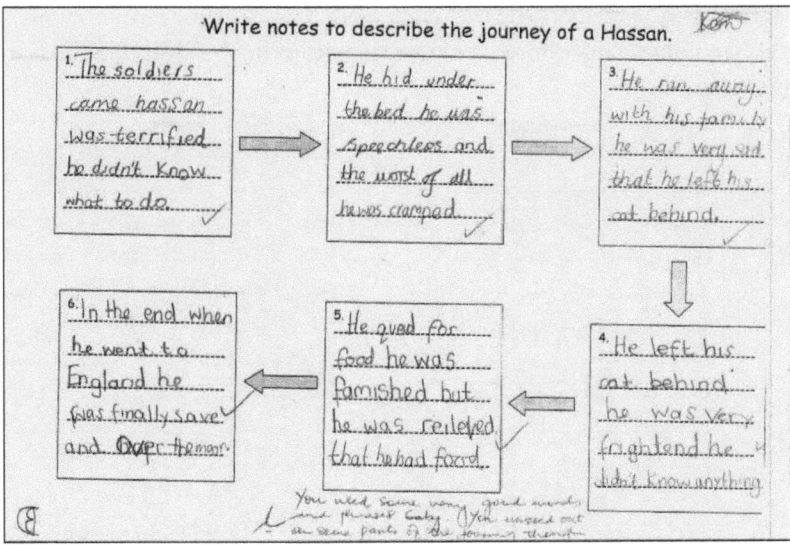

Figure 7.6: Izzy's description of Hassan's journey.

Figure 7.7: Izzy's diagram showing Hassan's outer life and inner feelings.

In Figure 7.7 Izzy produces a highly evocative diagram that depicts the events of Hassan's life and demonstrates all three parts of the refugee experience, but particularly the post-migration ecology. These surround a silhouette shape of his head and shoulders, with corresponding feelings inside: 'sad, guilty, depressed, frightened, awful, horrified, confused, startled, heartbroken, petrified, heart wrenched, tearful, shocked, nervous'. Such emotive vocabulary shows great compassion for the situation Hassan finds himself in.

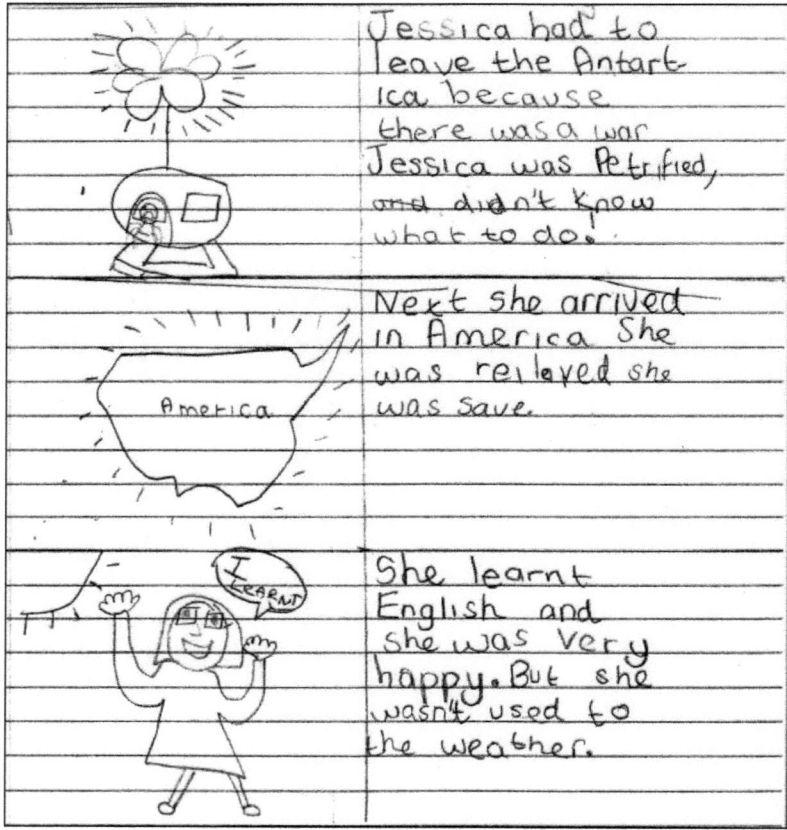

Jessica had to leave the Antartica because there was a war Jessica was Petrified, and didn't know what to do.

Next she arrived in America She was reileved she was Save.

America

She learnt English and she was very happy. But she wasn't used to the weather.

Figure 7.8: Izzy's storyboard beginning.

Figure 7.8 shows Izzy's first three pictures in her storyboard, which contributed to the making of her own book. She decided to start with a war, an escape to safety – via a well-drawn helicopter – and adapting to new circumstances. The rest of the story (not shown here) talks of her character making friends but missing home, despite living in a lovely house, 'in fact a Mansion!' The fact that Izzy's character still misses home shows her sensitivity to the attendant problems of settling in a new country as part of the migration/refugee experience. Furthermore, all three pieces of work show a deep and perceptive engagement with the refugee situation from a child who has not directly experienced it herself, but has enough knowledge, imagination and perhaps some personal perspectives to demonstrate an impressive response.

Reaction to violence

Comparing two girls in Year 3's drawings and written work is also useful in interrogating approaches to violence in the text. Peliona speaks Albanian/Shqip and her country of origin is Kosovo. She cannot relate directly to the refugee experience – the Kosovan crisis happened before she was born – but is almost certainly from a refugee background. Peliona demonstrates a deep empathy with Hassan and a heightened sensitivity to the effects of violence.

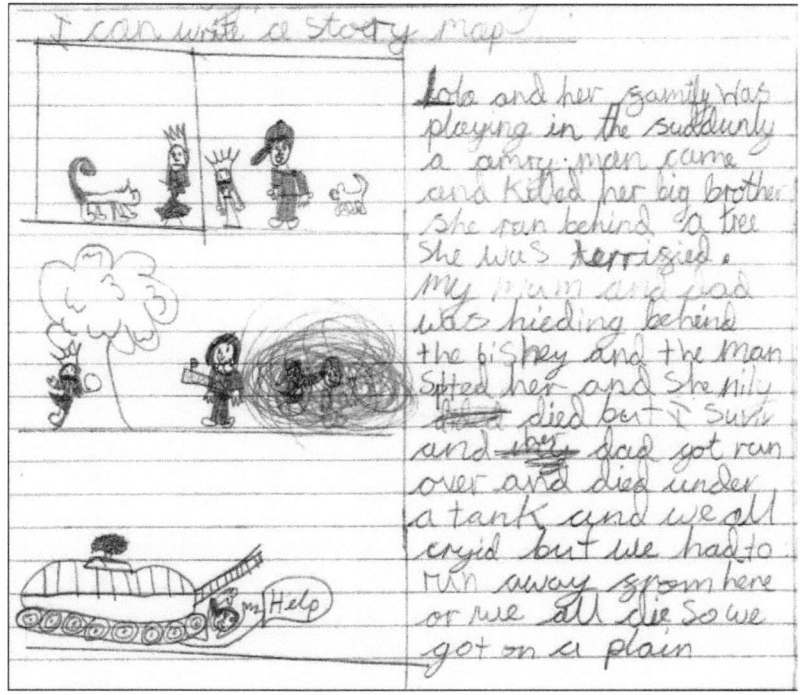

Figure 7.9: Peliona's story map.

Lola and her family was playing in the suddenly an army man came and killed her big brother. She ran behind a tree. She was terrified. My mum and dad was hiding behind the bushes and the man spotted her and she nearly died but I survived and her dad got run over and died under a tank and we all cried but we had to run away from here or we all die so we got on a plane.

When asked to construct a story map for her book, Peliona's writing is descriptive and her pictures graphic (Figure 7.9). The vividness with which she describes the scene suggests a familiarity with the subject matter and her change from third person to first person narration suggests her complete involvement. The final image of a person crushed under a tank is chilling in its detail and adds further evidence that the violence in Hassan's story resonates with her.

Figure 7.10: Amalia's story map.

Stefeny and her family live happily together in Spain. Their house burnt down. Stefeny was scared. She hid in a BOX! They had to move to LA. Stefeny was the saddest girl in the world. She went on a plane and she cried not tears of joy but sadness ones. She got to LA and she did not feel at home at her new home.

Amalia, partly from a Portuguese-speaking African background, who perhaps had an indirect experience of the wars in Angola or Mozambique, depicts a character who has to move because her house has been burnt down (Figure 7.10). That the family had to flee the country suggests that they were subject to war or persecution. The story continues in an extremely sad vein, with the subject (Stefeny) unable to find happiness in her new home. The graphic depictions by Amalia and Peliona, probably both from a refugee background, in their reflections on *The Colour of Home* and through their choice of violent catalysts in their own books, show a grim, and possibly familiar, engagement with the themes of war and flight.

Mashad, from Afghanistan, had been in the UK for four years, and was therefore likely to be a refugee. Despite his limited level of English, he showed good understanding of the story and a close identification with Hassan. In class discussion, Mashad mentioned that he didn't like the 'war part', but in a small group with me, when asked which part he liked best, he remarked surprisingly:

> I like the story (very animated) because when they smudge the picture and ruined it ... and the bullets (said with gusto!) came and guns came ... Because I like guns and I like blood.

Mashad's teacher felt strongly that he had not been disturbed by the subject matter of *The Colour of Home*. My own impressions of his participation in class discussions confirmed this, along with his enthusiasm to write about the book, and his comments in the more intimate situation of the group discussion, where such a disclosure might have come out. He related the events in the book to his own experience when he arrived in the UK:

> He can't talk English ... He talk to the Somali translator, and the translator talk to the children ... So Hassan can't talk ... Yeah ... when first time when I came to London ... I saw the clouds, grey and I saw my cousin.

My field notes record that when asked to write a diary entry about his first day at school in the role of Hassan, Mashad wrote two paragraphs, a lot for someone with limited English. This could have been due to his personal engagement with the text. In an insightful observation, Mashad pointed out to me that 'Hassan can talk, but the other children think he can't speak.'

Ahmed, from Egypt, was well aware of the civil war there and had strong reactions to the book. These could have stemmed from close connections he still had with people in his country. Ahmed was enthusiastic about *The Colour of Home* and seemed interested and motivated by the book, but in the group discussion his reaction was particularly extreme:

> My favourite part is when he smudged out his uncle ... I love the horrible bits! Because I'm a boy! Cool Stuff are horrible stuff for boys. I don't like the calm stuff in stories ... I like the killing.

However, Ahmed's teacher commented that he was proud of his homeland, despite its ongoing problems, and noticed a high level of awareness in him, clearly due to his home influences. Despite his relish of violence, the following quote demonstrates Ahmed's understanding of his own position, and of the horror of war:

> There's people firing all the places ... at the moment. And one person fired a school, um, burned a school ... and children died. I'm lucky that I'm ... I escaped before the war ... and I wish the war stops before Eid comes because ... people will die then.

After the discussion ended Shanaye said to me quietly: 'Boys think war is good but it's not, because people get killed and they get evacuated to other countries.'

Debora was from the Ivory Coast, another country with a turbulent recent history of civil war. She revealed that she had experienced significant family dislocation and loss, which still had echoes of sadness for her, and she was adamant that the book was not to her taste because of its violent content: 'Because it has blood in it and they're talking about war. Who wants to listen to war?'

There was a marked gender divide in reactions to violence in Year 3, with one boy commenting: 'I like the war part.' This appears to confirm the findings of the Children's Reading Choices project (Coles and Hall, 2002): reading patterns and practices are highly gendered, even from a very young age, and particularly prey to gendered peer pressure. While girls were more compassionate and humane in their responses to the problems of war, boys appeared to relish the elements of violence in the story, which became difficult to handle during the group discussion as they got excited by talk of guns and mimed shooting around the table. This 'resistant' reading is described by Sipe as a 'performative response' (2008: 173), whereby children playfully manipulate the text for their own creative purposes. Similarly

Pearson (2010) noticed that children 'acting out' in response to a text, using mimicry and other voices, was part of their engagement with literature.

Isolation, belonging and strategies of welcome

Children in Year 3 clearly related to wider issues that can affect any newcomer to the class, and in carefully planned activities were focused on engaging with prior experiences and empathy. When imagining Hassan's feelings as he stood in the doorway of his new class, they wrote:

> Scared because they might bully me.

> I think they are saying horrible things.

The vocabulary the children use in their books later echoes this understanding: 'apprehensive', 'frustrating', 'nostalgia'. They comment that he could be 'feeling lonely', and 'feeling angry'. I asked John, who had only just moved from another school in the area, how he felt when he arrived. 'Scared', he replied. John remembered missing everybody from his old school, and not knowing anyone in his new class. His writing reflects these memories, through Hassan's feelings of missing his family and cat: 'I wish I could just hug them once more or two.'

When Amalia writes in role, imagining herself in Hassan's position on his first day in school, she says: 'I fealt like I was a panyata and candy was going to pore out of me. Because it was like I was going to explode of shynes.' Amalia, who has one parent of Portuguese-speaking African heritage, may have had experience of piñatas filled with candy and is using this evocative simile to relate to Hassan's feelings. Clearly children in Year 3 can feel empathy with a refugee child depicted in a story, and can relate the character's story to their own life experiences.

In her own version of the start of the book, Izzy wrote this descriptive, empathetic piece, using a rich vocabulary:

> 'We have a new boy joining us at school today,' said Mrs Eljona. 'he is called Victor and he is from North Irealnd. (sic) I want you to make him feel at home.' Standing next to Mrs Eljona, while his legs shaking, nervously and his hair frizzing up, stood a tall wimpy boy, his bright green eye's shimmering to the class. 'can I have three caring people to volintere (sic) to make Victor observe around the school?' Mrs Eljona asked. Victor stared up at him, I'm so spooked out, he thought why are they observing me? (While they're mouth's (sic) agape.) I wish I could understand.

As well as being evocative and emotive, Izzy's writing conveyed practical strategies for welcoming a new child in the class. Peliona's diary entry, writing in role as Hassan after his first day at school, likewise demonstrates how crucial is the teacher's role in communicating with new arrivals, in this account by the use of hand signals. She describes how children observe their peers and copy their behavior, to accomplish the tasks expected of them:

> Then Miss Kelly gave me a paint brush and a pot. I didn't understand the first time but then she did actions with her hand. For a second I saw the kids, what they painted. Then I painted house, a cat, and nine people and a goat, a bunch of sheep.

Somalia in the spotlight

Reading *The Colour of Home* in the classroom obviously puts Somali children in the spotlight, since it names the country on the first page. When I asked Jill Rutter, expert on Refugee Education, whether she thought there was a danger of negatively portraying Somalia for children of Somali heritage, she replied:

> There's an embarrassment and I think among children who come from Africa, the media portrayals of Africa are so negative, and teasing children about their origins is an issue. It's not so much the refugee experience, as its origins in Africa that are problematic, and most of the media stories about Somalia at the moment are about pirates or about starvation ...

The two Somali children in Charlie's class were also both second-generation migrants – probably from a refugee background – and neither had visited the country. Although she had read the book before, Asma was ambivalent about it being read in front of the whole class:

> They've got headscarves on like me ... All the other children will look at me ... I get shy when it is about my country, because everyone looks at me on the carpet, because of what I'm wearing.

On my next visit Asma's ambivalence about being put in the spotlight was clear again:

> JH: Do you like having a book about Somalia read to the class?'

> Asma: No ... Because it's embarrassing me ... Because everyone just looks at me. Remember last time ... oh my God, oh my God, oh my God!

JH: But you like the book don't you?

Asma: I loved it ... It's really interesting. I would read it again ...
I really understand what Hassan meant.

Later in an individual interview, Asma talked to me animatedly about the book and how it connected directly with her family experience:

He wants to go back to his country. It's really sad, the war in Somalia, because they're giving children guns. My aunty ran away. She had to run all the way to London. Her feet really hurt. That must be hard.

This highly sensitive comment is remarkably insightful, coming as it does from an 8-year-old. Although born in the UK, Asma was able to relate directly to the situation in Somalia because of her family background, and demonstrated an affective emotional response.

It took a long time for Kadiye to open up to me in an interview, as he was inarticulate, and lacked appropriate vocabulary to express himself. He expressed a very negative view of Somalia, having no relatives there, only in Kenya: 'They're a poor country, and there's not much people. It's not a nice country to ... It's a dangerous country. It's not nice to go there.' Kadiye was ambivalent about the text, 'cause there are not many books that come from Somalia'. Like Asma, he found it embarrassing because other children looked at him, but also said: 'every time I hear the story I like it'. Rather than having it shared with the whole class in the Literacy hour, Kadiye said 'I would read it by myself'. But he thought it a good idea for other children to learn about Somalia.

Many Somali children in the UK have only a second-hand knowledge of the country, even though they would respond to it as familiar, as Somali parents, in common with most refugee communities, retain strong, emotional ties to their place of origin (Kahin, 1997). However, *The Colour of Home* depicts a view of a simple farming lifestyle, which might feed into stereotypes from the media and which can be very different to the Somalia parents talk about. Putting Somali children in the spotlight through a book with negative images of Somalia, may be worse than nothing, as Bishop (1990: n.p.) endorses:

When children cannot find themselves reflected in the books they read, or when the images they see are distorted, negative, or laughable, they learn a powerful lesson about how they are devalued in the society of which they are a part.

However, Demie *et al.* (2007) identified that including Somali language and cultural images in the curriculum was important for raising Somali children's self-esteem and achievement. Kruizenga (2010) also pointed out that Somali students, like others, should have opportunities to learn about and research their own identities. But as Botelho and Rudman (2009: 266) point out: 'One text cannot do it all; it is the reading of multiple texts and the juxtaposition of these texts against lived experience and secondary sources that is central.'

The 'constructed' text

> When readers perceive texts as motivated, rather than innocent, they position themselves within an alternative discourse of reading, participating in a critical literacy.
>
> (McDonald, 2004: 17)

Although the children were sometimes asked to think about the 'message' of the book and the author's motive or purpose for writing it, teachers rarely departed from reader response to critical literacy, where children consider whether the text is successful in achieving its purpose and whether this could have happened otherwise. This is something, as Comber (2001) suggests, that children can do, even when young:

> As readers, students must evaluate the social construction of a text and question the factors that may have influenced the author to create the text in a specific manner.
>
> (Coffey, 2008)

In a Year 3 discussion group Mashad showed his interest in the book, by raising the question of the author's motivation for writing. He was the only child to do so, and at one point he asked me whether I was the author. He also asked in a class discussion: 'Why did she write the story?' It is interesting that it was a child who asked this question, rather than the teacher, and other children made suggestions:

> To make her famous. (a perceptive thought here!)

> It might have happened to her before.

Charlie, the teacher, suggests, 'or someone she knows', and then adds: 'Maybe she read an article in the paper and that was a spark.' The children go along with the idea of 'intertextuality' by adding: 'Maybe she saw it in a TV programme and thought of something to write.'

In a discussion group outside the class afterwards, Shanaye, Debora, Peliona and Asma surmise about the motivations of the author:

Maybe she had an uncle or dad who died and who was fighting in the war and one of his mates accidently shot him ... To never forget about her dad.

Maybe they did this story because some people are very sad about war and who died and who was part of the family and who died.

I think she did that story to show how people can get frightened and in the end after it they can show the expressions on their faces how they are in their actions ...

To tell the people about what happened to Somalia that day.

Here we see a return to the idea of direct experience motivating the author, or a desire to communicate to others how people can be affected by civil war and the refugee experience.

Charlie's class were fortunate to have the opportunity to communicate directly with the author, interviewing Mary Hoffman on Skype. Charlie felt it gave the class 'the sense of a writer and a reader', a comment that could well be related to Rosenblatt's transactional theory of reading (1978). The children also had the opportunity to frame questions themselves – an important part of critical literacy (Fisher, 2008). However, in practice their questions were prepared in advance and chosen by the teacher. And rather than being about the creation of *The Colour of Home,* they tended to focus more on the generalities of authorship, such as: 'What is your favourite story?', 'Where do you write?' and 'Where do you get your ideas?'

Hoffman was asked about her favourite colour, food etc., although some asked what she like about being an author, when she started writing and finally what inspired her to write *The Colour of Home.* To the last question she answered that her publisher had asked her to write about refugees, but then she 'got really interested in it'. In terms of helping the children understand the wider significance of the text, this left a lot to be desired, although it was clearly tailored to the age-group of the class. Hoffman's response points again to the role of the teacher rather than the author, in locating the book within the larger themes and currents in society, which spawn, as in this case, challenging texts that counter populist media messages. In the words of Cervetti *et al.* (2001: n.p.):

Textual meaning is understood in the context of social, historic, and power relations, not solely as the product or intention of an author. Further, reading is an act of coming to know the world (as well as the word) and a means to social transformation.

Reflections

Picturebooks, as Nodelman and Reimer (1992) suggest, can evoke emotional reactions to texts beyond pure words – see Chapter 3. Illustrations can convey a book's overall 'meaning' far more powerfully than words do (as in Littlewood's interview in Chapter 5), carrying with them extra dimensions of interpretive possibilities (Nodelman, 2005). As refugees or children from a refugee background, some of the children in Year 1 and Year 3 had experienced voluntary migration. Some had only moved school within the area, while others had never moved at all. Yet all the children created meaning about the refugee experience from *The Colour of Home*, responding powerfully by creating their own multimodal texts.

Across the year groups reader responses varied. Some were unexpected – when certain boys indulged in a violent 'acting out', for example, displaying a resistant reading, unlike the girls who showed more empathy and in some cases were distressed by the content. Arizpe and Styles (2003) found that even at a young age girls tend to express their feelings more openly. The text and illustrations served as a catalyst for many children to talk about their own experiences, with some from refugee or migrant backgrounds relating the story to their own lives. While in general, Somali children welcomed a book that reflected them, they were ambivalent about it being read aloud to the whole class. To this extent the reader 'provides a context: this is drawn from his own past experience, and depends on his attitudes and values' (Rosenblatt, 1978: 97–8). However, it seemed that children from refugee backgrounds included contextual details that seemed to draw on personal experience or wider knowledge. Across the classes, however, response to the story depended more perhaps on individual sensitivities and personalities.

Even children in Year 1 showed understanding of the three parts of the refugee experience (Hamilton and Moore, 2004), identified with language barriers, empathized with 'newness' and suggested good welcoming strategies. However, it was clear that teacher input had a strong influence on response in building a 'community' of readers (Chambers, 1993). Significant moments in the book were represented in writing and drawing, but these were often at odds with each other and suggested that the children needed the opportunity to enact their responses in a variety of ways.

Critical literacy proposes that children should be encouraged to investigate the world of the text in relation to their own lived reality. But it should also go beyond mere reflections to discuss other possibilities (Hall, 1998). In Year 1 attempts to grapple with the overall 'message' in the writing were difficult, whereas in Year 3, ideas flowed somewhat better in discussion groups. This suggests that age is a factor in critical engagement, that dialogue rather than written work might be a better forum for critical literacy, and that teachers have a key role to play in enabling children to view the text as authored, partial and arbitrary, and to link it to larger themes.

Chapter 8

The 'enabling' teacher

Introduction

During my interview with Beverley Naidoo – see Chapter 5 – she mentioned the teacher specifically as a person in a pivotal position to introduce children to literature about the refugee experience: 'There are ... teachers who talk with the young people who they see every day about the themes that are in those books ... They can have the most interesting conversations with them.' These are useful starting points from which we can examine the role of the teacher as an 'enabling adult' when mediating between a text and the class, to engage in critical discussion (Chambers, 1991).

This chapter looks at two Year 5 classes who studied *The Other Side of Truth* over six weeks as part of the Literacy curriculum. I interviewed their two teachers, Violet and Sophie, evaluated their plans and made classroom observations. The sections follow the overall format of Chapter 6, but the themes that emerged emphasize that teachers had a slightly different role in Year 5 than Year 3. To generalize briefly: teachers mediated the text less directly at this stage, and planned for more class discussion, role play and written response. They also made more links with the wider world around the text.

Planning for reader response and critical literacy

Although Violet had used *The Other Side of Truth* in the classroom before, Sophie planned the scheme of work as the two teachers worked in partnership. Both were enthusiastic about the book, but Sophie immersed herself deeply in research for her planning and produced high-quality, attractive and stimulating lesson resources, which she later posted up on the *TES* website for other teachers to access. Accordingly, much of the focus of this section is on Sophie's planning.

Sources of inspiration

Sophie used a website from another Primary School in North London (no longer available) as her primary source of inspiration. This school had a history of engaging with refugee texts, and had produced a scheme and examples of children's work on *The Other Side of Truth*, all of which were available to share. As well as inventive ideas for written responses to the text, the school had taken a cross-curricular approach, incorporating drama, art, geography, maths and ICT into the study of the text. When tackling the issue of bullying, which arises in *The Other Side of Truth*, they showed children how to access the Childline website – a valuable lesson in itself – and asked them to compare the definitions of bullying found there with the treatment of the principal character, Sade, in the book. They also took the class on the actual 'Number 36' bus that Sade and Femi would have travelled on when they first arrived in the UK, and were visited by the author, Beverley Naidoo. Such inventive work, put on a website for others to use, is a gift for teachers who struggle with time when planning and producing resources. Furthermore, it promotes 'reading the word and the world' (Freire and Macedo, 1987), as it moves from the text to embrace issues in the environment of particular concern for children.

By chance, week 5 of the work on *The Other Side of Truth* coincided with Refugee Week, and Sophie was inspired to contact the Refugee Week organization via their website. They sent a representative to the school, who delivered a lesson on what causes people to become refugees and explained the Simple Acts initiative, which invites people to take positive social action to welcome and help refugees. Sophie also used a drama scenario – Everyone Everywhere: Refugees and Asylum – similar to the one in Year 3, which she obtained from the Amnesty website. Here a fictional situation where a family is threatened builds up to the decision to flee. In groups children role play the discussion that might have taken place amongst the family before they flee and then prepare a list of ten things to take with them. Involving other organizations and speakers broadened the 'voice' beyond just that of the teacher, to add authenticity and depth and to make connections with the real world.

Providing context and tackling challenging issues

Before the children in Year 5 even started looking at *The Other Side of Truth*, Sophie had planned to lay the groundwork for it in important ways. First, she had a display in her classroom of books about refugees, to prepare the children for the concepts they would encounter in the reading. This is an example of 'intertextuality' (Kristeva, 1966). Second, she chose to read *Gervelie's Journey* (Robinson and Young, 2008) to the class, a real-life story of a refugee child from the Congo. The book contains pictures and photographs and could be covered in its entirety in one lesson as a warm-up.

In sharing a short version of a refugee story as a swift introduction Sophie demonstrated from the outset that the experiences in both books happen to real children (Rutter, 1994). She skilfully introduced concepts to aid understanding of asylum, illegal entry and the use of fake identification documents, as in *The Other Side of Truth*. Sophie then asked the children to match such terms such as refugee, war, to flee, visa, passport, asylum, immigration control, Refugee Council, hostel and lawyer to given definitions. She thus demonstrated her own in-depth contextual knowledge of immigration control, a factor crucial to the success of such lessons, which I deal with more thoroughly later in the chapter. As Freire states: 'The starting point is what the teacher knows about the object and where the teacher wants to go with it' (Shor and Freire, 1987: 103). Dolan (2014a, 2014b) proposes a framework of 'Respect-Understanding-Action' for promoting development and intercultural education. With the above, Sophie clearly introduces the first two concepts, leaving the third for the more in-depth study of *The Other Side of Truth*.

As a follow-up lesson, Sophie planned for the children to use non-fiction sources such as books, atlases, photos and magazine articles to research Nigeria in general. She gave them a variety of headings: people, countryside, cities, school and education, landscape and climate, culture and food. Here we see further 'intertextuality', this time with non-fiction texts, and further 'reading of the world'. The activity also highlighted famous Nigerians such as Ken Saro-Wiwa's daughter and the pop star Tinie Tempah. Furthermore a map of Nigeria was provided in the centre of the sheet the children were going to work on, providing initial knowledge about the country's location. In a later session the children were encouraged to use the internet to access wider sources of information when gathering facts about Ken Saro-Wiwa, whose death was a major inspiration for writing *The Other Side of Truth* (discussed in Chapter 4). All this background work set the book in a worldwide and national context that children could find out more about, linked with real people, dead or alive, who had inspired the book. It also established positive images of Nigeria from the outset.

During the six weeks spent studying *The Other Side of Truth*, Year 5 children addressed many challenging concepts and issues and had opportunities to focus on socio-political territory. The story itself engages with bribery and corruption by police and government, a difficult concept for some children, but all too familiar for others. The class also discussed children going into care and what fostering actually means, the idea of emergency housing, hostels and the role of social workers in society. They were asked to contemplate the death of a parent and how they would deal with bereavement, which brought an affective reading of the text to the fore. The children also learnt about the deportation of failed asylum seekers by making a link with *X Factor* contestant, Gamu Nhengu. Nhengu had been fighting the decision that she had to return to Zimbabwe, an issue the children may well have been aware of. No wonder Sophie commented: 'so much that we did try and go into, but you feel like you are just tapping the very surface'.

Dovetailing with the Literacy curriculum

Among primary school children, reading a text such as *The Other Side of Truth* by themselves will be beyond the ability of some in the class, so the whole book has to be shared in class time. In her interview, Violet mentioned that the book was very long and Sophie spoke about the tensions between reading a class novel in its entirety while meeting the National Curriculum in England learning objectives for Literacy, which tended to focus on written responses – see Chapter 6:

> I had to read more out of the Literacy lesson, because too many of my Literacy lessons were just reading at them and I didn't therefore get to teach the objective and they didn't do enough work themselves so it was just a lot of listening and copying down words they liked.

Sophie's use of vocabulary is interesting here. She bemoans 'reading *at* them', because she couldn't 'teach the objective', and also that the children 'didn't do enough work themselves'. However, reading the whole book together does provide an opportunity for discussion about and beyond the book (Chambers, 1991; Barrs and Cork, 2001; McDonald, 2004), and allows critical literacy and dialogic pedagogy to play out. Furthermore, the full implications of a text like *The Other Side of Truth* would be lost if dealt with only through extracts. The story builds into a climax, with heightened tension, and issues grow larger as the book progresses.

The opening scene of *The Other Side of Truth* is detailed in Chapter 4, and could be described as one of the most dramatic story openers in any children's novel. It contains a short, sharp, enigmatic description of Mama being shot on the drive, written in italics in the present tense. The next paragraph switches to plain type and the past tense, as the children sit in the living room while the doctor comes to examine Mama, and pronounces her dead. Using an idea from the primary school website I mentioned, Sophie asked Year 5 to respond to the juxtaposition of the present and the past tense and examine its effect, instead of asking them to pick out what literary features cause the heightened sense of drama, which would have empowered them to come up with their own answers. My field notes state: 'Two ways of looking at this – killing the text by reducing it to a grammar lesson, OR good to base a grammar lesson on such a radical text.'

At this point in my observations I was unsure whether the book was being used to fit the Literacy targets, or if the learning objectives were being manipulated to fit in with the text's emotional weight. As we have seen, critical literacy is entirely contingent 'on educators' professional ingenuity in navigating the enabling and disenabling local contexts of policy' (Luke, 2012: 9). As the weeks rolled out, I grew to admire these two teachers increasingly for their skill and expertise in drawing out an appreciation of language from the text. They also developed Literacy tasks that aimed to improve the children's writing without detracting from the power and meaning of *The Other Side of Truth*. My field notes show details whilst in Violet's class:

> A prepared diary entry by Femi. At the airport, opened their bags, X-rayed suitcase and him. Very imaginative … Written by T? Have to find synonyms for his feelings – adjectives. Using dictionaries. Children come up with good synonyms.

> T. points out language devices as she reads – simile, metaphors, etc. They have to write speech bubbles for six characters – what they might be thinking, using connectives – Sade, Femi, Robert, Mrs Graham, Kevin, Jenny.

Furthermore, a sample of week 3's learning objectives show how the dull language of the National Curriculum in England was transformed to encourage a more active response. These were linked to the Literacy curriculum to justify their inclusion:

- Learning objective: I can choose form and content for a purpose. In pairs typing (Marlowe School) Chronicle article about Beverley Naidoo's visit. Winning article to be published in newsletter.
- Learning objective: I can engage in challenging subject matter. Discussing terms: 'asylum', 'refugee' and stereotypes of each. Looking at facts about Ken Saro-Wiwa.
- Learning objective: I can identify different question types and evaluate their impact. In pairs, children write questions to ask Sade and Mr Nathan as immigration officers.

The first activity involves writing for a real purpose and a real audience – the school community, and gives children a chance to report a first-hand experience. The second is certainly challenging, tackling aspects of the refugee process, and finding facts about the man who influenced the book's inception. The final activity used questioning to simulate a highly contentious area: the attitude of immigration officials when dealing with asylum seekers. This led on to a role play, using the questions the children developed, in which the teacher and the teaching assistant played the parts of immigration officers, interrogating Sade and Mr Nathan, who were acted by the children.

In week 4, children accessed the Childline website, as previously mentioned, under the learning objective of 'I can retrieve information from a text'. They then created a poster encouraging children experiencing bullying to get help from Childline, with the learning objective of 'I can use persuasive language'. These are further examples of transforming the functional language of the NLS into purposeful and creative activities. Finally in this week, under the learning objective of 'I can imagine and explore feelings', the children rewrote the story of Mariam, another refugee in the book, from third person to first person, detailing her harrowing journey on foot from Somalia to Kenya and thence to the UK. This task led the children to identify directly with Mariam, clearly evoking an affective response to the text, and providing an alternative refugee story.

Making connections

Sophie pointed out in her interview that *The Other Side of Truth* had made many connections around the world, and with the international and multicultural make-up of her Year 5 class:

> The book covering Nigeria, Somalia, the UK aspect and also even Jamaica with the foster family and then you've got Beverley's background of South Africa and apartheid, so there are all of those issues. You know, in this class I've got Olu from Nigeria, Hedley who's Jamaican and Dawo who's Somali and a few others … it's really good for them to have that extra link into the book as well …

Sophie's planning encouraged interrogating multiple viewpoints, an important component of critical literacy. Through various activities she stimulated the children to respond through the eyes of the many characters, representing different perspectives in the story. For example, she asked the children to write in role as Femi, thinking about his feelings on the aeroplane, and his diary entry when he arrived at Heathrow, considering issues such as bribery, trafficking and false passports. My field notes taken in Violet's class record:

They all have to imagine they are Femi: ...

- Having their passports checked
- Customs officers take an hour to check all their bags.
- Uncle Dele not meeting them in Arrivals hall.

As already mentioned, children also compiled questions for the immigration officers, which gave them an opportunity to investigate the reasons behind UK Border Agency discourses, and to understand the arguments against allowing free access to immigration. These are prevalent in the media and also now in government. It is important for children to access controversial, contradictory and interdependent discourses, and to make up their own minds on challenging issues. This is the kind of dialogue Beverley Naidoo wanted her books to stimulate. While watching an improvised drama sketch where children acted out an interview with immigration officials in small groups, I recorded:

> Children's answers demonstrate clear understanding of the reasons why the family are claiming asylum. Into role as different characters. Able to see it from different perspectives. Some of the questions are probing and very directly to the point – e.g. 'Why do you have the right to stay here?'

Drama often functions well in providing the opportunity to interrogate multiple viewpoints (Lewison *et al.*, 2002). It also 'disrupts the commonplace' and engages with 'socio-political issues', dealing with difficult questions of legality and obligation with regards to asylum seekers. Here the book reflects the underlying 'climate of belief' (Hollindale, 1988: 37) of the society of which it is a part, opposing the systematic silencing of asylum seekers in contemporary discourse (Kushner, 2003: 26).

Towards the end of the time spent studying the book, my field notes record:

> They are to act the interview with Uncle Dele, Sade and Femi outside the detention centre where their father is. Shown on news. Create questions first. Children come up with ideas of questions really quickly. They are well into the situation.

Again, the use of drama is particularly effective when interrogating multiple viewpoints, as pupils enter into other situations and roles, and can become very involved with the characters they are representing. After this activity, the children wrote up a news report of the interview, taking conflicting positions, arguing for and against offering Papa refugee status, and could again see why this is a contested and controversial issue.

The 'constructedness' of the text

At the side of the classroom Sophie had set out a selection of other books by Beverley Naidoo, making a direct connection to the author via 'intertextuality' and highlighting the 'constructedness' of the text. She downloaded a video from the BBC website of Naidoo reading the opening paragraph of the book, to give the children a visual and auditory impression of the author, and arranged for Naidoo herself to visit.

Figure 8.1: Beverley Naidoo reading to Year 5 on her visit to the school.

Naidoo, as the quotes from her interview at the beginning of this chapter show, is passionate about entering into dialogue with readers and making connections between 'the word and the world'. She frequently visits schools and is expert at engaging an audience of children. Myhill (2007: 62) suggests that: 'Questioning the author alters the nature of the task from open-ended enquiry to critical thinking about authors and texts and how every text is an artefact, something created which has a purpose.'

Obviously the questions Comber suggests – 'Who has produced the text, under what circumstances, and for which readers?' (2001: 1) – can be optimally addressed when the author is met in person. When Naidoo visited the school, the children were fully immersed in dialogic pedagogy

(Skidmore, 2000), and thus able to see that her author's discourse is subjective and, since she outlined the myriad of influences on her writing, 'contingent' (Aukerman, 2012). My field notes recorded part of her assembly:

> BN ... begins talking about S. Africa. She shows her notebook from Feb–Dec 1997 in which she did her research for The Other Side of Truth. BN talks about Ken Saro-Wiwa. Novel begins day after weekend that he was executed. She relates Saro-Wiwa to Papa. Both writers ... Shows pictures of Nigeria she took on her research trip. Lagos, forest, Ife. 'Sade's hill.' 'Mama's lemon tree.' Picture of immigration office. Explains how she went to Croydon, Lunar House.

The children had the chance to hear Naidoo talk about her life and work in an assembly, and in direct contrast to the typical 'pedagogical dialogue', where the teacher is usually the questioner (Skidmore, 2000 – see Chapter 3), were then able to ask her authentic questions. As Sophie commented, 'the idea was to stage it like a news conference.' The children had looked at Naidoo's website prior to her visit, to gather information and to prepare their questions. This resulted in intelligent and penetrating questions. Naidoo then joined them in the classroom for a more intimate encounter, where she engaged closely in personal dialogue, allowing the children to direct the topic and to build on her answers to ask more probing questions.

After the event Naidoo wrote about the visit in her blog, thanking the children as 'I was reminded yesterday of the pleasure of visiting young readers in school' (Naidoo, 2012). She included the photograph of her reading to the children in the assembly hall (Figure 8.1). All of this was collective, reciprocal, supportive, cumulative and purposeful, the key ingredients Alexander (2008) identified as essential to good dialogic teaching. As Sophie commented in her interview:

> I think they really felt that the book was very important in the year ... For the author to come in really kind of raised the significance of it and raised its profile, and that not only are they then seeing the book from Sade's point of view, but they are sort of seeing it from Beverley's point of view. Why she chose to write it. I think that's really brilliant to be able to hear from the author about her writing style, what her background is and then to try and pick up that as you are continuing to read the book.

Teachers mediating the text
Sharing the script

Sophie transferred the whole of *The Other Side of Truth* to the Interactive White Board (IWB), so that the text was displayed large for the children to follow while both teachers read it aloud to the class. Like the other teachers in my study, she mediated the text during the reading, occasionally 'translating' it into more accessible language, but kept this to a minimum.

Violet, the other Year 5 teacher, was also able to display the text on her IWB and saw this as a huge asset for the class. She stated in her interview:

> Thanks to Sophie, it made it easier for the children to understand because they had it, visualized it. I think if … I just stood in front of the class and read the book, I think I would have lost them ages ago and they wouldn't have really understood what was going on in the book, but because it was on the board and had images, I think that really helped.

The use of IWBs has been hugely contested since they were adopted in British schools through large-scale government investment between 2003 and 2005. In this context, Levy argued that the scale of IWBs meant that visual information could be more easily shared, thereby 'drawing the class together' (2002: 11). Both Year 5 teachers, as confident ICT users, were able to use the IWB to great effect to enhance their teaching and the students' learning.

Questioning and discussion

Three extracts from my field notes highlight teacher and class interaction during my observations in Year 5, showing that teacher questioning can serve a variety of purposes. The first is an example of simple recall: Violet asked the children to recap the story so far, possibly partly for my benefit. It shows the children's enthusiastic engagement with the story:

> T. asks for recap of the story.

> Ch: Two ch, brother and sister. Their Dad was telling the Truth about something …

> T: About what?

> Ch: There's a war on. The people are coming after the Dad. The people they are telling the truth about.

T: Who decided they should go?

Ch: Their Aunty.

T: Who do they go with? Who is Mrs Bankole? Are they happy?

Ch: No

T: What happened?

Ch: She abandoned them.

T: Where?

Ch: Victoria Station café.

The questions and answers continued, but this is sufficient to demonstrate the use of questioning for recall, and to check that children have understood the narrative. Later on my field notes record that Violet encourages varied reader response explicitly, while building a 'community' of readers, as described by Chambers (1991): 'Questioning as she reads, T. shapes understanding. But she repeats that they can have their own interpretation and each may be different.'

The next extract shows a clear example of questioning and discussion that draw the class's attention to the author's writing style and its effect on the narrative. I have mentioned linking the opening page of the novel to the present tense to heighten drama, and my field notes of the session in action record Sophie's class tackling this idea:

T. highlights verbs on board.

Discussion of how to change present to past: add –ed

T: What effect does the switch in tenses have? How does it make the reader feel?

Ch: Emotional, because somebody dies in there.

T: Good. It makes the reader connect because it is in present tense.

Ch: It brings a tear to your eye – the gun, the screams.

Ch: It makes it feel like it's happening right now.

Here the teacher plants the seed of the lesson and follows this by open questioning. The children respond with excellent ideas and make a fruitful connection between content and style, building on each other's ideas through 'chaining'. The teacher strengthens the connections they make by reminding them of the stylistic device that promotes this – the use of the present tense.

Sophie also used a drama scenario – *Everyone Everywhere: Refugees and Asylum* (Amnesty International, n.d.). This dialogic activity is collective, reciprocal, supportive, cumulative and purposeful (Alexander, 2008 – see Chapter 3), similar to the work devised by the LA advisor for Year 3 – see Chapter 6). It also invites the children to empathize with the refugee experience through drama and creative thinking. My field notes record this process:

> They work through *Everyone Everywhere: Refugees and Asylum*, reading a section at a time.
>
> T. explains that it is a similar situation. She explains each piece carefully. Map of the journey drawn on the board including desert and high forest with trees.
>
> T: Might be snakes, foxes, ants, spiders, wolves. Dangerous by car. Imagine what you have to carry. What would you do? Imagine you are four characters.
>
> T: What might the mum say?
>
> Ch: It's dangerous for the kids.
>
> T: What would the 12-year-old girl say?
>
> Ch: She might be frightened and that they might not have enough food.
>
> T: What would the boy say?
>
> Ch: I don't want to go. I will miss my friends.
>
> T: What might the dad say?
>
> Ch: 'We have to go because it's too dangerous.

Here we see the teacher supplying information and context, setting up the situation and then structuring the activity through open-ended questioning. This prompts an 'affective' response, demanding a high degree of empathy. The lesson is also notable in using all the dimensions of critical literacy Lewison *et al.* (2002) proposed – see Chapter 3: it disrupts the commonplace, interrogates multiple viewpoints, focuses on socio-political issues and even promotes taking social action (which is, in Lewison's view, the most difficult aspect to achieve).

Teachers' own experiences

To introduce *The Other Side of Truth* to her class, Sophie found covers of the book translated into many languages with varied illustrations which she displayed on the IWB. It was a good way to demonstrate how the book has been read around the world, a point Beverley Naidoo also made in connection with all her books during her school visit. Sophie drew attention to one in German and told the class that she would be able to read this, as she speaks German. Such an explicit statement of multilingualism recognizes that this is a personal asset, one that some of the children had too.

However, in conversation with Sophie later, I discovered that she had a much closer personal connection with the book, as my notes record: 'Sophie talked about her own background. She told me how her grandparents were Jewish refugees from Germany, escaping through Sweden in 1939 and that this had had a lasting effect on her father.' This snippet of information is significant. It revealed that Sophie herself was from a refugee background, albeit nearly 75 years ago, an experience that can have a lasting legacy for a family, as discussed. Sophie's personal connection to the subject matter may have motivated her further to connect the children to the messages and themes in the book, fuelling her enthusiasm and the enormous amount of effort she put into planning the lessons, thinking of innovative and purposeful ideas and gathering and producing high-quality resources. It was striking that Sophie had not felt it opportune to share her family story with the class, so they could see yet more teacher experiences that linked with the text. Teachers may be reticent to share personal details with their class, but possibly Sophie simply didn't realize how she could have engendered a connection with the book via her own family story.

Teachers' contextual knowledge

Linked to teachers' own experience is the importance of contextual knowledge when leading discussions, particularly about challenging and controversial issues like those raised by *The Other Side of Truth*. We saw that during the reading of *Gervelie's Journey* Sophie had shown an in-depth understanding about immigration control. Dolan (2012: n.p.) stresses that 'educators need to be well versed themselves in the complexities of these perspectives and the political frameworks underpinning these concepts'. Where Sophie admitted to struggling with explanations was in the area of institutionalized bribery and corruption:

> … explaining to the children about, for instance the Nigerian dictatorship 'cause I find it hard maybe to imagine a government

that's doing the wrong thing in such a massive way, or corrupt soldiers, or policemen who are taking bribes. For me, it's not something I know. Some of the children said they'd seen it or they'd heard about it, but they were asking questions like 'Why don't you ... in Nigeria, why didn't you just go to the police?' and that sort of thing, and it was hard to explain it.

Finally, a comment in Sophie's interview shows how a project such as reading *The Other Side of Truth* with a class can spark the interest of teachers, leading them on to further learning. As Freire commented: 'the ability of the educator to know the object is remade every time' (Friere and Macedo, 1987: 100).

Linking with the Refugee Week website, I was then just looking through local events and I found the Weiner Library in London had an Austrian film that I went to see during the Refugee Week and they mentioned the Kindertransport, which I don't know a lot about, and I wonder if that's sort of similar because I guess all these children arrived in London and they couldn't all have been met by social services and families.

Sophie thus built on her experience of teaching the text to increase her own contextual knowledge. This dynamic relationship between teacher and pupils in the learning process is exactly what Freire propounds; it produces the best teaching and learning experiences for all involved.

Teachers' perceptions
Awareness of refugee children in the class

Teachers are sometimes unaware of the number of refugee children in their class and do not always make connections between a child's country of origin and their immigration status. However, Violet did not shy away from embracing the idea of migration in a child's background, as my notes record:

T. challenges assumptions that children from other countries can't speak English, mentioned in text. She asks how many born elsewhere? Three out of 16. One from Romania. T. points out that they all speak English. Relaxed manner of referring to those not born here.

Violet also knew the children in her class who had migrated and were possibly refugees. She told me: 'I think I've got about four in my class, they have been refugees. They've come over from another country.'

During Beverley Naidoo's visit to Year 5 one child came forward and spoke to the author, making an important disclosure, which Naidoo later recorded in her blog:

> Yesterday, when it was time to go home, a girl with deep enquiring eyes came up to me. 'Have you ever written a story about a child in a refugee camp?' she asked. I replied, 'Have you ever been in a refugee camp?' Yes, she said softly. She had stayed in a camp when she was 5 years old.

The child may have told the author this in confidence, but I wondered if she was happy about her disclosure being revealed so publicly in a blog. Violet observed that this child did not seem disturbed in any way when the book was read in class and had not talked to the teacher about her situation, reinforcing the notion that refugee status carries with it such stigma that students are reluctant to divulge it, even to their teachers. Coupled with the problems of teachers' access to data on individual children's migration status, this indicates the difficulties teachers have in knowing who in their class might be a refugee.

Sophie was candid about the fact that she had no idea. After I took several of her class out to participate in a discussion group, I wrote the following observations in my field notes:

> Discussion with Sophie afterwards. She is really surprised that so many children come from refugee backgrounds. She hadn't realized before. We discussed how this has an effect on children ... Also talked about how hard it is for Ts to know all this about the children in their classes as they never get a chance to work in a small group with them.

Using and understanding the term 'refugee'

In contrast to *The Colour of Home, The Other Side of Truth* uses the term 'refugee' several times, and invites discussion of its meaning. Right from the start, while the class were reading the blurb, looking at the covers and discussing what the book might be about, one child made the connection, as my field notes show:

T: From the covers, what do you think this might be about?

Ch: Telling lies. Telling the truth.

T. reads the blurb. Gives away a lot of the story!

T: Given the blurb and glossary, predict what book might be about.

Ch: It's about refugees.

T. very praising. They discuss in pairs …

T. (reading) 'Sade and Femi will flee the country at once and alone.

T: 'escaping, getting away.'

Ch: They might go through tough times with immigration because they are foreigners and they weren't born here. There will be some lies told.

Chapter 16 is entitled 'Refugees?' In it, the social worker tries to find out more of the children's story and suggests that they will have to apply for asylum, 'you know, to be treated as refugees' (Naidoo, 2000: 77). Sade, the main character, looks surprised at this. After the social worker has gone we are made privy to her thoughts:

> Refugee? They were those winding lines of starving people, with stick-thin children. People who carried their few possessions in dusty cotton bundles, struggling across deserts and mountains. Refugees were people trying to escape famine and war. You saw them on television. Were she and Femi really refugees?
>
> (ibid.: 78)

Clearly the book aims to combat the stereotypical view of refugees, but this negative image is not one that would inspire refugee children to identify as such and needs, I suggest, to be challenged immediately during the reading. Later when Sade and her foster carer are being shown round her new school by a young teacher, 'Miss Harcourt's cheeks had flushed a deep crimson when Aunt Gracie mentioned "refugees"' (ibid.: 104). Again the term appears to be stigmatizing and embarrassing, and should inspire further discussion about why this might be.

Children's engagement and understanding
When asked if the issues raised by the book were potentially disturbing for children in Year 5, Violet was adamant that this had been an important feature of the reading:

> It wasn't difficult to deal with. In fact, it was quite the opposite. It was good that it was brought up because we had really good discussions about bullying and about racism and applying to

issues that had been going on in like today's world, so it was a
good thing. There wasn't anything negative about it.

Sophie also felt that the children might have been moved by the difficult
issues the book raises, but not upset by them in the long term:

> They were kind of shocked in the moment of reading it, like the
> mugging and … but I don't really think they were disturbed …
> I liked the way all those issues were built into the book, and
> the children already feel sympathy, or understand Sade from the
> beginning, so anything difficult, they are sort of seeing it through
> Sade's eyes. … Somehow I think it cushions it.

In terms of pupils' understanding of the term 'refugee', Sophie felt her class
hadn't had a clear idea of the meaning before they read the book. Violet felt
that apart from the four refugees she had identified in her class, 'the others,
I don't know if they had any real views. Any views that they did have, they
would have got from family, or things that they've overheard, they maybe
didn't know the truth …'

Neither teacher identified any anti-refugee prejudice amongst either
the children or the wider community, and Violet felt the book had had a
powerful effect in connecting children to the concept. The fact that that the
refugees in *The Other Side of Truth* are a similar age to the children was
particularly supportive in this regard, as it helped the children identify and
empathize with them. As Violet observed: 'I think they're more aware of
how refugees are.'

Taking 'social action'

Sophie discussed the possibility that learning about the refugee situation
through *The Other Side of Truth* would lead to reflection and a long-
term change in attitudes and behaviour, the 'social action' that might be a
consequence of good critical literacy. However, she questioned whether this
was realistically possible:

> Once you have done all the definition work, and you hope that
> they've got the right idea, that it is someone whose life is in
> danger, then for me it was more if there was a refugee in their
> class, say in secondary school, the way they would treat them …
> However, I feel that a lot of it is so short term, with your memory
> as a child and how much impact a book has … I don't know …
> how much they would apply that to their own experience in the
> classroom in two years' time.

This echoes Mallan's (2013) work on fostering narrative empathy and Naidoo's own thesis (1992), which found that working with texts that challenge racism yielded no evidence of attitudinal change and was almost impossible to quantify.

Sophie had also been unhappy about the visit from the Refugee Week representative. She felt that too much time had been devoted to defining 'refugeeness' – which she had already covered adequately – and not enough to what Simple Acts, or social action, could be taken:

> I thought they were coming in just to talk about Simple Acts and going through what the kids could be doing that week ... I think it's 20 things, ... for instance reading a book about exile. Well, we've all done that ... Things like smiling at a refugee, having a cup of tea with a refugee, possibly playing football with a refugee, in which case you would have to know a local refugee ... And they were invited to ... local events that were run by the people on the website. So we all wrote a blog entry that I posted off ... I don't know if it will end up on their website.

I was critical of this visit too because when talking about acts that could be done to help refugees, and local events that could be attended explicitly for non-refugees to meet refugees, it was assumed that none of the children in the class were from a refugee background themselves. The speaker therefore seemed to be 'othering' refugees, a surprising oversight for a representative of such an organization.

Reflections

Jill Rutter, the respected writer about refugee education, told me in her interview:

> A lot of teaching that aims to make children think about refugee movement and migration, and also race more broadly is quite crude ... And you have to approach the attitudes that children have already ... I think that *The Other Side of Truth* is much more effective in changing ... children's attitudes because it enables teachers to look at exercises that build empathy and because it's a much richer literature. You can get children to imagine what it would be like being those two Nigerian children in a much more roundabout and perhaps less crude way.

Sophie had noticed this distancing effect already. It shows the crucial role that fiction can play in tackling controversial and potentially disturbing subject matter with young children in the classroom.

As 'enabling adults', when sharing *The Other Side of Truth* in the classroom both Year 5 teachers demonstrated how to mediate skilfully between text and readers, making the experience informative and positive and carefully balancing the 'aesthetic' and 'efferent' aspects of reader response. The teachers navigated curriculum objectives to devise purposeful classroom practice, giving the children opportunities to 'read the world', carry out activities with a real-life objectives and take action on a small scale. However, both were frustrated by the lack of opportunities for small-group discussion with their pupils. As a researcher, I benefited from this, as I discuss in the next chapter.

The author visit was particularly rich in terms of critical pedagogy and dialogic possibilities, Naidoo skilled in instigating 'reading the word and the world' through both her books and persona. In focusing on socio-political issues, making connections and interrogating multiple viewpoints (Lewison *et al.*, 2002), she and the teachers gave the children opportunities for optimal critical literacy. Pre-planning and follow-up lessons were important in making the most of this event and ensured that the refugee experience was brought into the classroom in high profile, via the medium of good literature.

Clearly, studying *The Other Side of Truth* for six weeks had been a treat for Year 5. If enthusiasm to read the sequel is proof of good engagement with a book, which it probably is, then Sophie had the perfect response:

> All of the children at the end were desperate to read *Web of Lies* and one of them went to the library, and two of them have already started it. I said to them 'Well I've only read half of it so I'm not giving you the book yet,' and they were saying 'Oh come on read it quick, so we can have it!'

Chapter 9

Listening to children's voices

Introduction

In her interview Beverley Naidoo suggested that:

> If it's a well-told story, the child will then ask questions, and you
> are then in a position to say, well I wonder if that might not be
> the answer to that. What do *you* think? And you engage in a
> much more open ended way in exploring what is going on, than
> in a didactic way.

To encourage this kind of exploratory dialogue, I had to gather much of the
data for this chapter from small group discussions outside the classroom
during weeks 4, 5 and 6 of Year 5's study of *The Other Side of Truth*. It is
often the case that the 'community' of readers (Chambers, 1993) is built
up in whole class sessions, but uncovering older children's opinions is not
easy through their written work, driven as it is by curriculum constraints
to meet pre-determined learning objectives. However, as we saw with Year
3, children may be prepared to speak out in groups of two to four. In this
milieu their thoughts can be unearthed and their voices heard, whereas in
one-to-one interviews they cannot build on the responses of others and may
feel under pressure to deliver the 'right' answer. In whole class discussions
expressing one's point of view can feel too intimidating, and some children's
voices might not be heard at all.

Early work by Cochran-Smith (1984) identified types of adult–
child verbal interactions around story reading. These included 'life-to-text'
interactions – those that helped story-listeners use their knowledge to make
sense of texts – and 'text-to-life' interactions, which enabled them to use
textual knowledge to make sense of their lives. Keene and Zimmerman
(1997) refined this paradigm to purport that students comprehend better
when they make different kinds of connections to a text, namely: 'text-to-
self', 'text-to-text', and 'text to world'. In this chapter, I classify children's
responses under the first and third headings, having briefly addressed 'text-
to-text' comparisons in Chapter 8. The final section deals with 'author-
to-text' reflections, or the 'constructedness' of the text, connecting with a
central tenet of critical literacy.

Text to self
Talking about their own lives

From my discussions with Year 5 about *The Other Side of Truth* I gained a powerful sense that several children were stimulated by the book to reflect on their own lives, or that of their parents and grandparents, many of whom were migrants and also refugees. The following examples give a sense of the range and diversity of experience in the class. Some children talked about the reasons their parents had come to the UK. These were not to do with extreme 'push factors' of fleeing from war or persecution, but more with 'pull factors' (Richmond, 1993) such as employment and educational opportunities, which would classify the children's parents as 'economic migrants'. Other children, however, made personal links with refugee themes of forced migration, violence and dislocation, as portrayed in Naidoo's book.

Amisha was specific about the details and motivations behind her parents' story:

> My mum and dad come from Bangladesh, but they come from different states. My mum and dad met in my country. They married each other and then they came to London for us, for the children to have a better future.

Dana was also clear in her account of her own migration. The break-up of her family precipitated the move, but for her mother the pull factor was personal connection, as well as the idea of a 'better life':

> My mum, my dad and I ... I was born in Romania ... And we came here when I was seven and a half. We came because my mum and dad were divorced, ... my mum lost her job and we decided that we should come to London ... And now my mum stays with a friend, and then we just came here ... not for a real specific reason, I don't think there was war or nothing. We just came for a better life, so my mum could get a job and I could get like ...

Further on in the conversation Dana discloses that her education was also a factor in her mother's decision to come to the UK. Her mother saw schooling as less formal than in Romania, and the UK system as offering more opportunities.

Interestingly, children were happy in the discussion groups to mention that their parents or grandparents had been refugees, but not they themselves. Solange spoke of her parents coming to the UK to seek sanctuary from the Democratic Republic of Congo, a notoriously violent and politically unstable country where the many shifts in power over decades have precipitated much forced migration:

> When my parents came here, they were seeking for asylum and then they got it but after like one year or two that's when they got their passport and their visa and all that stuff to be able to live here. So because my parents had me and my sister to look after, lucky my dad got a job already, so that he could provide, but it was still quite hard, because if, like, if the police found you they would deport you.

Solange's account shows an understanding of the stages of the asylum process. Later she spoke volubly about the fact that no sense of shame should be associated with the term 'refugee'.

Idil, whose ethnicity was described as Somali on the school database, but who had never been to Somalia, similarly shared details of her grandmother's migration experience:

> They were having a war at that time, and then they had to bring my grandma all the way to London ... but my grandma couldn't stay here, but she was a refugee here, but ... the government finally said she could stay, and then she stayed.

Dawo was happy to talk about her father's experiences of arriving in Italy, a common first stop for Somali migrants because southern Somalia had been colonized by Italy in 1889. Dawo made direct links between her father's story and that of the children in *The Other Side of Truth*:

> My dad, he was a bit like Sade and Femi, 'cause when he came to Italy he didn't know how to speak Italian. He only knew how to speak a little bit of Somalian and English ... and he had some friends that were living in Italy, and then he was looking for them, and then he couldn't find them ... and he had like £200 and then he went on the taxi and then do you know what happen? The taxi man only needed £40 – that's a lot actually ... And my dad gave him £100 cause he didn't know ... And then he had to keep moving houses, his cousin's house one time and then his friend's house ... He went to lots of houses and then when he had £100, £50 left he gave it to this old woman that would let him have his

137

own bedroom in the house ... and then he found himself a home to stay in.

Dawo gave me great detail of a kind derived from recounting personal experience, based closely on what her father had been prepared to share with her. She engaged with issues of language barriers, unfamiliarity with currency and value, poverty and homelessness all within her short account.

From these disclosures it seemed that *The Other Side of Truth* had been a powerful catalyst for children to talk about their own and their parents' backgrounds, and reasons for migrating. All the responses I've quoted are from girls, as they were more willing, and maybe more able to talk about family circumstances, women and girls having traditionally been the keepers of family history (Fiese *et al.,* 1995). Freire maintained that finding out about students' background circumstances and lives is an essential prerequisite for the 'dialogical method': it is 'a moment where humans meet to reflect on their reality as they make and remake it' (Shor and Freire, 1987: 98).

My discussion groups seemed to achieve this purpose and generally opened up a discourse about 'refugeeness' that children were willing to engage in, particularly in a small-group setting outside the classroom. However, it is not easy to make the space and time for this kind of interaction during the primary school day, and teachers may be frustrated by a lack of such opportunity.

Considering the refugee perspective

My discussion groups, class observations and interviews with the teachers did not show that any children identified as a refugee, although they were happy to talk about their parents and grandparents in such terms. Neither did they address the 'message' of the book from a refugee reader's point of view. Asking children about a hypothetical situation in their class was therefore the only way I could garner their opinion. This was important, as reservations about how refugees will react are constantly given as reasons against using such potentially disturbing books in the classroom. So I asked the discussion groups whether they thought this book would present difficulties if there were a refugee child in the class. Abdi and Moussa both said they thought it would, Abdi relating it to himself:

Abdi: 'Cause this sort of stuff has happened to me, and I wouldn't like to talk about it that much ... 'Cause it reminds me of all the bad stuff that has happened.

Moussa: If that happened to me, that my dad died, it would have reminded me and I wouldn't like it.

Solange referred to the potential for a refugee child in the class to shrink from the spotlight, and Amisha returned to the theme of evoking difficult memories:

Solange: Yes, it would. 'Cause it would be really tough to, like, take in the book. She would feel exposed, in a way.

Amisha: Yes, because if they're hearing the story it will make them remember what happened to them.

Olu and Kye had different opinions, but felt confident to voice them. They saw that in discussion groups multiple viewpoints were allowed and respected:

Olu: I don't think so ... Because the book is about a refugee and if a child in our class is a refugee I think they would understand properly what is happening.

Kye: I think 'yes' because they might have just reminded them that they were in the situation and then it would make them feel different from other people.

Amechi demonstrated a sophisticated ambivalence to the question, and approached the answer from both angles (despite using 'yes' and 'no' the opposite way round). It was noticeable that despite all the work and discussion around the book, she still hesitated before using the word 'refugee':

I'd say 'yes' and 'no'. 'No', because the (hesitation) refugee, the person might not really like people to read it and start feeling sorry for her, and ... 'Yes' because her or him would like ... well when they're reading the book they feel like they can say stuff more openly to their friends and people around them, cause people will understand after reading the book.

Dana talked about the stigma associated with 'refugeeness', but also a possible resistance to being labelled. As Zetter (1991) points out, being a refugee is only a bureaucratic entity:

It would be a little bit difficult, and then I'm thinking of what happened to them maybe. They will feel a little bit ashamed because it will be like 'Oh! You're a refugee! How was it?' ... And they were like thinking 'I don't want to be called a refugee. I'm a person. It's not like I'm a different human. I'm still a human, but I'm just a refugee.' And then, like, they won't really like it.

Here the children demonstrate reflection and analysis, raising issues that teachers need to be aware of when introducing a text such as *The Other Side of Truth* in the primary classroom, especially with regards to refugee children in the class. Their opinions differed about whether the book would present difficulties for a refugee child in the class, which was to be expected as this is debated by student teachers and teachers themselves. I would suggest that there is no right answer to the question, and that each child's situation needs to be taken into account. However, as we have seen, it is not easy to know the details of everyone's circumstances in the class. What proved useful was the debate engendered by this question, in which children felt able to offer contrasting points of view and differing arguments within their own response. Here we see 'dialogic engagement' in practice (Aukerman, 2012): children's voices and opinions were heard and listened to.

Suitability of the text

I also asked the discussion groups whether they thought the teacher should not read the book to the class, if a refugee child would be upset by it. Abdi, Moussa, Kye and Thomas all thought it would be better not to. As Thomas put it:

> 'Cause, every time, if you read a book and a refugee is in the school ... that means they might think, the refugee person might think ... might be embarrassed ... that even he's a refugee.

Olu took a different approach and answered from conflicting viewpoints. This impressed me, as his English language skills were not particularly strong:

> I've got 'yes' and 'no'. Because 'yes' ... it's a good book and maybe there's a refugee in our class and he might see this book as more interesting and be happier, or 'no', they shouldn't because that will make the child, the refugee child angrier.

Like those in Arizpe and Styles's study (2003), the girls were more eloquent than the boys, and spoke at length on the issue. They were generally in favour of reading the book to the class, on the grounds that it was 'for the greater good'. As Dana explained:

> Yes ... she should read it to us because ... just because one person's a refugee, then it can't ... if it affects them, it can't really affect

all our learning, because it kind of depends … To them it could be good because, for example, if we have to write something about how you feel … how would you feel being a refugee? they will really put all their effort inside then because they know how you've been through it. Like not just stop everything for one person.

With a platform from which to offer their opinions, the groups put forward contrasting perspectives, discussed points of view amongst themselves and even changed their minds as a result of the atmosphere created, in which they felt able to take risks in their arguments and demonstrate divergent thinking. The following exchange, given in full, shows the process in action. It begins with the girls offering practical examples of how problems could be overcome:

Solange: Because most of the children already are excited to hear the book, maybe the refugee child could be taken out and do a private session, or something, to read another book, or the teacher, or assistant teacher, TA could be, like, reading with them.

Amisha: The teacher should read another book and keep that book, and then in the spare time, when the child isn't here, they could read it.

Dawo: Also, the teacher shouldn't read it, because there might be another class with a big mouth, and when its playtime and they're playing with the refugee child, whatever the name is, they might tell him and then he might remember and then he might cry, and then he might get bullied, just like Sade.

Solange: Miss, Miss, I just changed my mind. I think it is good because it will open their eyes more, not to be afraid because you are a refugee. It doesn't matter, or you can't go back in the past and change everything – you are a refugee.

Amisha: They should get that experience.

Dawo: I think the teacher should read it now. I've changed my mind again.

As we've seen, Beverley Naidoo is herself a fierce spokesperson for children being engaged with controversial and socio-political issues, even if this challenges some in the class to deal with their own histories and experiences. It occurred to me that she would be pleased to hear this exchange in defence of her book, by children from Bangladeshi, Congolese and Somali backgrounds. During her visit to Year 5 I recorded in my field notes: 'She talks about the potential problem for refugee children dealing with the emotional side of the books.' Naidoo's argument was that, far worse than talking about the refugee experience is making it a taboo area, one that a refugee child might be ashamed of and other children be denied access to.

Nigeria in the spotlight

Three children in my discussion groups had themselves migrated from Nigeria, and I wondered how they would relate to the characters and view their country's depiction in *The Other Side of Truth*. Amechi and Ade made direct connections with the location and experiences in the book and were keen to share this commonality. Amechi told me that her father had left the family and returned to Nigeria. However, Ade, who had disclosed to Beverley Naidoo during her visit that she had been in a refugee camp for a short time when she was 5, did not open up about her experience, either in class or in the discussion group, where only Amechi and I were present. Despite a clear push factor of violence, she seemed unclear of the circumstances and only alluded to her experience mysteriously:

> Amechi: Because we are both Nigerian, we know ... we come from very close to where they came from so we know what it would be like ...

> Ade: So we know what it would feel like for them, cause of everything they've been going through, it's like what I've been through with my family ... Well, it's like we had to leave, 'cause they nearly killed my mum, because some people didn't like her ... and ... We came here and we became safe. And like, when I was two we went back to Nigeria and everything was ok and ... it's like nothing ever happened, and something did happen, and some people still don't put their past behind them.

Ade's last sentence suggests that she knew far more about the circumstances she was alluding to than she was prepared to discuss. It is also interesting that Amechi became visibly sad during the discussion, which I attributed to her missing her father. It is important to consider that children who are not refugees can also be affected by the subject matter of the book; it could touch their lives in many ways. The duality of 'mirrors' and 'windows' is misleading (see Chapter 3), as links between *The Other Side of Truth* and children's lives are far more nuanced than this.

Nevertheless, reading the book in class clearly had a powerful effect on Ade, and had seemingly disturbed her in its closeness to a location and experience she was familiar with:

> I can still remember it cause it's like vivid in my head, cause whenever I go to bed, um, I've read the book at school, um, it makes me have dreams at night about what ... about my journey here and Nigeria.

The 'affective' side of the reading transaction, in Rosenblatt's terms, is clear here. It raises questions about the responsibilities of teachers, who may engender these feelings by reading the book in class, but offer children no opportunity to talk about or deal with them. The idea of 'bibliotherapy' (Shrodes, 1950) – discussed in Chapter 3 – is pertinent here, and is thought to include identification, catharsis and insight. Later in the discussion Ade said that the book had had a positive effect too, evoking pleasant memories of her childhood in Nigeria. The three phased model had apparently been realized here:

> It kind of makes me feel like I'm back in Nigeria, 'cause when I was one, my mum used to take me to this park and I used to have so much fun there and then the picture, it just makes the memories come all back to me.

Olu, who arrived from Nigeria in 2005, told me that his parents spoke Yoruba at home, and that he had memories of using the Nigerian currency, Naira. He displayed obvious pride in his nationality but spoke with insight about corruption, bribery and violence in Nigeria, such as is vividly portrayed in the book:

> Yes, there are some soldiers that if they want to go in cars, if they want to go to the shop, they hand over 1,000 Naira to them to go to the shop and there's soldiers stopped them, and they take the 1,000 pounds ... 1,000 Naira but they can't go back. They can't go back because they block the way.

It was unclear whether Olu was talking from personal knowledge, but he did not seem to be negatively affected by the image of Nigeria presented in the book. By contrast he appeared empowered by the cultural relevance of the story to him personally.

Text to world
Attitudes to migration and seeking asylum
I detected negative attitudes in Year 5 of Marlowe School when I asked three boys what they had learned from the book. The following discussion took place between Olu, Thomas from Uganda and Kye, who has a Caribbean background:

> Thomas: That some people can get past with fake passports.
>
> JH: Yeah, right, they can, can't they? … Do you think it's right to do that?
>
> All: No.
>
> JH: No. Not ever?
>
> Thomas: They try to trick people …

Despite the fact that his own family may have come to the UK to seek asylum, Thomas's negative attitude towards refugees generally spilled out when he considered that Olu might be a refugee. Thomas challenges him:

> Thomas: You were a refugee?
>
> Olu: No refugees here.
>
> Thomas: Were you one?
>
> Olu: No. Never. (laughs) My grandma was. My grandma was.

Olu's repeated denial shows an unwillingness to identify with refugees that was noticeable throughout the class. The children were able to acknowledge that their parents or grandparents had been refugees, however, as this allowed some distance from the situation.

In general Dana, from Romania, displayed great sensitivity to the situation of refugees and migrants, probably because she had arrived in the UK a few years ago:

> It could happen to anybody … pretend there's a big war in the whole of London, people would have to go to another country. Let's say I need to go to Greece, and then they'll be like 'Excuse me, you're a refugee!' and then I'll be, like, 'I am from Romania, from London, now I came here. How am I a refugee?' and they'll be like 'you're a refugee cause you're from another country', and really that could happen to anybody.

Dana's point that 'it could happen to anybody' chimes with Jill Rutter's observation that 'refugees are ordinary people, who had to go through extraordinary experiences' (1991: 4). Her way of dramatizing the situation in simple speech shows that she understands the issues at stake even though she might not have the vocabulary to express herself more precisely.

The conversation in one discussion group, mainly with Solange, suggested attitudes I was unable to glean directly that refugee children might themselves have about issues of migration:

> JH: So do you think children are embarrassed to say that they are refugees?
>
> Solange: No, it's not embarrassing ... Some people are rude so they shouldn't know the word refugee and use it in the wrong way, cause when they know it, that's when they take advantage of it, and it's like being rude to children who are refugees ...
>
> JH: So you don't think reading this book would help people ...
>
> Dawo: It would make them know about refugees and it would teach them not to bully people, or threaten people ...
>
> Solange: In the classroom, yeah, I'm not a shy person. I would actually say ... 'I am refugee. I came from another country because of the way it was.... People were getting killed, and there were bad things, and that's why I came here.

Solange had mentioned earlier that her parents were refugees, so she is not far from the experience herself. In this exchange she gives us an intriguing view of how she deals with the possible stigma by talking about her situation and defending it.

Dawo also remarks that reading *The Other Side of Truth* might be useful in changing attitudes to refugees. However, in her interview, Jill Rutter was sceptical about how effective one book can be in challenging negative perceptions, although she still felt that fiction was an appropriate starting point, especially for younger children:

> I think you need to understand the limitations of changing attitudes, and that one story in a term is probably not going to have a huge impact. I think drama, literature and the arts are more effective in unpicking attitudes to newcomers ... it enables you to look perhaps in a more creative way and perhaps go deeper into the issues.

Defining the term 'refugee'

Judging by the discussions during the last three weeks of studying *The Other Side of Truth,* many children had a clear idea of what the refugee experience entailed, if not a concise definition of the term 'refugee'. Amisha, a highly empathetic girl who had soaked up the book and was reading the sequel, showed a deep understanding when she said: 'I think refugee means when somebody or someone, their home is lost, or something very terrible has happened to them, they really have to come here or the same thing will happen to them.'

This 'hypothetical modality' of talk (Barnes and Todd, 1995), beginning with 'I think ...', kept the space open for dialogue between speakers, as they listen to each other and extend their ideas, along the lines of Mercer's (2000) 'exploratory talk'. As Maine (2013: 154) points out: 'Their ideas were suggestions and therefore up for debate, offering the possibility of further exploration or connection to their existing world.' We see this in Solange's attempt to clarify the explanation further: 'So basically what she said is that when you are a refugee means that something has happened in your home place and then you have to evacuate or leave from your country.'

When I tried to add more depth to the definition by saying, 'a refugee is someone who has had to go to another country because in their own country they've been persecuted', Dawo asked, 'What's persecuted? I know executed, but not persecuted.' I put forward my own contributions tentatively, as in 'pupil framed' discourse (John, 2009: 127) feeling that explaining the meaning of 'persecution' was important for children to understand the refugee situation, and that Year 5 might be able to engage with it. Building a community of readers is best achieved sensitively, as a didactic approach can inhibit some children from speaking.

Understanding the refugee experience

Generally the children in the discussion groups displayed a good understanding of the nature of the refugee experience, developed during the reading of *The Other Side of Truth*. They were clear on all three aspects of 'refugeeness' – the pre-, trans- and post-migration ecologies – as detailed by Hamilton and Moore (2004). Kye, from a Caribbean background, focused mainly on the shooting and killing that precipitated the flight of the two children in Naidoo's story, and the possible danger they would face by staying (the pre-migration ecology):

> Your parents might not want you to die and they might send you
> to another country so you can stay there ... Because some people

were trying to kill her dad so … they accidently killed the mum. They might accidently kill Femi or Sade.

Mariam's story, a tale-within-a-tale device, is presented by Naidoo to give another refugee's account that contrasts to that of Sade and Femi. Two Somali boys, Abdi and Moussa, made real connections with this story and had just written their own retelling of it:

Moussa: And Mariam was just the girl that her dad died for feeding rebels and they had to walk all the way from Hargeisa to … to … to … Kenya and they got a letter from their dad …

Abdi: Their dad. The dad's brother …

Moussa: Their uncle, and they said, bad news is their dad died. But they had … they wanted to come to London to stay with their uncle, but the brother said he will go back, but they didn't heard from him ever again.

Abdi: They never heard from him.

Moussa: They had to walk … 15 days …

Abdi: No. It took them a long time. They went on a boat … It was 15 days.

Moussa: It was very crowded.

JH: Um, yes. That was from Somalia, wasn't it?

Abdi: Yes, and their feet were swollen. They didn't have shoes on.

The manner in which they boys interrupt and echo each other in response reveals their identification with the subject matter. This evokes a graphic description, requiring minimal input from me. Their empathy with the family is striking as they describe in detail the gruelling journey they undertook. They also show an understanding of how refugee experiences intersect with the ordinary events in people's lives:

Moussa: The sad part was it was on her birthday that her dad got taken away.

Abdi: And birthdays are supposed to be happy days.

Maine and Waller (2011: 364) argue that 'feelings of empathy do more than assist readers in comprehending the text; they act as a tool of engagement'. Here we can see this 'deepening' of the dialogic space between text and reader.

In another group the boys recalled with relish the (trans-migration) journey – using fake passports and being smuggled out of the country – that Sade and Femi had made, dwelling on the brushes with customs, passport officers and the police. Again the way they interrupt each other shows their eagerness in retelling aspects of the story, seemingly appealing to their sense of adventure and possibly resonating with films, TV programmes or video games they had seen or played.

> Olu: … when Uncle Tunde shouted to go and Mr Bankole and Mrs Bankole, treat them really badly and called them different names … And the Passport Officer kept looking at the passport, and Sade called him 'Googly Eyes' or something else.
>
> Kye: She calls him 'Cool Gaze'.
>
> All three boys: Miss Police Business.
>
> Olu: Yeah and they got searched for drugs.
>
> Kye: They got searched. They did a crime … the police think it was them that did the crime and it wasn't them. Some teenagers broke into a shop and they were next to it …
>
> Olu: The police office got mostly about the money.
>
> Kye: And I like the part when Mrs Bankole put the money inside the suitcase and they bribed the police officer who got the money …

Here the boys demonstrate a process of joint discovery and 'a commitment to the principles of collectivism rather than individualism' (Bignall, 2012: 53). Open-ended discussion and the exchange of ideas like this are crucial if children are to respond aesthetically to literature (Nystrand, 2006). Such discourse is not easily achieved, however.

As the two Year 5 classes read through the book, their understanding of the problems asylum seekers face on arriving in the host country, and the process for claiming sanctuary deepened – all part of the post-migration ecology. What stood out most in Idil's mind was the scene when the abandoned children first had to fend for themselves in London, a frightening scenario, but one perhaps that also conveyed a sense of adventure: 'I think when they got on the bus and they didn't know what to do. They didn't know the buses or anything.'

For Dana, it was more the discovery that the children's uncle – the only person they knew in London – was not there to meet them. This is indeed a traumatic point in the text:

> Well the bit that really stands out to me is when they went to the college and didn't find Uncle Dele cause they were expecting a hand to help them when they got to London, but being nowhere, knowing that your closest person trying to help you is not there, just stands out.

Solange took a more sophisticated approach, both in her vocabulary and manipulation of language, as well as her ability to summarize and analyse a situation:

> I think what was really frightening is the way that they want to have a good life here in London, but like there are so many barriers, like the bullies at school and they can't tell the bullies or Aunty Gracie and Uncle Roy their real names to help them like find their family back home.

The book had many significant moments that affected the children, and interestingly their spread reflected all aspects of the refugee experience, from pre-migration catalyst, to trans-migration stressors and finally to post-migration nightmares – quite literally in Sade's case – as predicated by Hamilton and Moore (2004).

The effectiveness of 'drawing on personal testimony and asking 'how would you feel if …' questions' (Rutter, 2006: 9) drew the children into the reading and follow-up activities, instead of confining discussion to statistics and hard facts, which have a more limited impact.

Addressing other issues

When asked what they had learnt from reading the book, children made explicit links to bullying and racism, recognizing the problems refugees regularly encounter when they arrive in a new country. This is covered fulsomely in the book and is the source of much dramatic tension. Kye wanted to talk about what he had learnt from the Childline website. He was keen to link this to his own indirect experience of the effects of bullying:

> … that you get bullied, and that you get bullied so badly that you might die … They can't run away but they commit suicide. We was talking about Childline … One of my brother's friends … he died because people were teasing him, and so someone stabbed him at the end. And then there was my cousin's cousin … people

were stretching her and calling her names and her heart actually stopped … it was tightened, because she was so mad. She had to go hospital.

In the same group, Olu and Thomas followed this by discussing instances in the book where Sade is bullied, and link this explicitly to racism.

Olu: Ya, people in Sade class they think her name is wrong. They spell it like S H A Y D A Y but actually her name is S A D E.

Thomas: They say she's called …

Olu: 'Shadayaday'…

Thomas: Yes. 'Shadayaday.' They are being racist to her.

For Moussa and Abdi it was the bullying and racism at school that were uppermost in their minds, perhaps because they had just then been focusing on this part of the book. They also made connections with racism in their own lives:

Moussa: One time I was at this park and two boys came up to me and they said I'm a Paki …

Abdi: My mum has been racially abused.

Idil and Dana felt that the book contained a 'do-as-you-would-be-done-by' message, and they wanted to use this to formulate a blueprint for the future:

Idil: Never let someone boss you around, cause what happened to Sade? … So, um, never boss someone around.

Dana: … don't make yourself be unhappy, just to make other people happy. You need to stand up for yourself and say that 'No! I am not doing this. I am bossing myself around, not you, not nobody'.

Finally, Dawo and Solange felt that they had gained important understandings about Nigeria, or Africa in general, and linked this to themes of war, contrasting standards of living and language use – all important issues in their own right:

Dawo: I learnt that in Nigeria, in Africa, actually, there's a lot of wars …

Solange: I've learnt that in Nigeria it seems really nice and not everyone has the same riches as each other, but some people live at high standards, and others quite low.

Dawo: I learnt that, if you're from Africa, doesn't mean that you can't speak English.

Freire asserts that 'reading ... is preceded by and intertwined with knowledge of the world' (Freire and Macedo, 1987: 29). In this way he highlights the way students do not just learn *from* the text, but bring their prior understanding of the world *to* the text. Children in Year 5 brought their preconceived ideas to the book, and through 'collaborative' discourse (John, 2009) created an atmosphere in which they listened to each other and felt confident to contribute their own ideas.

The 'constructedness' of the text
Engaging with the author

When Beverley Naidoo visited Marlowe School during the research period, she gave an assembly about her writing to both Year 5 classes, and joined them in their classrooms for more intimate question-and-answer sessions afterwards. This gave the children a perfect chance to interrogate the 'constructedness' of the text in action, and to find out about the author's personal story and her underlying 'climate of belief' (Hollindale, 1988: 37), her motives for writing and the research she undertook in preparation for the book. A selection from my field notes is telling:

Ch: How did you feel when you first came to this country?

BN: Very much like Sade, my head was in one place, but my body was in another.

Ch: Did you feel emotions when you wrote the book?

BN: Yes, I cried at some parts (in very emotional voice!)

Ch: Is it a true book?

BN: The things that happened really could happen.

Ch: Do you write from your own experience?

BN: No. I have had similar experiences, but I also have many friends with similar experiences. I also read a lot and find out that way about other people's lives.

After the visit, the children wrote a newspaper article for the school journal about their encounter with Naidoo. The best were chosen to be published in the weekly newsletter – see Figure 9.1.

A Visit from a Captivating Spirit

Famous children's novelist, Beverley Naidoo, made the effort to travel over 100 miles to meet Year 5 at (Marlowe School). When she arrived half of Year 5 crowded around her, asking about her brilliant books. The visit took place in the Main Hall on Friday 25th May and even her husband joined us. Year 5 have been reading one of her most popular books, "The Other Side of Truth" and some children have read another of her texts, "Out of Bounds" during guided reading.

Beverley grew up in South Africa, but her time there was short. Due to her fight against racism, during the apartheid, England became her home, where she lived in exile. Her writing is extraordinary and has opened people's eyes and hearts for years. The saying, 'One person can change the world' is true.

I think she is a truly wonderful woman.

Figure 9.1: Winning article about Naidoo's visit for the school newspaper.

This piece pays tribute to Beverley Naidoo, after meeting her and finding out about her life. But it also refers to the power of literature as a transformative force via 'efferent' and 'aesthetic' means – 'people's eyes and hearts' – and the power of the author to effect change through their writing. We can see that Year 5's engagement with the writer was more complex than the younger children's (see Chapter 7), perhaps because of their age or because Naidoo visited the school in person, spending much more time explaining the backstory to the text, or perhaps a combination of both. If such contact is not possible, Myhill suggests an activity called Questioning the Author (2007: 62), where children devise a series of questions they would ask the author were they given the chance. This builds on critical literacy skills, focusing on the 'why?' and 'how?' choices that have been made in creating the text as an artefact.

Discussing the 'message'

Through the medium of literature Naidoo invites children to engage with socio-political issues in the world around them and to question what is generally taken for granted or commonplace. Although she resists the idea that her writing has a 'message', the children appeared to relish the opportunity in their small groups after her visit, to discuss why she had written *The Other Side of Truth*. Maine (2013) considers that rather than a single transaction between text and reader, as described by Rosenblatt (1978), there needs to be conversations between the readers as they co-construct meaning from text, thus deepening their reading experience. This process had started in the classroom, and in their discussion groups the children explored the significance of the text from a range of perspectives, demonstrating their awareness that multiple interpretations and responses are possible 'and more valuable as such' (Maine, 2013: 155).

Abdi felt that the message of the book was simply expository: 'To show everyone how it feels to be a refugee … 'Cause some people might want to come to this country for a reason, but they haven't got passports and stuff.' Amisha linked understanding the refugee experience with a plea for action, embracing kindness and tolerance and exhorting against bullying: 'She wrote these books so when people read it, they will understand why refugees come here, and to be more kind to them, and if they are a bully, whoever reads the book will learn the lesson not to bully.'

Characteristically Solange saw the message as a moral, cautionary tale, appealing for tolerance and understanding:

> I think she wrote the book because you know the way people say 'don't judge a book by its cover' …? You could use it as a metaphor, like 'don't judge people for the way they are'. … You never know what's happened to them and they might be in a terrible state, maybe they just lost someone, and they've had to become a refugee to be safe, like Sade and Femi, so it's not good to judge people and be rude to them.

Dana brought the message back to her previous theme: the refugee experience is not exclusive to children in other parts of the world but could happen to any of us at any time:

> Well, I think she wrote this book because the experience of what happens with children, it could happen to anyone, like their parents got shot. Let's hope that wouldn't happen, but that could

happen and it could even be that you're getting bullied or have to have foster parents, all of that story can be based on life.

Then Amechi broadened the discussion to muse on the role of literature in general, opening up unexplored pathways. She focused on the importance of children being aware of the world around them from an early age, and thought that school might play a role in developing this, over and above that allowed at home:

> I think she wrote it to make sure all the other world knows what happens in other countries, for instance, parents might keep these things away from children, but when children grow up and they still don't know it, it can come as a really big shock to them, when they find out.

Kundnani (2001: 59) calls for 'initiatives in schools to explain to young people from where and why refugees come' while pulling apart prevailing discourse. It is interesting that all the children saw the message in terms of a 'window' onto the refugee situation, or even a 'sliding glass door' (Bishop, 1990) through which to experience it vicariously. No one saw it as a 'mirror' to hold up and see themselves and their own lives in so they might gain comfort and reassurance. Despite both authors' insistence that such books have a dual function (see Chapter 5), it seems that the 'implied reader' (Iser, 1976) responded to by the children is still a non-refugee, even though the 'actual reader' may well be.

Reflections

Meeting Beverley Naidoo was highly significant in the children's appreciating the 'constructedness' of the text. Finding out about the author's own personal history, and having the opportunity to ask direct questions of an unfamiliar adult is something children are seldom able to do. The children also enjoyed questioning me, capitalising on the informal nature of our conversations to ask about my relationship with and opinion of the author: 'How did you meet Beverley Naidoo?', 'Are you a fan of the author, by the way? Do you read her books?' I was able to offer my own opinion, and acknowledge it as equally partial, whereas the teacher does not usually explicitly reveal their point of view.

Children were keen to talk to me about the story in discussion groups, and to feel that their voices were heard and their opinions listened to (an unusual occurrence, despite it being a cornerstone of the United Nations Convention of the Rights of the Child (Unicef, 1989), (James, 2007). Carey-

Webb (1996: 16) reminds us of the need for teachers 'to meet their students where they live', a laudable aim, but hard to achieve with class management demands as they are. Teachers can plan and teach high quality lessons, but what they lack is teacher time to really find out how their students have received a book. This ingredient is key to the pedagogical process, and we must seek ways that it can be achieved. Teachers are too often missing out on the pleasure of literary discussion with their students, and children's opinions and ideas are often passing by unheard.

Chapter 10

Conclusion and ways forward

The reading transaction

Rosenblatt (1978) identified the reading experience as like a circuit created between writer, text and reader, each one a different 'event' to the last. She saw reading as a 'transaction' between the three parts, but never developed a diagrammatic model of her idea. I imagine it would look something like this: the author has a direct relationship with the text, the reader/text interaction is a two-way process – the reader brings their own lived experience to the text and develops new horizons through it – and the direct reader to author exchange would be the weak link in the circuit, see Figure 10.1.

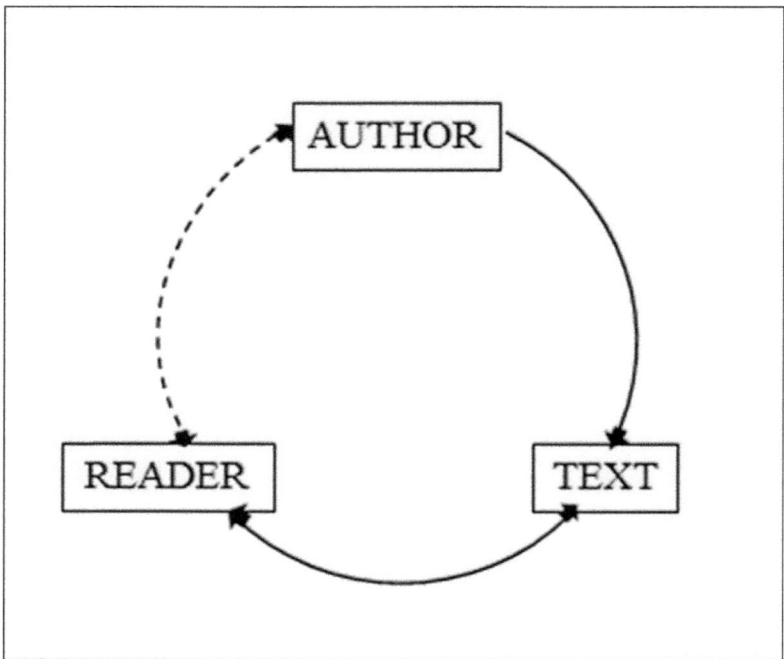

Figure 10.1: The Reading Circuit, adapted from Rosenblatt (1978).

Authors' websites, articles and interviews afford them several ways to communicate with readers, but, as we have seen, an author visit to a school offers a particularly rich opportunity for children to meet and interact with them directly, by listening to them talk and asking valuable questions.

The author obtains feedback from adult readers, in the form of reviews and comment, but this is less easily garnered from children. While visits to schools may not be possible, other avenues need to be encouraged to develop the writer/reader connection. Perhaps it can be done virtually: children could access authors' websites, for instance, where details might be provided to allow young people to share reviews of the author's books, or display written and drawn responses to texts. This would be of value to a range of people: authors, teachers and other children alike.

I suggest that authors and illustrators of children's literature about the refugee experience, have, by 'giving voice to the voiceless', a substantial and dynamic responsibility towards their readers. These authors need to think of the 'actual' readers of these texts – refugee children, those from a refugee background, as well as other migrants, and children who might have had related experiences, such as the death of a parent or being bullied or subjected to racism. While acknowledging the possible trauma asylum seekers have been through, it is important to present scenarios of resilience, so that child readers can be inspired by affirmative images, rather than patronizing pity or destructive self-pity. Meeting young readers in person is a rewarding experience for authors, and it also gives them a rare chance to find out what young readers really think of their work. Judging by how much value Hoffman, Littlewood and Naidoo gave to positive feedback from child readers, this is a necessary part of the reading circuit, and also, I suggest, part of the responsibility of writers and illustrators of children's literature especially that deals with challenging and controversial issues. Children are deeply impressionable and may be more open to positive influences than adults are.

Teachers as mediators

This study amply demonstrates that as a mediator, the teacher is in a pivotal position in the reading of a class text. Chambers (1991) saw the 'enabling adult', be they teacher, parent or carer, as having a very powerful role in building a 'community' of readers (Chambers, 1993), but criticized teachers who take control over the reading process, steering the class to a reading *they* want to reconstruct. In his 'Tell Me' model, he introduced the idea of a 'Reading Circle' whereby the 'enabling adult' selects the text, reads it and then encourages response through talk, which leads to the selection of further books. I have redrawn the Reading Circle (clockwise this time!), although I think that it would be a spiral, as the teacher moves on to select a new text. I therefore call it a 'cycle' – see Figure 10.2.

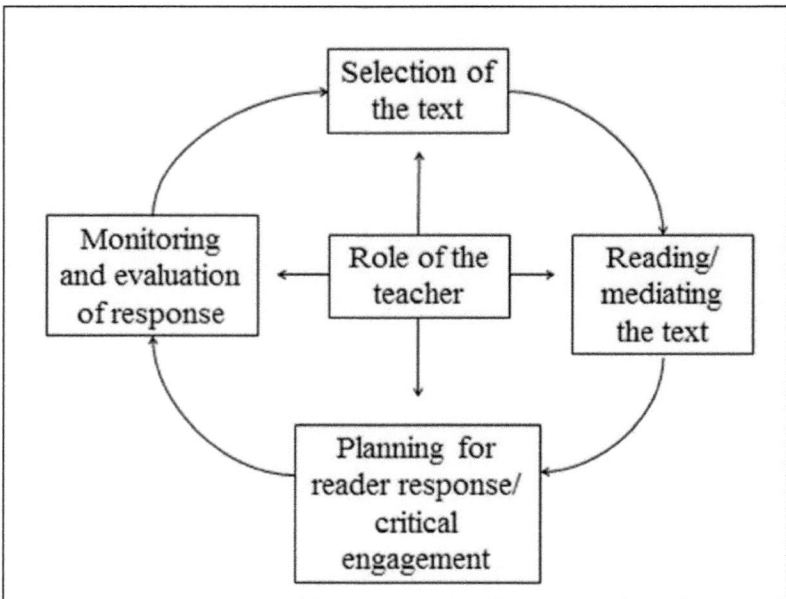

Figure 10.2: The role of the teacher in the reading cycle, adapted from Chambers (1991).

My study shows that teachers rarely select the text independently, their choices contingent on many competing factors. But in undertaking to teach a book about refugees, they take a brave step towards tackling a controversial and challenging area. Dolan (2014b: 24) asserts that:

> Choosing high-quality authentic (picture)books is the first step. It is important that we, as educators, approach this task with a critical eye to ensure that the (picture)books used in class are accurate, dispel or challenge stereotypes, avoid generalizations and provide authentic setting and language.

When reading such a book, teachers invite children to 'read the word and read the world'. Through the dialogue they initiate, they can create greater or lesser engagement, and by the tasks and activities they plan, they can move children beyond merely recalling the story to developing their own 'critical perception, interpretation and rewriting of what is read' (Freire and Macedo, 1987: 36). However, a key role of all teachers is also to monitor and evaluate the responses, to assess children's understanding of the text and to inform future choices of suitable and challenging books that would engage the class, lead to powerful dialogic encounters and offer transformatory possibilities.

Furthermore, the teacher might inspire praxis/social action because of what is read, and although this is impossible to quantify, it is worth saying that encouraging open-mindedness and a welcoming attitude is a good start:

> As teachers, we may be able to assess to some degree the meaning of a text in our classroom, yet we will never be fully aware of its long-lasting impact on our individual students, as they may ... reconnect with the themes of the novel in later life.
>
> (Habib, 2008: 50)

It is part of a teacher's responsibility not to 'other' refugee children in the reading, and to be aware and informed about the lives of the children in their class so they can make a professional judgement about the effect the texts might have. What did emerge was a feeling that the teacher plays a key role in introducing children's literature in the primary classroom about the refugee experience. Indeed the Centre for Literacy in Primary Education write as a caveat at the top of their list of 'books focusing on identity, belonging, conflict, migrant and refugee experiences', produced for Refugee Week: 'As these books deal with strong and emotive themes, it's important that teachers, parents and carers share them with children' (CLPE, n.d.).

What also became clear was the importance of small group discussion that allows children to ask questions, develop ideas and critique the books they are reading. It was also vital to ensure that all responses are valued. This 'collaborative' discourse (John, 2009) and co-construction of meaning from the text through conversations between readers, adds depth to the reading experience, and provide an opportunity to engage with 'critical literacy', not just reader response. Such activity demonstrates to children that multiple interpretations are possible and valuable, and that the opportunity to change viewpoints through discussion is crucial. This is what 'literature circles', and what is now known as 'guided reading', should be about (see Chapter 3), involving more discussion about the holistic meaning and purpose of the text, and putting an end to 'bite-size chunks for short amounts of time, with an emphasis on filleting them for phonic or punctuation potential' (Arizpe and Styles, 2003: 239). As well as benefiting children, it is clear that the teachers in my study were frustrated by the lack of opportunity for this kind of discussion, to engage with their students' responses to the text, and generally to find out more about the children in their class.

More research is clearly needed into the genre identified, and more studies made of the impact of such texts in the classroom, observing, listening to and reading children's responses. Meanwhile, I would like to suggest a seven-point framework for 'the enabling adult' sharing a book that raises controversial, sensitive or socio-political issues – for example, about refugees. This should include responsible pedagogy and critical literacy and would require:

- awareness (prior to selection of the text) of children in the class who may have a connection with the themes of the book
- sensitivity (when reading the text) to those who might have similar, and maybe unknown, circumstances, thereby creating a climate of trust within the classroom
- researching the context (prior and during the reading) on the part of teachers and pupils, so that surrounding geo-political themes and issues can be made explicit
- fostering inclusive dialogue (during and after the reading) that accepts many points of view, and does not 'other' any of the community of readers
- inviting a variety of forms of response, so that children of all ages and varying linguistic and cognitive levels can react to texts in ways that challenge an overemphasis on writing
- deconstructing the 'constructedness' of the text, leading to an awareness of author standpoint and the overt or subliminal ideological influences of the wider world
- encouraging social action that empowers children to carry the text forward and use it as an emancipatory force, both in the classroom and in the world at large.

Children making meaning

Freire and Macedo (1987) see reading as a process of engagement through one's own lived experience, but also as a process that takes the reader on journeys beyond (see Figure 10.3). Literature fills gaps that real life sometimes cannot, and by virtue of this, can be emancipatory. Meeting the author in person was a high point for Year 5, but an opportunity the younger classes did not get to enjoy, and understanding the 'constructedness' of the text is much easier when encountering the originator of the work. Children may also make connections during the reading that the author has not thought of themselves.

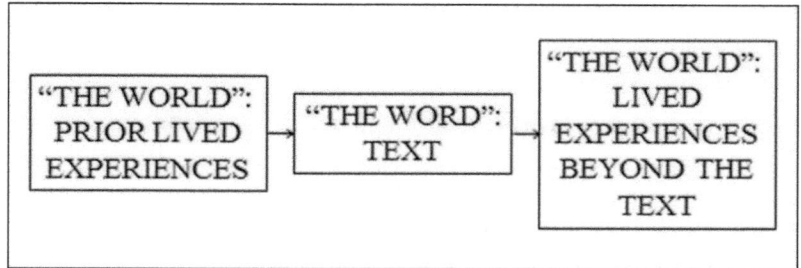

Figure 10.3: 'Reading the word and the world', adapted from Freire and Macedo (1987).

My study demonstrated how hard it is to understand the real nature of children's feelings about a text, and this may be why it is such an unreported area. Children's voices need to be heard in critiquing children's literature. As part of the politics of voice (Spivak, 1988; hooks, 1990) we should consider the responses of 'actual' rather than 'implied' readers (Iser, 1972), as I have tried to do. Bishop (1990) uses the metaphor of 'mirrors, windows and sliding glass doors' in relation to reader response, to describe how children see themselves reflected in literature or learn about the lives of others, entering into them for the duration of the reading.

However, children's responses to *The Colour of Home* and *The Other Side of Truth* demonstrated that a simple dichotomy between refugee and non-refugee children in their reactions, was a blunt and unworkable instrument. Apart from being unable to tell which children were refugees, who was from a refugee background and who had simply migrated to the UK – very few children being of White British origin in all the classes I researched – it seemed from children's own stories that the boundary between forced and voluntary migration was blurred, 'push' and 'pull' factors creating more of a continuum than a reactive/proactive contrast (Richmond, 1993).

Postmodern identities are multiple, hybrid and fractured (Bhabha, 1994; Hall, 1992), and children cannot be viewed simply as refugees or non-refugees. Their backgrounds are complex, which affects their reaction to a text. As Arizpe *et al.* (2014a: 319) note:

> While generating discussion of migration in the classroom is vital, a conscious effort must also be made to avoid treating new arrivals as ambassadors of a coherent, essentialized culture. This runs the risk of cementing their alterity by valuing migrants for their ability to represent difference, instead of valuing them for their more realistic, hybrid identities.

161

For some, the books discussed had the added value of helping them understand their own histories – that of their parents and families – and through this, their own stories. Yet there was still a degree of stigma to the term 'refugee', which persisted through discourse from beyond the classroom and the school. For others, such readings can help children decide what sort of person they want to choose to be, and what sort of social action they want to take in relation to others.

The wider context

> The skills of analysis applied to different levels of a text should form part of teacher training in any society which hopes for adequate literacy. (Hollindale, 1988: 31)

ITE courses need to introduce students to a wide range of children's literature and how to teach it, and should involve critical literacy and dialogic pedagogy. Teachers also need guidance on how to deal with controversial, violent and potentially distressing content in the classroom, and to learn strategies to counter prejudice and challenge the unexpected reactions from 'resistant readers'. Schools need to provide CPD that promotes an ongoing exposure to high-quality children's literature – such as the Power of Reading project – and continually encourage teachers to tackle controversial issues through the medium of quality literature. Sources of inspiration in planning for strong textual engagement are available, and other agencies such as the Amnesty and Childline websites can stimulate ideas. However, such resources need to be highlighted to help teachers amid pressing time constraints. Moreover teachers need refresher courses on how to promote critical literacy, not just reader response, and how to continually employ dialogic pedagogy, such as that suggested by Chambers (1991).

All institutions involved in education need to recognize that the classroom is not an independent space, isolated from broader agendas, but is heavily influenced by the political, cultural and historical forces of the wider world. We need to campaign for a more 'literature-based' rather than a 'literacy-based' curriculum, that encourages children to criticize the books we present them with in order to gain 'textual power' (Scholes, 1985). However, with a government that seeks to control and anaesthetize the texts children read, and that introduced a new National Curriculum in England in September 2014 (DfE, 2013), with a strong Literacy focus on spelling, punctuation and grammar, and on word recognition over comprehension in reading, the future for 'reading the world and the word' looks bleak. Here I found only one hidden line of enthusiasm for literature: 'Reading also feeds pupils' imagination and opens up a treasure-house of wonder and joy for curious young minds' (DfE, 2013: 4). In this book I have presented an alternative view of the power of reading, apart from pleasure, wonder or joy. Literature can contain all these elements, but importantly, as this book shows, it can provide global awareness and connections, enable the reader to shape what sort of person they want to be and help them understand their responsibility to others.

Further research

I chose to focus my study exclusively on the primary age range when encountering books about refugees. I looked at the complexity of ideas presented, and the suitability of the subject matter for children of this age. While Habib (2008) has discussed using *Refugee Boy* by Benjamin Zephaniah (2001) with secondary-aged children, there are a wealth of refugee texts written for the primary age group that have not been researched in the classroom context. Obviously in a case study of two books, the field is limited by the choice of books themselves. Would other texts about refugees by different authors and telling different stories, have provoked the same responses? Then there is the choice of setting. Would the same texts read in other schools with different pupil profile – perhaps in a predominantly mono-cultural, monolingual and mainly stable population, unused to migration and refugee issues – have produced an alternative reading?

My focus is restricted to the UK context in terms of the books chosen, the authors interviewed, and the schools visited. A wider comparative study, such as that conducted by Arizpe *et al.* (2014b) which looked at immigrant children's responses to the wordless picturebook *The Arrival* by Shaun Tan (2006) in several cities, across various countries in three continents, offers a richness of situation and perspective. To take my initial question into other countries to find answers and responses that are conditioned by regional factors and contrasting historical, cultural and social perspectives, would be an exciting proposition, and could uncover implications for international educational contexts, especially at this time of refugee crisis. This would also involve research into the kinds of refugee stories that are available in other languages and other places.

Sipe asks 'What good is literary understanding?' (2008: 247). He suggests that more longitudinal research into how it develops over time, from the first years of school to the later years, is imperative (ibid.: 242). This is another possible trajectory: to ascertain whether children in my study were influenced in the long term by the books they read and the ideas they discussed in the classroom as a consequence of sharing those texts.

Both Beverley Naidoo and Sophie, one of the teachers in my study, raised the question: does reading books such as *The Other Side of Truth* have a direct impact on students for the future, or is the relationship more subtle than that?

Sipe helpfully answers his own question:

> Literature thus allows us to perceive our lives, the lives of others, and our society in new ways, expanding our view of what is possible, serving as a catalyst to ignite our capacity to imagine a more just and equitable world. (2008: 247)

However, unless we follow young people through from their early encounters with books that might suggest 'praxis' or 'social action', how can we fully understand the possibilities reading and sharing such texts might offer?

Although understanding international power relations seems an enormous challenge in the primary classroom, the emergent school of cognitive literary criticism suggests that by stimulating mirror neurons in our brains that activate emotionally charged memories, literature can develop a range of feelings in children. This, according to (Nikolajeva, 2012: 289) 'suggests a neurological basis for the value of reading: it provides a way of helping us understand other human beings'. Nikolajeva calls for 'scholars who work with books and children to test the ideas developed here' (ibid.: 290). I hope that my study offers a contribution in investigating the capacity of children's books about refugees to generate empathy, as well as the possibility of stimulating emotions – such as sadness, fear, anger, guilt and love, that Nikolajeva mentions – through an affective response. It also demonstrates an idea that resonates especially strongly with me:

> Solidarity, quite distinct from sympathy, is the recognition of common interest: 'your struggle is our struggle.'
>
> (Yandell, 2008: 39)

List of children's literature about refugees published in English

	Author	Date	Title	Publisher	Place
1.	Ahmedi, F.	2005	*The Story of My Life*	Simon and Schuster	NY, USA
2.	Aliki	1998	*Marianthe's Story: Painted Words and Spoken Memories*	Greenwillow	NY, USA
3.	Almond, D.	2008	*Jackdaw Summer*	Hodder	London, UK
4.	Almond, D.	2014	*Klaus Vogel and the Bad Lads*	Barrington Stoke	Edinburgh, UK
5.	Al-Windawi, T.	2004	*Thura's Diary*	Puffin	London, UK
6.	Aman	1994	*Story of a Somali Girl*	Bloomsbury	London, UK
7.	Anderson, R.	1984	*The War Orphan*	OUP	Oxford, UK
8.	Anderson, R.	2000	*Warlands*	OUP	Oxford, UK
9.	Anderson, R.	2011	*Asylum*	Hodder	London, UK
10.	Applegate, K.	2007	*Home of the Brave*	Square Fish	NY, USA
11.	Argueta, J.	2003	*Xochitl and the Flowers*	Children's Books	San Fran, CA, USA

12.	Argueta, J.	2007	*Alfredito Flies Home*	Groundwood	Toronto, Can
13.	Armstrong, J.	2002	*Shattered: Stories of Children and War*	Knopf	NY, USA
14.	Asgedom, M.	2001	*Of Beetles and Angels: A Boy's Remarkable Journey from a Refugee Camp to Harvard*	Little, Brown	NY and Boston, USA
15.	Ashley, B.	1990	*Boat Girl*	Harcourt	San Diego, CA, USA
16.	Ashley, B.	1999	*Little Soldier*	Orchard	London, UK
17.	Ashley, B.	2014	*Nadine Dreams of Home*	Barrington Stoke	Edinburgh, UK
18.	Avery, T.	2011	*Too Much Trouble*	Frances Lincoln	London, UK
19.	Baillie, A.	2004 (Orig 1985)	*Little Brother*	Penguin	NY, USA
20.	Barakat, I.	2007	*Tasting the Sky*	Farrar, Straus and Giroux	NY, USA
21.	Bawden, N.	1969	*The Runaway Summer*	1969, Lippincott 1972, Puffin	Phil, PA, USA Middx, UK
22.	Beah, I.	2007	*A Long Way Gone*	Farrar, Straus and Giroux	NY, USA
23.	Beckwith, K.	2005	*Playing War*	Tilbury House	ME, USA
24.	Bergman, T. trans: Swirsky, M.	1988 1991	*Along the Tracks*	Schocken Publishing Houghton Mifflin	Tel Aviv, Israel NY, USA

25.	Bessora and Barroux (trans: Sarah Ardizzoni)	*Alpha: Abidjan to Gare du Nord*	2016 (orig 2014)	Barrington Stoke Gallimard	Edinburgh, UK Paris, France
26.	Bilkuei, C.	*Cola's Story*	2008	Macmillan	London, UK
27.	Bondoux, A-L.	*A Time of Miracles*	2010	Random House	NY, USA
28.	Booth, A.	*Girl with a White Dog*	2014	Catnip	London, UK
29.	Booth, A.	*Refuge*	2016	Nosy Crow	London, UK
30.	Borden, L.	*The Journey That Saved Curious George: The True Wartime Escape of Margret and H.A. Rey*	2005	Houghton Mifflin	Boston, MA, USA
31.	Bradman, T. (ed)	*Give Me Shelter*	2007	Frances Lincoln	London, UK
32.	Brahmachari, S.	*Artichoke Hearts*	2011	Macmillan	London, UK
33.	Bunting, E.	*How Many Days to America?*	1988	Clarion	NY, USA
34.	Bunting, E.	*Gleam and Glow*	2001	Harcourt	San Diego, CA, USA
35.	Bunting, E.	*One Green Apple*	2006	Clarion	NY, USA
36.	Calcines, E.F.	*Leaving Glorytown*	2009	Farrar, Straus and Giroux	NY, USA
37.	Carmi, D.	*Samir and Yonatan*	2000	Arthur A. Levine	NY, USA
38.	Cavouras, C.	*Rainbow Bird*	2007	Wakefield	Adelaide, S. Aus
39.	Cha, D.	*Dia's Story Cloth*	1996	Lee and Low	NY, USA
40.	Coates, J.	*A Hare in the Elephant's Trunk*	2010	Red Deer	Ontario, Can

41.	Cohen, S.	2005	*Mai Ya's Long Journey*	Wisconsin Historical Society	Madison, WI, USA
42.	Cooney, C.	2007	*Diamonds in the Shadow*	Waterbrook	Colorado Springs, CO, USA
43.	Cornwell, N.	2006	*Christophe's Story*	Frances Lincoln	London, UK
44.	Cornwell, N.	2011	*Armel's Revenge*	Frances Lincoln	London, UK
45.	Cottrell Boyce, F.	2011	*The Unforgotten Coat*	Walker	London, UK
46.	Crew, L.	1989	*Children of the River*	Delacourt	NY, USA
47.	Cross, G.	2010	*Where I Belong*	OUP	Oxford, UK
48.	Cross, G.	2013	*After Tomorrow*	OUP	Oxford, UK
49.	Davidow, S.	1998	*The Red Shadow*	Macmillan	London, UK
50.	Dalton, D.	2006	*Living in a Refugee Camp: Carbino's Story*	World Almanac Library	Milwaukee, WI, USA
51.	Dechian, S., Millar, H. and Sallis, E. (eds)	2004	*Dark Dreams: Australian Refugee Stories by Young Writers Aged 11–20 Years*	Wakefield	Adelaide, S. Aus
52.	De Groen, E. trans: Compton, P.	1997	*No Roof in Bosnia*	Spindlewood	
53.	Deitz Shea, P.	1995	*The Whispering Cloth*	Boyds Mill	Homesdale, PA, USA
54.	Deitz Shea, P.	2003	*Tangled Threads*	Clarion	NY, USA
55.	Deitz Shea, P.	2010	*Abe in Arms*	PM	Oakland, CA, USA

56.	Deng, B., Deng, A., and Ajak, B., with Bernstein, J.A.	2005	They Poured Fire On Us From the Sky: The True Story of Three Lost Boys from Sudan	Public Affairs	NY, USA
57.	Dhondy, F.	2000	Run	Bloomsbury	London, UK
58.	Diaz Gonzalez, C.	2011	The Red Umbrella	Yearling	NY, USA
59.	Diaz Gonzalez, C.	2012	A Thunderous Whisper	Yearling	NY, USA
60.	Dickenson	1992	A K	Delacorte	NY, USA
61.	Do, A. and Do, S.	2011	The Little Refugee	Allen and Unwin	Sydney, NSW, Aus
62.	Dorros, A.	2006	Under the Sun: A Novel Based on True Stories of Survival During War	Amulet	NY, USA
63.	Dunmore, H.	1996	Amina's Blanket	Egmont	London, UK
64.	Durant, A.	2009	Game Boy Galactic	Barrington Stoke	Edinburgh, UK
65.	Ellis, D.	2001	The Breadwinner	OUP	Oxford, UK
66.	Ellis, D.	2002	Parvana's Journey	OUP	Oxford, UK
67.	Ellis, D.	2004	Mud City	OUP	Oxford, UK
68.	Ellis, D.	2004	Three Wishes: Palestinian and Israeli Children Speak	Groundwood	Toronto, Can
69.	Ellis, D.	2009	Children of War: Voices of Iraqi Refugees	Groundwood	Toronto, Can, and Berkeley, CA, USA
70.	Ellis, D.	2010	No Safe Place	Groundwood	Toronto, Can
71.	Engle, M.	2009	Tropical Secrets	Henry Holt	NY, USA

72.	Evans, A.	2004	*Walk in My Shoes*	Penguin	Melbourne and Sydney, Aus
73.	Farish, T.	2012	*The Good Braider*	Marshall Cavendish	NY, USA
74.	Filipović, Z.	1994	*Zlata's Diary*	Viking	London, UK
75.	Fitzgerald, W.	2010	*The Go-Away Bird*	HarperCollins	London, UK
76.	Flores-Galbis, E. and Chaghatzbanian, S.	2010	*90 Miles to Havana*	Roaring Brook	NY, USA
77.	Fraillon, Z.	2016	*The Bone Sparrow*	Orion	London, UK
78.	Francis, V	1999	*Letters to Grandma Grace*	Macmillan	London, UK
79.	Frank, A.	1953	*The Diary of Anne Frank*	Pan	London, UK
80.	Friedman, D.	2006	*Escaping into the Night*	Simon and Schuster	London, UK
81.	Garay, L.	1997	*The Long Road*	Tundra	Toronto, Can
82.	Garland, S.	1993	*Lotus Seed*	Harcourt	San Diego, CA, USA
83.	Garland, S.	2012	*Azzi In Between*	Frances Lincoln	London, UK
84.	Geda, F.	2010	*In the Sea There Are Crocodiles*	Doubleday	NY, USA
85.	Geras, A.	1997	*A Candle in the Dark*	A and C Black	London, UK
86.	Gerdner, L. and Langford, S.	2008	*Grandfather's Story Cloth*	Shen's Books, Lee and Low	NY, USA
87.	Gervay, S.	2012	*Ships in the Fields*	Ford Street	Abbotsford, Vic, Aus
88.	Gibbons, A.	1999	*A Fight to Belong*	Save the Children	London, UK
89.	Gibbons, A.	2003	*The Dark Beneath*	Orion	London, UK

90.	Gibbons, A.	2011	*An Act of Love*	Orion	London, UK
91.	Gibbons, A.	2014	*A Strange Land*	Barrington Stoke	Edinburgh, UK
92.	Gleeson, L.	2008	*Mahtab's Story*	Allen and Unwin	Sydney, NSW, Aus
93.	Gleitzman, M.	2002	*Boy Overboard*	Penguin	Camberwell, Vic, Aus
94.	Gleitzman, M.	2004	*Girl Underground*	Penguin	Camberwell, Vic, Aus
95.	Golabek, M. and Cohen, L.	2002	*The Children of Willesden Lane*	Warner	NY, USA
96.	Goode, K.	1997	*Jumping to Heaven*	Wakefield	Adelaide, S. Aus
97.	Graber, J.	2009	*Muktar and the Camels*	Henry Holt	NY, USA
98.	Grant, N.	2012	*The Ink Bridge*	Allen and Unwin	Sydney, NSW, Aus
99.	Greder, A.	2008	*The Island*	Allen and Unwin, 2002	Crows Nest, Aus Germany
100.	Halahmy, M.	2011	*Hidden*	Gardners	Eastbourne, UK
101.	Halilbegovich, N.	2008	*My Childhood Under Fire*	Kids Can	Toronto, Can
102.	Hampton, M.J.	2001	*The Cat From Kosovo*	Nimbus	Halifax, Nova Scotia, Can
103.	Harris, C. and Ong, H.	1994	*The Silver Path*	Boyds Mills	Honesdale, PA, USA
104.	Hawke, R.	2004	*Soraya the Storyteller*	Lothian	Melbourne, Aus
105.	Heffernan, J.	2001	*My Dog*	Margaret Hamilton	Blackheath, NSW, Aus
106.	Hest, A.	2003	*When Amy Came Across the Sea*	Candlewick	Somerville, MA, USA
107.	Hiçyilmaz, G.	1997	*And The Stars Were Gold*	Orion	London, UK

108.	Hiçyilmaz, G.	1998	*Smiling for Strangers*	Orion	London, UK
109.	Hiçyilmaz, G.	2000	*The Girl in Red*	Orion	London, UK
110.	Ho, M.	1991	*The Clay Marble*	Farrar, Straus and Giroux	NY, USA
111.	Hoffman, M.	2002	*The Colour of Home*	Frances Lincoln	London, UK
112.	Holliday, L. (ed)	1998	*Children of Israel, Children of Palestine: Our Own True Stories*	Pocket	NY, USA
113.	Holm, A.	1963	*I Am David*	Gyldendal 1965, Methuen	Copenhagen, Den London, UK
114.	Howard, H.	2006	*Living as a Refugee in America: Mohammed's Story*	World Almanac Library	Milwaukee, WI, USA
115.	Huynh, Q.N.	1999 (Orig 1982)	*The Land I Lost: Adventures of a Boy in Vietnam*	HarperCollins	NY, USA
116.	Jal, D. and Jacobs, L.	2012	*David's Journey*	Khor Wakow School	Sioux Falls, SD, USA
117.	Jansen, H. (2002). (Trans: Elizabeth D. Crawford)	2002	*Over a Thousand Hills I Walk With You*	Carolrhoda	Minneapolis, MN, USA
118.	Johnston, T.	2008	*Voice from Afar: Poems of Peace*	Holiday House	NY, USA
119.	Kadohata, C.	2006	*Weedflower*	Simon and Schuster	London, UK
120.	Keidel, L.	1979	*Caught in the Crossfire*	Herald	Scottdale, PA, USA

List of children's literature about refugees published in English

121.	Kemp, C.	1999	*My Brother is a Soldier*	Macmillan	London, UK
122.	Kerr, J.	1971	*When Hitler Stole Pink Rabbit*	Collins	London, UK
123.	Kerz, A.	2010	*The Gnome's Eye*	Orca	Custer, WA, USA
124.	Khan, R.	1998	*The Roses in My Carpets*	Holiday House	NY, USA
125.	Kidd, D.	1991	*Onion Tears*	William Collins	Aus
126.	Kiely, K.	2005	*A Horse Called El Dorado*	O'Brien	Dublin, Ire
127.	Kilborn, S.	1999	*Leaving Vietnam: The Journey of Tuan Ngo, a Boat Boy*	Simon and Schuster	NY, USA
128.	Koralek, J.	2004	*War Games*	Egmont	London, UK
129.	Kramer, L.	1998	*Cry Baby*	Macmillan	London, UK
130.	Krishnaswami, U.	2003	*Chachaji's Cup*	Children's Book	NY, USA
131.	Kurtz, J.	2000	*Faraway Home*	Gulliver	AK, USA
132.	Lai, T.	2011	*Inside Out and Back Again*	HarperCollins	NY, USA
133.	Lainez, R.C.	2004	*Waiting for Papa*	Pinata	El Paso, TX, USA
134.	Lainez, R.C.	2010	*My Shoes and I*	Boyds Mills	Honesdale, PA, USA
135.	Laird, E.	1991	*Kiss the Dust*	Heinemann	London, UK
136.	Laird, E.	1997	*On the Run*	Mammoth	London, UK
137.	Laird, E.	2003	*A Little Piece of Ground*	Macmillan	London, UK
138.	Laird, E.	2017	*Welcome to Nowhere*	Pan Macmillan	London, UK
139.	Landowne, Y.	2004	*Sélavi: A Haitian Story of Hope*	Cinco Puntos	El Paso, TX, USA

140.	Landowne, Y.	2010	Mali Under the Night Sky: A Lao Story of Home	Cinco Puntos	El Paso, TX, USA
141.	Latifa	2002	My Forbidden Face	Virago	London, UK
142.	Layburn, J.	2008	Ghostscape	Frances Lincoln	London, UK
143.	Levitin, S.	1970	Journey to America	Atheneum	NY, USA
144.	Levy, D.	2010	The Year of Goodbyes	Disney-Hyperion	NY, USA
145.	Lingard, J.	1989	Tug of War	Lodestar	London, UK
146.	Lobel, A.	2008 (Orig 1998)	No Pretty Pictures: A Child of War	HarperCollins	NY, USA
147.	Lofthouse, L.	2007	Ziba Came on a Boat	Viking	Melbourne, Aus
148.	Lombard, J.	2006	Drita, My Homegirl	Putman's Sons	NY, USA
149.	Lord, M.	2008	A Song for Cambodia	Lee and Low	NY, USA
150.	Lottridge, C.B.	2010	Home Is Beyond the Mountains	Groundwood	Toronto, Can
151.	Lowry, L.	1989	Number the Stars	HarperCollins	London, UK
152.	Manivong, L.	2010	Escaping the Tiger	HarperCollins	NY, USA
153.	Marin, G.	2007	A True Person	New Frontier	Sydney, NSW, Aus
154.	Marsden, J.	2008	Home and Away	Lothian	Melbourne, Aus
155.	Martin, S.	1999	On the Other Side of the Hill	Macmillan	London, UK
156.	Martin, S.	1998	The Lost Children	Macmillan	London, UK
157.	Marx, T.	2000	One boy from Kosovo	HarperCollins	NY, USA

158.	Matthews, L.	2003	Fish	Hodder	London, UK
159.	Mattingley, C.	1993	No Gun for Asmir	Penguin	London, UK
160.	MacPhail, C.	2007	Under the Skin	Barrington Stoke	Edinburgh, UK
161.	MacPhail, C.	2013	Mosi's War	Bloomsbury	London, UK
162.	McDonnell, V.	2002	Out of the Flames	O'Brien	Dublin, Ire
163.	McKay, L.	1998	Journey Home	Lee and Low	NY, USA
164.	McQuinn, A.	2008	My Friend Jamal	Alanna	Slough, UK
165.	Mead, A.	1996	Adem's Cross	Farrar, Straus and Giroux	NY, USA
166.	Mead, A.	2001	Girl of Kosovo	Random House	NY, USA
167.	Mead, A.	2003	Year of No Rain	Random House	NY, USA
168.	Mikaelsen, B.	2002	Red Midnight	HarperCollins	NY, USA
169.	Mikaelsen, B.	2004	Tree Girl	HarperCollins	NY, USA
170.	Miller, D.	2003	Refugees	Lothian	Melbourne, Aus
171.	Miller-Lachmann, L.	2009	Gringolandia	Curbstone	Evanston, IL, USA
172.	Mitchell, P.	2004	Petar's Song	Frances Lincoln	London, UK
173.	Mobbin-Udin, A.	2007	The Best Eid Ever	Boyds Mills	Honesdale, PA, USA
174.	Mochizuki, K.	1997	Passage to Freedom: The Sugihara Story	Lee and Low	NY, USA
175.	Molnar, H.L.	2010	Under a Red Sky	Donnelley and Sons	Harrisonburg, VI, USA
176.	Morgan, M.	2008	Night Flight	Frances Lincoln	London, UK

177.	Morley, B.	*The Silence Seeker*	2009	Tamarind	London, UK
178.	Morpurgo, M.	*Waiting for Anya*	1990	Heinemann	London, UK
179.	Morpurgo, M.	*Shadow*	2010	HarperCollins	London, UK
180.	Munsch, R.	*From Far Away*	1995	Annick	Buffalo, NY, USA
181.	Naidoo, B.	*The Other Side of Truth*	2000	Penguin	London, UK
182.	Naidoo, B.	*Web of Lies*	2004	Penguin	London, UK
183.	Naidoo, B. (ed).	*Making it Home*	2004	Puffin	London, UK
184.	Nanji, S.	*Child of Dandelions*	2008	Boyds Mills	Honesdale, PA, USA
185.	Nye, N.S.	*Sitti's Secrets*	1994	Four Winds	NY, USA
186.	Osman, A.Y.	*In the Name of Our Fathers*	1996	Haan	Svedala, Swe
187.	Park, F. and Park G.	*My Freedom Trip: A Child's Escape from North Korea*	1998	Boyds Mills	Honesdale, PA, USA
188.	Park, L.S.	*A Long Walk to Water*	2010	Clarion	NY, USA
189.	Partridge, E.	*Dogtag Summer*	2011	Bloomsbury	NY, USA
190.	Paterson, K.	*The Day of the Pelican*	2009	Clarion	NY, USA
191.	Pellegrino, M.	*Journey of Dreams*	2009	Frances Lincoln	London, UK
192.	Perkins, M.	*Bamboo People*	2010	Charlesbridge	Watertown, MA, USA
193.	Pirotta, S.	*The Best Prize of All*	2001	Hodder	London, UK
194.	Pressler, M.	*Malka*	2001	Beltz 2002 – Picador	Weinheim, Germ London, UK
195.	Powers, J.L.	*That Mad Game*	2012	Cinco Puntos	El Paso, TX, USA

	Author	Year	Title	Publisher	Place
196.	Refugee Council	1998	*Why Do They Have to Fight?*	Refugee Council	London, UK
197.	Refugee Trauma Recovery	2010	*Beyond the Dark Journey*	Refugees as Survivors Trust	Wellington, NZ
198.	Riordan, J.	2005	*Escape From War*	Kingfisher	London, UK
199.	Robert, N.	2008	*From Somalia With Love*	Frances Lincoln	London, UK
200.	Robinson, A.	2009	*Hamzat's Journey*	Frances Lincoln	London, UK
201.	Robinson, A.	2010	*Meltem's Journey*	Frances Lincoln	London, UK
202.	Robinson, A. and Young, A.	2008	*Gervelie's Journey*	Frances Lincoln	London, UK
203.	Robinson, A. and Young, A.	2009	*Mohammed's Journey*	Frances Lincoln	London, UK
204.	Ross, S.	2001	*Only a Matter of Time*	Hodder	London, UK
205.	Rosselson, L.	2002	*Home is a Place Called Nowhere*	OUP	Oxford, UK
206.	Rosenberg, L.	1999	*The Silence in the Mountains*	Orchard	NY, USA
207.	Rutter, J.	1998	*Why Do They Have To Fight?*	Oxfam	London, UK
208.	Ruurs, M.	2016	*Stepping Stones: A refugee family's journey*	Orca Book Publishers	Victoria, BC, Canada
209.	Sanna, F.	2016	*The Journey*	Flying Eye	London, UK
210.	Satrapi, M.	2003	*Persepolis*	Jonathan Cape	London, UK
211.	Satrapi, M.	2004	*Persepolis 2*	Pantheon	NY, USA
212.	Say, K.P.	2011	*Karenni Strength*	Yates	Omaha, NE, USA
213.	Schmidt, G.	2008	*Trouble*	Clarion	NY, USA

214.	Schumer Chapman, F.	2010	*Is It Night or Day?*	Farrar, Straus and Giroux	NY, USA
215.	Senzai, N.H.	2010	*Shooting Kabul*	Simon and Schuster	NY, USA
216.	Sepetys, P.	2011	*Between Shades of Gray*	Philomel	NY, USA
217.	Serraillier, I.	1956	*The Silver Sword*	Jonathan Cape	London, UK
218.	Shah, S.M.	2010	*Peace in my World*	Tate	Mustang, OK, USA
219.	Shoveller, H.	2006	*Ryan and Jimmy*	Kids Can	Toronto, Can
220.	Shulevitz, U.	2008	*How I Learned Geography*	Farrar, Straus and Giroux	NY, USA
221.	Skrypuch, M.F.	2012	*Last Airlift*	Pajama	Ontario, Can
222.	Smith, I.	2010	*Half Spoon of Rice*	East West Discovery	Manhattan Beach, CA, USA
223.	Strachan, I.	1991	*Journey of 1000 miles*	Mammoth	London, UK
224.	Staples, S.F.	2005	*Under the Persimmon Tree*	Farrar, Straus and Giroux	NY, USA
225.	Swindells, R.	2004	*Ruby Tanya*	Doubleday	London, UK
226.	Szymanik, M.	2013	*A Winter's Day in 1939*	Scholastic	Auckland, NZ
227.	Tan, S.	2007	*The Arrival*	Arthur A. Levine	NY, USA
228.	Testa, M.	2005	*Something about America*	Candlewick	Cambridge, MA, USA
229.	Thor, A. trans: Schenck, L.	1996	*A Faraway Island*	Bonnier Carlson 2009 – Random House	Stockholm, Swe NY, USA

230.	Thor, A. trans: Schenck, L.	1997	The Lily Pond	Bonnier Carlson 2011 – Random House	Stockholm, Swe NY, USA
231.	Turner, B.	2003	One Small Suitcase	Puffin	London, UK
232.	Unicef	2003	Lines in the Sand	Frances Lincoln	London, UK
233.	Van Leeuwen, J. (trans Nagelkerke, B.)	2013	The Day My Father Became a Bush	Gecko	Oxford, UK
234.	Veciana-Suarez, A.	2002	Flight to Freedom	Orchard	NY, USA
235.	Walgren, J.	1998	The Lost Boys of Natinga	Houghton Mifflin	NY, USA
236.	Walker, B.	2011	A Safe Place to Live	Ashburton	Vic, AUS
237.	Warren, A.	2004	Escape from Saigon: How a Vietnam War Orphan Became an American Boy	Farrar Straus Giroux	NY, USA
238.	Watkins, Y.	1994	My Brother, My Sister, and I	Aladdin	NY, USA
239.	Watts, I.	1998	Goodbye Marianne	Tundra	Toronto, Can
240.	Watts, I.	2000	Remember Me	Tundra	Toronto, Can
241.	Watts, I.	2002	Finding Sophie	Tundra	Toronto, Can
242.	Whelan, G.	1992	Goodbye, Vietnam	Yearling	NY, USA
243.	Williams, M.	2005	Brothers in Hope	Lee and Low	NY, USA
244.	Williams, M.	2011	Now is the Time for Running	Little, Brown	NY, USA
245.	Williams, K. and Mohammed, K.	2007	Four Feet, Two Sandals	Eerdmans	Grand Rapids, MI, USA

246.	Williams, K. and Mohammed, K.	2009	*My Name is Sangoel*	Eerdmans	Grand Rapids, MI, USA
247.	Wilkes, S.	1994	*One Day We Had to Run!*	Evans Bros	London, UK
248.	Wilson, L.	2005	*Last Train from Kummersdorf*	Faber	London, UK
249.	Woodruff, E.	1999	*The Memory Coat*	Scholastic	NY, USA
250.	Youme	2010	*Mali Under the Night Sky: A Lao Story of Home*	Cinco Puntos	El Paso, TX, USA
251.	Zephaniah, B.	2001	*Refugee Boy*	Bloomsbury	London, UK
252.	Zoya with Follain, J.	2002	*Zoya's Story: An Afghan Woman's Struggle for Freedom*	HarperCollins	NY, USA

This list has been compiled with reference to the following sources:

Australian Refugee Week Resources (n.d.). Online. www.refugeeweek.org.au/resources/2012_RW_ResourceKit_Ch5.pdf (last accessed 09/12/16)

Booktrust: Books about Refugees and Asylum Seekers. Online. www.booktrust.org.uk/books/children/booklists/408/ (last accessed 09/12/16)

Coughlan, M. (2010) *Caught Up in Conflict: Refugee stories about and for young people.* Online. www.papertigers.org/personalViews/archiveViews/MCoughlan4.html (last accessed 09/12/16)

Coughlan, M. (2012) *Escaping Conflict, Seeking Peace: Picture books that related refugee stories, and their importance.* Online. www.papertigers.org/personalViews/archiveViews/MCoughlan9.html (last accessed 09/12/16)

List of children's literature about refugees published in English

Gangi, J. (2009) 'Annotated bibliography of children's literature resources on war, terrorism, and disaster since 1945: By continents/ countries for grades K-8'. *Childhood Education*, 85 (6), 390–94. Online. http://cell.msmc.edu/wp-content/uploads/2014/03/gangi-annotated-childhood-pdf1.pdf (last accessed 09/12/16)

Letterbox Library Refugee and Migration Booklist (n.d.) Online. www.letterboxlibrary.com/cgi-bin/ss000001.cgi?RANDOM=NETQUOTEVAR%3ARANDOMandPAGE=SEARCHandTB=Aan dPR=-1andS_BookTheme0_0=Refugees+and+MigrationandS_AgeRange0_1=andGB=AandSS=andACTION.x=74andACTION. y=24andACTION=Search (last accessed 09/12/16)

Mason, E. (2009) *Collecting Children's Refugee Literature: A bibliography*. Online. http://forcedmigrationguide.pbworks.com/w/ file/fetch/6884748/ChildrensRefugeeLiteratureBibliogr-2013.pdf (last accessed 09/12/16)

Refugee Week (2015) 'Fiction resources'. Online. http://refugeeweek.org.uk/info-centre/educational-resources/fiction-resources/ (last accessed 09/12/16)

Toft, Z. (2015) *Recent Children's Books about the Refugee Experience*. Online. www.playingbythebook.net/2013/06/19/refugee-week-recent-childrens-books-about-the-refugee-experience/ (last accessed 09/12/16)

University of Strathclyde (n.d.) 'Children's literature resources: Refugees'. Online. www.strath.ac.uk/library/eresources/subjecthelp/childliteratureresources/childrensbookliststhemes/refugees/ (last accessed 09/12/16)

References

Agnew, K. and Fox, G. (2001) *Children at War: From the First World War to the Gulf*. London: Continuum.

Ahmed, S. (2000) *Strange Encounters: Embodied others in post-coloniality*. London: Routledge.

Alexander, R. (2001) *Culture and Pedagogy: International comparisons in primary education*. Oxford: Blackwell.

— (2008) *Towards Dialogic Teaching: Rethinking classroom talk*. Cambridge: Faculty of Education.

Amazon (n.d.) *Bernard Ashley Biography*. Online. www.amazon.co.uk/Bernard-Ashley/e/B001HOJO6Y/ref=ntt_athr_dp_pel_1 (accessed 22 October 2014).

Amnesty International (n.d.) *Everyone Everywhere – Refugees and Asylum*. Online. www.amnesty.org.uk/resources/lesson-refugees-and-asylum (accessed 22 October 2014).

Anne Frank Museum (n.d.) 'Anne Frank's diary is published'. Online. http://www.annefrank.org/en/Anne-Frank/Publication-of-the-diary/Anne-Franks-diary-is-published/ (accessed 18 September 2014).

Arizpe, E. (2009) 'Sharing visual experiences of a new culture: Immigrant children's reponses to picturebooks and other visual texts'. In Evans, J. (ed.) *Talking Beyond the Page: Reading and responding to picturebooks*. Abingdon: Routledge.

Arizpe, E., Bagelman, C., Devlin, A.M., Farrell, M. and McAdam, J.E. (2014a) 'Visualizing intercultural literacy: Engaging critically with diversity and migration in the classroom through an image-based approach'. *Language and Intercultural Communication*, 14 (3), 304–21.

Arizpe, E., Colomer, T. and Martinez-Roldan, C. (2014b) *Visual Journeys through Wordless Narratives*. London and New York: Bloomsbury.

Arizpe, E. and Styles, M. (2003) *Children Reading Pictures: Interpreting visual texts*. London: Routledge.

Arnot, M. and Pinson, H. (2005) *The Education of Asylum-Seeker and Refugee Children: A study of LEA and school values, policies and practices*. Cambridge: General Teaching Council for England (GTC), Faculty of Education.

Ashley, B. (1974) *The Trouble with Donovan Croft*. Oxford: Oxford University Press.

— (1999) *Little Soldier*. London: Orchard.

Aukerman, M. (2012) '"Why do you say yes to Pedro, but no to me?" Toward a critical literacy of dialogic engagement'. *Theory Into Practice*, 51, 42–8.

Bader, B. (1976) *American Picturebooks from Noah's Ark to The Beast Within*. New York: Macmillan.

Baker, C. (1991) 'Literacy practices and social relations in classroom reading events'. In Baker, C. and Luke, A. (eds) *Towards a Critical Sociology of Reading Pedagogy: Twelfth world congress on reading: Revised selected papers*. Amsterdam/Philadelphia: John Benjamins.

Baker, R. (1983) 'Refugees: An overview of an international problem'. In *The Psychosocial Problems of Refugees*. London: Refugee Council.

Bakhtin, M. (1934) 'Discourse in the novel'. In *The Dialogic Imagination*. Austin, TX: University of Texas Press.

Barnes, D. and Todd, F. (1995) *Communication and Learning Revisited: Making meaning through talk*. Portsmouth, NH: Boynton/Cook.

Barrs, M. and Cork, V. (2001) *The Reader in the Writer*. London: CLPE.

Barthes, R. (1968) 'The death of the author'. In *Image Music Text*. New York: Hills and Wang.

Beard, R. (1999) *National Literacy Strategy: Review of research and other related evidence*. London: DfEE.

Beckwith, K. (2005) *Playing War*. Gardiner, ME: Tilbury House.

Behrman, E.H. (2006) 'Teaching about language, power, and text: A review of classroom practices that support critical literacy'. *Journal of Adolescent and Adult Literacy*, 49 (6), 490–8.

Bhabha, H. (1994) *The Location of Culture*. Abingdon: Routledge.

Bickford, D.M. (2008) 'Using testimonial novels to think about social justice'. *Education, Citizenship and Social Justice*, 3 (2), 131–46.

Bignall, C. (2012) 'Talk in the primary curriculum: Seeking pupil empowerment in current curriculum approaches'. *Literacy*, 46 (1), 48–55.

Bishop, R. (1992) 'Multicultural literature for children: Making informed choices'. In Harris, V. (ed.) *Teaching Multicultural Literature in Grades K-8*. Norwood, MA: Christopher Gordon.

Bishop, R.S. (1990) *Mirrors, Windows and Sliding Glass Doors*. Online. www.rif.org/us/literacy-resources/multicultural/mirrors-windows-and-sliding-glass-doors.htm (accessed 22 October 2014).

Bolloten, B. and Spafford, T. (1998) 'Supporting refugee children in east London primary schools'. In Rutter, J. and Jones, C. (eds) *Refugee Education: Mapping the field*. Stoke-on-Trent: Trentham.

Bolloten, B. and Spafford, T. (n.d) *Refugee and Asylum Seeker Children in UK Schools*. Online. www.naldic.org.uk/eal-teaching-and-learning/outline-guidance/ealrefugee (accessed 22 October 2014).

Bond, M. (1958) *A Bear Called Paddington*. London: William Collins and Sons.

Botelho, M. and Rudman, M. (2009) *Critical Multicultural Analysis of Children's Literature: Mirrors, windows, and doors*. New York and Abingdon: Routledge.

Britton, J. (1993) *Literature in its Place*. London: Cassell.

Bronfenbrenner, U. (1979) *The Ecology of Human Development. Experiments by nature and design*. Cambridge, MA: Harvard University Press.

Burns, C. and Myhill, D. (2004) 'Inactive or interactive?' *Cambridge Journal of Education*, 34 (1), 35–49.

Cameron, D. (2000) *Good to Talk?* London: Sage.

Carey-Webb, A. (1996) 'Transformative voices'. In Carey-Webb, A. and Benz, S. (eds) *Teaching and Testimony: Rigoberta Menchu and the North American classroom*. Albany, NY: State University of New York Press.

Castles, S. and Loughna, S. (2005) 'Trends in asylum migration to industrialised counties, 1990–2001'. In Borjas, G.J. and Crisp, J. (eds) *Poverty, International Migration and Asylum*. London: Palgrave.

Cervetti, G., Pardales, M. and Damico, J. (2001) 'A tale of differences: Comparing the traditions, perspectives, and educational goals of critical reading and critical literacy'. *Reading Online,* 4 (9). Online. www.readingonline.org/articles/cervetti/ (accessed 24 October 2014).

Chambers, A. (1991) *The Reading Environment: How adults help children enjoy texts.* Stroud: Thimble.

— (1993) *Tell Me: Children, reading and talk.* Stroud: Thimble.

— (1995) *Booktalk: Occasional writing on literature and children.* 2nd ed. Stroud: Thimble.

Claire, H. (2004) *Teaching Citizenship in Primary Schools.* Exeter: Learning Matters.

Clarke, J. and Postle, E. (1988) *Reading Therapy.* London: Clive Bingley.

Cliff Hodges, G. (2010) 'Reasons for reading: Why literature matters'. *Literacy,* 44 (2), 60–8.

Centre for Literacy in Primary Education (CLPE) (n.d.) *Booklists.* Online. www. clpe.org.uk/page/52 (accessed 25 October 2014).

Cochran-Smith, M. (1984) *The Making of a Reader.* Norwood, NJ: Ablex.

Coffey, H. (2008) *Critical Literacy.* Online. www.learnnc.org/lp/pages/4437 (accessed 24 October 2014).

Coles, M. and Hall, C. (2002) 'Gendered readings: Learning from children's reading choices'. *Journal of Research in Reading,* 25 (1), 96–108.

Collins, F.M. (2005) '"She's sort of dragging me into the story!" Student teachers' experiences of reading aloud in Key Stage 2 classes'. *Literacy,* 9 (1), 10–17.

Comber, B. (2001) 'Negotiating critical literacies'. *School Talk,* 6 (3), 1–7.

Cornwell, N. (2006) *Christophe's Story.* London: Frances Lincoln.

— (2011) *Armel's Revenge.* London: Frances Lincoln.

— (n.d.) *About Me.* Online. http://nickicornwell.com/about_me.htm (accessed 6 September 2014).

Coughlan, M. (2010) *Caught up in Conflict: Refugee stories about and for young people.* Online. www.papertigers.org/personalViews/archiveViews/MCoughlan4. html (accessed 17 July 2015).

— (2012) *Escaping Conflict, Seeking Peace: Picturebooks that relate refugee stories, and their importance.* Online. www.papertigers.org/personalViews/ archiveViews/MCoughlan9.html (accessed 17 July 2015).

Cowan, P. and Maitles, H. (2012) *Teaching Controversial Issues in the Classroom: Key issues and debates.* London and New York: Continuum.

Crago, H. (1996) 'Healing texts: Bibliotherapy and psychology'. In Hunt, P. (ed.) *International Companion Encyclopedia of Children's Literature.* London and New York: Routledge.

Crawford, P.P. and Hade, D.D. (2000) 'Inside the picture, outside the frame: Semiotics and the reading of wordless picture books'. *Journal of Research in Childhood Education,* 15 (1), 66–80.

Crothers, S.M. (1916) 'A literary clinic'. *Atlantic Monthly,* 118, 291–302.

Cullingford, C. (1998) *Children's Literature and its Effects: The formative years.* London: Cassell.

Daniels, H. (1994) *Literature Circles: Voice and choice in the student-centered classroom.* York, ME: Stenhouse.

Day, L. (2002) '"Putting yourself in other people's shoes": The use of Forum theatre to explore refugee and homeless issues in schools'. *Journal of Moral Education,* 31 (1), 21–34.

Demie, F., McLean, C. and Lewis, K. (2007) *Raising Achievement in Somali Pupils: Challenges and school responses.* London: Research and Statistics Unit, London Borough of Lambeth.

Department for Education (DfE) (2011) *Teachers' Standards: Guidance for school leaders, school staff and governing bodies.* Online. https://www.gov.uk/government/publications/teachers-standards (accessed 22 October 2014).

— (2013) *The National Curriculum in England: Key stages 1 and 2 framework document.* Online. www.gov.uk/government/uploads/system/uploads/attachment_data/file/210969/NC_framework_document_-_FINAL.pdf (accessed 22 October 2014).

Department for Education and Employment/Qualifications and Curriculum Authority (DfEE/QCA) (1999) *The National Curriculum: Handbook for primary teachers in England.* Online. www.educationengland.org.uk/documents/pdfs/1999-nc-primary-handbook.pdf (accessed 22 October 2014).

Dolan, A. (2012) 'The potential of picture story books for teaching migration'. In *Crossing Boundaries: Translations and Migrations.* Proceedings of the 33rd IBBY International Congress held at Imperial College London, 23–26 August 2012.

— (2014a) *You, Me and Diversity.* London: Trentham at Institute of Education Press.

— (2014b) 'Intercultural education, picturebooks and refugees: Approaches for language teachers'. *Children's Literature in English Language Education,* 2 (1), 92–109.

Doll, B. and Doll, C. (1997) *Bibliotherapy with Young People: Librarians and mental health professionals working together.* Englewood, CO: Libraries Unlimited.

Duffy, P. (1995) 'Literary reflections on Irish migration in the 19th and 20th centuries'. In King, R., Connell, J. and White, P. (eds) *Writing Across Worlds: Literature and migration.* London and New York: Routledge.

Eagleton, T. (1983) *Literary Theory: An introduction.* Oxford: Blackwell.

Ellis, D. (2000) *Women of the Afghan War.* Westport, CT: Praeger.

— (2001) *The Breadwinner.* Oxford: Oxford University Press.

— (2002) *Parvana's Journey.* Oxford: Oxfor Foucault, M. (1969) 'What is an author?'. In d University Press.

— (2004) *Mud City.* Oxford: Oxford University Press.

— (2005) *Three Wishes: Palestinian and Israeli children speak.* Sydney: Allen and Unwin.

— (2010) *No Safe Place.* Toronto, ON: Groundwood.

English, E., Hargreaves, L. and Hislam, J. (2002) 'Pedagogical dilemmas in the National Literacy Strategy: Primary teachers' perceptions, reflections and classroom behaviour'. *Cambridge Journal of Education,* 32 (1), 9–26.

European Council on Foreign Relations (2015) *European Foreign Policy Scorecard 2015.* Online. www.ecfr.eu/scorecard/2015/issues/57 (accessed 25 June 2015).

Fazel, M. and Stein, A. (2002) 'The mental health of refugee children'. *Archives of Disease in Childhood,* 87 (5), 366–70.

Fiese, B.H., Hooker, K.A., Kotary, L., Schwagler, J. and Rimmer, R. (1995) 'Family stories in the early stages of parenthood'. *Journal of Marriage and Family,* 57 (3), 763–70.

Filipović, Z. (1994) *Zlata's Diary.* London: Viking.

Fish, S. (1980) *Is There A Text in this Class?* Cambridge, MA, and London: Harvard University Press.

Fisher, A. (2008) 'Teaching comprehension and critical literacy: Investigating guided reading in three primary classrooms'. *Literacy,* 42 (1), 19–28.

fishpond.co.uk (n.d.) *Three Wishes: Palestinian and Israeli children speak.* Online. www.fishpond.co.uk/Books/Three-Wishes-Deborah-Ellis/9781741146325 (accessed 23 October 2014).

Foucault, M. (1969) 'What is an author?'. In Harari, J. (ed.) *Textual Strategies: Perspectives in poststructuralist criticism.* Ithaca, NY: Cornell University Press.

Fox, C. (2001) 'Conflicting fictions: National identity in English children's literature about war'. In Meek, M. (ed.) *Children's Literature and National Identity.* Stoke-on-Trent: Trentham.

— (2007) 'History, war and politics: Taking 'comix' seriously'. In Ellis, V., Fox, C. and Street, B. (eds) *Rethinking English in Schools: Towards a new and constructive stage.* London and New York: Continuum.

Frank, A. (1952) *Diary of a Young Girl.* London: Vallentine Mitchell.

Freebody, P. and Luke, A. (1990) 'Literacies programs: Debates and demands'. *Prospect: Australian Journal of TESOL,* 5 (7), 7–16.

Freire, P. (1970) *Pedagogy of the Oppressed.* New York: Herder and Herder.

Freire, P. and Macedo, D.P. (1987) *'Literacy: Reading the word and the world'.* South Hadley, MA: Bergin and Garvey.

Freud, A. and Burlingham, D. (1943) *War and Children.* New York: Medical War Books.

Galda, L., Ash, G. and Cullinan, B. (2001) 'Research on children's literature'. *Reading Online,* 4 (9). Online. www.readingonline.org/articles/art_index.asp?HREF=/articles/handbook/galda/index.html (accessed 23 October 2014).

Gamble, N. and Yates, S. (2008) *Exploring Children's Literature.* London: Sage.

Gangi, J.M. and Barowsky, E. (2009) 'Listening to children's voices: Literature and the arts as means of responding to the effects of war, terrorism, and disaster'. *Childhood Education,* 85 (6), 357–63.

Garland, S. (2012) *Azzi In Between.* London: Frances Lincoln.

— (n.d.) *Azzi in Between.* Online. www.sarahgarland.co.uk/azzi.html (accessed 17 September 2014).

Gibbons, A. (1999) *A Fight to Belong.* London: Save the Children.

— (2003) *The Dark Beneath.* London: Orion.

Giles, J. (2009) 'What is "The Other Side of Truth"?' In Montgomery, H. and Watson, N. (eds) *Children's Literature: Classic texts and contemporary trends.* Basingstoke: Palgrave Macmillan.

Gleitzman, M. (2003) *Boy Overboard.* London: Penguin.

— (2004) *Girl Underground.* London: Penguin.

Goleman, D. (1995) *Emotional Intelligence: Why it can matter more than IQ.* New York: Bantam.

Goodall, O. (2007) 'War and peace with young children'. In Claire, H. and Holden, C. (eds) *The Challenge of Teaching Controversial Issues*. Stoke-on-Trent: Trentham.

Gopalakrishnan, A. (2011) *Multicultural Children's Literature*. Thousand Oaks, CA: Sage.

Gordimer, N. (2002) 'Testament of the word'. *The Guardian*, 15 June. Online. www.theguardian.com/books/2002/jun/15/fiction.nadinegordimer (accessed 23 October 2014).

Graham, J. (2008) 'Picturebooks: Looking closely'. In Goodwin, P. (ed.) *Understanding Children's Books: A guide for education professionals*. London: Sage.

Grenby, M. (2008) *Children's Literature*. Edinburgh: Edinburgh University Press.

Grossfeld, J. (1993) 'Afterword'. In Serrallier, I. (1993) *The Silver Sword*. London: Penguin.

Gubar, M. (2013) 'Risky business: Talking about children in children's literature criticism. *Children's Literature Association Quarterly*, 38 (4), 450–7.

Habib, S. (2008) 'Refugee Boy: The social and emotional impact of the shared experience of a contemporary class novel'. *Changing English*, 15 (1), 41–52.

Halahmy, M. (2011) *Hidden*. Eastbourne: Gardners.

Hall, K. (1998) 'Critical literacy and the case for it in the early years of schooling'. *Language, Culture and Curriculum*, 11 (2), 183–94.

— (2003) *Listening to Stephen Read: Multiple perspectives on literacy*. Buckingham: Open University Press.

Hall, S. (1992) 'New ethnicities'. In Donald, J. and Rattansi, A. (eds) *'Race', Culture and Difference*. London: Open University Press/Sage.

Hamilton, R. and Moore, D. (2004) *Educational Interventions for Refugee Children*. London: Routledge Falmer.

Hammersley, M. and Atkinson, P. (1983) *Ethnography: Principles in practice*. London: Tavistock.

Harding, D.W. (1977) 'What Happens When We Read?' Originally 1962. In Meek, M., Warlow, A. and Barton, G. (eds) *The Cool Web: The patterns of children's reading*. London: Bodley Head.

Harste, J., Short, K. and Burke, C. (1989) *Creating Classrooms for Authors: The reading-writing connection*. Portsmouth, NH: Heinemann Educational.

Hiçyilmaz, G. (1998) *Smiling for Strangers*. London: Orion.

— (2000) *The Girl in Red*. London: Orion.

— (2003) *Pictures from the Fire*. London: Orion.

HMSO (2010) *The Equality Act*. Online. www.legislation.gov.uk/ukpga/2010/15/pdfs/ukpga_20100015_en.pdf (accessed 22 October 2014).

Hoffman, M. (1991) *Amazing Grace*. London: Frances Lincoln.

— (1995) *Grace and Family*. London: Frances Lincoln.

— (1997) *An Angel Just Like Me*. London: Frances Lincoln.

— (2002) *The Colour of Home*. London: Frances Lincoln.

— (2003) *Lines in the Sand: New writing on war and peace*. London: Frances Lincoln.

— (n.d.) Online. www.maryhoffman.co.uk/ (accessed 17 September 2014).

Hollindale, P. (1988) 'Ideology and the children's book'. *Signal, 55*, 3–24.

Holm, A. (1965) *I Am David*. London: Methuen.

hooks, b. (1990) 'Marginality as a site of resistance'. In Ferguson, N.R. (ed.) *Out There: Marginalization and contemporary cultures*. Cambridge MA: MIT.

Hope, J. (2007) 'Fightlines: Exploring early readers for children about the refugee experience'. *Forum, 49* (3), 289–99.

— (2008) '"One day we had to run": The development of the refugee identity in children's literature and its function in education'. *Children's Literature in Education, 39* (4), 295–305.

Hunt, P. (1991) *Criticism, Theory and Children's Literature*. London: Blackwell.

Hunt, P. and Sands, K. (2000) 'British empire and post-Empire children's literature. In McGillis, R. (ed.) *Voices of the Other: Children's literature and the postcolonial context*. New York and London: Garland.

Hyder, T. (2005) *War, Conflict and Play*. Maidenhead: Open University Press.

Information Centre about Asylum and Refugees (ICAR) (2012) *Asylum Seekers, Refugees and the Media*. Online. www.icar.org.uk/Asylum_Seekers_and_Media_Briefing_ICAR.pdf (accessed 22 October 2014).

Iser, W. (1972) *The 'Implied Reader'*. Baltimore, MD: John Hopkins.

— (1976) *The Act of Reading: A theory of aesthetic response*. London: Routledge and Kegan Paul.

James, A. (2007) 'Giving voice to children's voices: Practices and problems, pitfalls and potentials'. *American Anthropologist, 109* (2), 261–72.

John, C. (2009) 'Reading lessons: Teacher-pupil interactions with text during three KS1 shared reading sessions'. *Literacy, 43* (3), 123–33.

Johnson, L. (2003) 'The diversity imperative: Building a culturally responsive school ethos'. *Intercultural Education, 14* (1), 17–30.

Kahin, M. (1997) *Educating Somali Children in Britain*. Stoke-on-Trent: Trentham.

Kardiner, A. (1941) *The Traumatic Neuroses of War*. New York: Hoeber.

Keene, E. and Zimmerman, S. (1997) *Mosaic of Thought: Teaching comprehension in a reader's workshop*. London: Heinemann.

Kerr, J. (1970–2002) *The Mog Books*. London: HarperCollins.

— (1968) *The Tiger Who Came To Tea*. London: HarperCollins.

— (1971) *When Hitler Stole Pink Rabbit*. London: Collins.

Kidd, D.C. and Castano, E. (2013) 'Reading of literary fiction improves reading of mind'. *Science, 342*, 377–80.

King, C. (2001) '"I like group reading because we can share ideas": The role of talk within the literature circle'. *Literacy, 35* (1), 32–6.

King, C. and Briggs, J. (2005) *Literature Circles: Better talking, more ideas*. Leicester: United Kingdom Literacy Association.

King, M. (2003) 'Challenging attitudes to asylum seekers and refugees'. *Race Equality Teaching, 22* (1), 12–14.

King, R., Connell, J. and White, P. (1995) *Writing Across Worlds: Literature and migration*. London: Routledge.

Kingsley, P., Bonomolo, A. and Kirchgaessner, S. (2015) '700 migrants feared dead in Mediterranean shipwreck'. *The Guardian*, 19 April. Online. www.theguardian.com/world/2015/apr/19/700-migrants-feared-dead-mediterranean-shipwreck-worst-yet (accessed 25 June 2015).

Knowles, E. and Ridley, W. (2005) *Another spanner in the works: Challenging prejudice and racism in mainly white schools.* Stoke-on-Trent: Trentham.

Kress, G. and van Leeuwen, T. (1996) *Reading Images: The grammar of visual design.* London: Routledge.

— (2001) *Multimodal Discourse: The modes and media of contemporary communication.* London: Edward Arnold.

Kristeva, J. (1966) *Desire in Language: A semiotic approach to literature and art.* Paris: Editions du Seuil.

Kruizenga, T.M. (2010) 'Teaching Somali children: What perceived challenges do Somali students face in the public school system?' *International Journal of Education,* 1 (1), 1–17.

Kundnani, A. (2001) 'In a foreign land: The new popular racism'. *Race and Class,* 43 (2), 41–60.

Kushner, T. (2003) 'Meaning nothing but good: Ethics, history and asylum-seeker phobia in Britain'. *Patterns of Prejudice,* 37 (3), 257–76.

Laird, E. (1991) *Kiss the Dust.* London: Heinemann.

— (2017) *Welcome to Nowhere.* London: Pan Macmillan.

— (n.d.) *About Me.* Online. www.elizabethlaird.co.uk/#!bio/c1ktj (accessed 6 September 2014).

Lathey, G. (1999) 'Other sides of the story: War in translated children's fiction'. *Signal,* 88, 48–58.

— (2001) 'The road from Damascus: Children's authors and the crossing of national boundaries'. In Meek, M. (ed.) *Children's Literature and National Identity.* Stoke-on-Trent: Trentham.

— (2005) 'Autobiography and history: Literature of war'. In Reynolds, K. (ed.) *Modern Children's Literature: An introduction.* Basingstoke: Palgrave Macmillan.

Lehr, F. (1981) 'Bibliotherapy'. *Journal of Reading,* 25 (1), 76–9.

Lehr, S. (1995) 'Fourth graders read, write, and talk about freedom'. In Lehr, S. (ed.) *Battling Dragons: Issues and controversy in children's literature.* Portsmouth, NH: Heinemann.

Leland, C., Lewison, M. and Harste, J. (2013) *Teaching Children's Literature: It's critical!* New York and Abingdon: Routledge.

Lemon, L. and Reis, M. (1965) *Russian Formalist Criticism: Four essays.* Lincoln, NE: University of Nebraska Press.

Levi, P. (1988) *The Drowned and the Saved.* London: Abacus.

Levy, P. (2002) *Interactive Whiteboards in Learning and Teaching in Two Sheffield Schools: A developmental study.* Sheffield: Department of Information Studies, University of Sheffield.

Lewis, D. (1996) 'The constructedness of texts: Picture books and the metafictive'. In Egoff, S., Stubbs, G., Ashley, R. and Sutton, W. (eds) *Only Connect: Readings on children's literature.* Toronto, ON: Oxford University Press.

— (2001) *Reading Contemporary Picturebooks: Picturing text.* London: Routledge.

Lewison, M., Flint, A.S. and Van Sluys, K. (2002) 'Taking on critical literacy: The journey of newcomers and novices'. *Language Arts,* 79 (5), 382–92.

Lofthouse, L. (2007) *Ziba Came on a Boat.* Melbourne: Viking.

Lowry, L. (1989) *Number the Stars*. London: HarperCollins.

Lucas, C.V. and Soares, L. (2013) 'Bibliotherapy: A tool to promote children's psychological well-being'. *Journal of Poetry Therapy,* 26 (3), 137–47.

Luke, A. (2012) 'Critical literacy: Foundational notes'. *Theory Into Practice,* 51 (1), 4–11.

Luke, A., De Castell, S. and Luke, C. (1983) 'Beyond criticism: the authority of the school text'. *Curriculum Inquiry*, 13, 111–27.

Luke, C. and Luke, A. (1989) 'Beyond criticism: The authority of the school textbook'. In de Castell, S., Luke A. and Luke, C. (eds) *Language, Authority and Criticism: Readings on the school textbook*. London: Falmer.

MacSween, R. and Laird, E. (2010) 'Children in conflict: The significance of children's literature in relation to war'. In Plastow, J. and Hillel, M. (eds) *The Sands of Time: Children's literature, culture, politics and identity*. Hatfield: University of Hertfordshire.

Madura, S. (1998) 'An artistic element: Four transitional readers and writers respond to the picture books of Patricia Polacco and Gerald McDermott'. In Shanahan, T. and Rodriguez-Brown, F. (eds) *National Reading Conference Yearbook 47*. Chicago, IL: National Reading Conference.

Maine, F. (2013) 'How children talk together to make meaning from texts: A dialogic perspective on reading comprehension strategies'. *Literacy,* 47 (3), 150–6.

Maine, F. and Waller, A. (2011) 'Swallows and amazons forever: How adults and children engage in reading a classic text'. *Children's Literature in Education,* 42 (4), 354–71.

Mallan, K. (2013) 'Empathy: Narrative empathy and children's literature'. In Wu, Y., Mallan, K. and McGillis, R. (eds) *(Re)imagining the World: Children's literature reponse to changing times*. Berlin and Heidelberg: Springer-Verlag.

Marshall, B. (2006) 'The future of English'. *Critical Quarterly,* 48 (1), 105–13.

Marshall, J. (n.d.) *About I Am David*. Online. www.readingmatters.co.uk/articles/about-i-am-david-anne-holm (accessed 1 September 2014).

Masten, A.S., Best, K.M. and Garmezy, N. (1990) 'Resilience and development: Contributions from the study of children who overcome adversity'. *Development and Psychopathology,* 2 (4), 425–44.

Mattingley, C. (1993) *No Gun for Asmir*. London: Penguin.

Maybin, J. and Moss, G. (1993) 'Talk about texts: Reading as a social event'. *The Journal of Research in Reading,* 16 (2), 138–47.

McCulliss, D. (2012) 'Bibliotherapy: Historical and research perspectives'. *Journal of Poetry Therapy,* 25 (1), 23–38.

McDonald, J. (1998) 'Refugee students' experiences of the UK education system'. In Rutter, J. and Jones, C. (eds) *Refugee Education: Mapping the field*. Stoke-on-Trent: Trentham.

McDonald, L. (2004) 'Moving from reader response to critical reading: Developing 10–11-year-olds' ability as analytical readers of literary texts'. *Literacy,* 38, 17–25.

Meek, M. (1987) 'Symbolic outlining: The academic study of children's literature'. *Signal,* 53, 97–115.

— (1988) *How Texts Teach What Readers Learn*. Stroud: Thimble.

— (2001) *Children's Literature and National Identity*. Stoke-on-Trent: Trentham.

Melzak, S. and Warner, R. (1992) *Integrating Refugee Children into Schools.* London: Medical Foundation/Minority Rights Group.

Menter, I., Cunningham, P. and Sheibani, A. (2000) 'Safe at last? Refugee children in primary schools'. In Datta, M. (ed.) *Bilinguality and Literacy: Principles and practice.* London: Continuum.

Mercer, N. (2000) *Words and Minds: How we use language to think together.* London: Routledge.

Mercer, N., Wegerif, R. and Dawes, L. (1999) 'Children's talk and the development of reasoning in the classroom'. *British Educational Research Journal, 25* (1), 95–111.

Migration Observatory (2011) *Thinking Behind the Numbers: Understanding public opinion on immigration in Britain.* Online. http://migrationobservatory. ox.ac.uk/sites/files/migobs/Report%20-%20Public%20Opinion.pdf (accessed 22 October 2014).

— (2014) *Global International Migrant Stock: The UK in international comparison.* Online. www.migrationobservatory.ox.ac.uk/sites/files/migobs/ Briefing%20-%20Global%20International%20Migrant%20Stock_0.pdf (accessed 22 October 2014).

Miller, D. (2003) *Refugees.* Melbourne: Lothian.

Mitchell, C. (1984) 'Case studies'. In Ellen, R. (ed.) *Ethnographic Research: A guide to general conduct.* London: Academic Press.

Mitchell, P. (2004) *Petar's Song.* London: Frances Lincoln.

Moebius, W. (1986) 'Introduction to picturebook codes'. *Word and Image, 2* (2), 141–58.

Morley, B. (2009) *The Silence Seeker.* London: Tamarind.

Morpurgo, M. (1990) *Waiting for Anya.* London: Heinemann.

— (2010) *Shadow.* London: HarperCollins.

Morrice, L. (2011) *Being a Refugee: Learning and identity.* Stoke-on-Trent: Trentham.

Mroz, M., Smith, F. and Hardman, F. (2000) 'The discourse of the literacy hour'. *Cambridge Journal of Education, 30* (3), 379–90.

Myhill, D. (2007) 'Reading the world: Using children's literature to explore controversial issues'. In Claire, H. and Holden, C. (eds) *The Challenge of Teaching Controversial Issues.* Stoke-on-Trent: Trentham.

Naidoo, B. (1985) *Journey to Jo'burg.* London: Longmans.

— (1992) *Through Whose Eyes? Exploring racism: Reader, text and context.* Stoke-on-Trent: Trentham.

— (2000) *The Other Side of Truth.* London: Penguin.

— (2004a) *Out of Bounds: 'Witness literature' and the challenge of crossing racialised boundaries.* Online. www.beverleynaidoo.com/i/ boundsWitnessLiterature.pdf (accessed 30 September 2016).

— (2004b) *Web of Lies.* London: Penguin.

— (2009) 'A writer's journey: Retracing 'The Other Side of Truth'. In Montgomery, H. and Watson, N.J. (eds) *Children's Literature: Classic texts and contemporary trends.* Basingstoke: Palgrave Macmillan.

— (2012) *Readers of The Other Side of Truth.* Online. www.beverleynaidoo.com/ blog.htm (accessed 22 October 2014).

— (n.d.) *Imagining Change*. Online. http://www.beverleynaidoo.com/ (accessed 27 March 2017).

National Archives (1998) *Data Protection Act*. Online. www.legislation.gov.uk/ukpga/1998/29/contents (accessed 20 October 2014).

Needle, J. (1978) *My Mate Shofiq*. London: Andre Deutsch.

Nial, C. (2005) 'Teaching refugees and asylum seekers in an adolescent psychiatric unit'. *Race Equality Teaching*, 23 (2), 32–4.

Nicholson, C. (1999) 'Reading the pictures: children's responses to Rose Blanche'. In Goodwin, P. (ed.) *The Literate Classroom*. London: David Fulton.

Nikolajeva, M. (2006) 'Word and picture'. In Butler, C. (ed.) *Teaching Children's Fiction*. Basingstoke and New York: Palgrave Macmillan.

— (2012) 'Reading other people's minds through word and image'. *Children's Literature in Education*, 43 (3), 273–91.

Nikolajeva, M. and Scott, C. (2001) *How Picture Books Work*. New York and Abingdon: Routledge.

Nodelman, P. (1992) 'The other: Orientalism, Colonialism, and children's literature'. *Children's Literature Association Quarterly*, 17 (1), 29–35.

— (2005) 'Decoding the images: How picture books work'. In Hunt, P. (ed.) *Understanding Children's Literature*. London: Routledge.

Nodelman, P. and Reimer, M. (1992) *The Pleasures of Children's Literature*. Boston, MA: Allyn and Bacon.

Noll, E. (2003) 'Accuracy and authenticity in American Indian children's literature: The social responsibility of authors and illustrators'. In Fox, D.L. and Short, K.G. (eds) *Stories Matter: The complexity of cultural authenticity in children's literature*. Urbana, IL: National Council of Teachers of English.

Nystrand, M. (2006) 'Research on the role of classroom discourse as it affects reading comprehension'. *Research in the Teaching of English*, 40 (4), 392–412.

O'Sullivan, O. and McGonigle, S. (2010) 'Transforming readers: Teachers and children in the Centre for Literacy in Primary Education Power of Reading project'. *Literacy*, 44 (2), 51–9.

Ofsted (Office for Standards in Education) (2002) *The National Literacy Strategy: The first four years 1998–2002*. London: Ofsted.

Oulton, C., Day, V., Dillon, J. and Grace, M. (2004) 'Controversial issues: Teachers' attitudes and practices in the context of citizenship education'. *Oxford Review of Education*, 30 (4), 489–507.

Oxford Dictionaries (n.d.) *Validate*. Online. www.oxforddictionaries.com/definition/english/validate (accessed 18 September 2014).

Pearson, C. (2010) 'Acting up or acting out? Unlocking children's talk in literature circles'. *Literacy*, 44 (1), 3–11.

Pinsent, P. (1997) *Children's Literature and the Politics of Equality*. London: David Fulton.

— (2005) 'Language, genres and issues: The socially committed novel'. In Reynolds, K. (ed.) *Modern Children's Literature*. Basingstoke: Palgrave Macmillan.

Pinson, H., Arnot, M. and Candappa, M. (2010) *Education, Asylum and the 'Non-Citizen' Child*. Basingstoke: Palgrave Macmillan.

Rabey, K. (2003) 'Thinking aloud: Looking at children drawing in response to picture books'. In Arizpe, E. and Styles, M. (eds) *Children Reading Pictures*. Abingdon and New York: Routledge.

Rainey, K. and Campbell, R. (1997) 'Refugees—From a Small Issue to an Important Cause'. Unpublished Report to the Refugee Council. Cited in Rutter, J. (2003) *Supporting Refugee Children in 21st Century Britain*. Stoke-on-Trent: Trentham Books.

Rease, T. (2004) 'Inside the mind of a refugee child'. *Sankofa: A Journal of African Children and Adult's Literature*, 3, 62–7.

Refugee Council (2016) *Refugee Council Information: Asylum statistics*. Online. www.refugeecouncil.org.uk/assets/0003/6984/Asylum_Statistics_Annual_ Trends_Feb_2016.pdf (accessed 1 April 2016).

— (n.d.) *Who's who? Definitions*. Online. www.refugeecouncil.org.uk/policy_ research/the_truth_about_asylum/the_facts_about_asylum (accessed 22 October 2014).

Refugee Week (n.d.) *About Us*. Online. www.refugeeweek.org.uk (accessed 22 October 2014).

Reynolds, D. (1998) 'Schooling for literacy: A review of research on teacher effectiveness and school effectiveness and its implications for contemporary educational policy'. *Educational Review,* 50 (2), 147–62.

Reynolds, D. and Farrell, S. (1996) *Worlds Apart? A review of international studies of educational achievement involving England*. London: HMSO for OFSTED.

Reynolds, K. (2005) *Modern Children's Literature*. Basingstoke: Palgrave Macmillan.

Richman, N. (1998) *In the Midst of a Whirlwind: A manual for helping refugee children*. Stoke-on-Trent: Trentham.

Richmond, A.H. (1993) 'Reactive migration: Sociological perspectives on refugee movements'. *Journal of Refugee Studies,* 6 (1), 7–24.

Ringel, S. and Brandell, J. (2011) *Trauma: Contemporary directions in theory, practice, and research*. Thousand Oaks, CA: Sage.

Roalfe, R.K.C. (1997) 'Refugees: From a small issue to an important cause'. Unpublished report to the Refugee Council. Cited in Rutter, J. (ed.) *Supporting Refugee Children in 21st Century Britain*. Stoke-on-Trent: Trentham.

Robinson, A. (2009) *Hamzat's Journey: A refugee diary*. London: Frances Lincoln.

— (2010) *Meltem's Journey: A refugee diary*. London: Frances Lincoln.

Robinson, A. and Young, A. (2008) *Gervelie's Journey: A refugee diary*. London: Frances Lincoln.

— (2009) *Mohammed's Journey: A refugee diary*. London: Frances Lincoln.

Roche, M. (2015) *Developing Children's Critical Thinking through Picturebooks: A guide for primary and early years students and teachers*. Abingdon and New York: Routledge.

Rösch, H. (2004) 'Migrationsliteratur als neue Weltliteratur'. *Sprachkunst,* 35, 89–109.

Rose, J. (1984) *The Case of Peter Pan: Or the impossibility of children's fiction*. Philadelphia, PA: University of Pennsylvania Press.

Rosenblatt, L. (1938) *Literature as Exploration*. New York: Appleton-Century.

— (1978) *The Reader, the Text, the Poem: The transactional theory of the literary work*. Carbondale, IL: Southern Illinois Press.

Russell, D.L. (1997) 'Reading the shards and fragments: Holocaust literature for young readers'. *The Lion and the Unicorn,* 21 (2), 267–80.

Rutter, J. (1991) *Refugees: We left because we had to.* London: Refugee Council.

— (1994) *Refugee Children in the Classroom.* Stoke-on-Trent: Trentham.

— (1998) 'Refugees in today's world'. In Rutter, J. and Jones, C. (eds) *Refugee Education: Mapping the field.* Stoke-on-Trent: Trentham.

— (2003) *Supporting Refugee Children in 21st Century Britain.* Stoke-on-Trent: Trentham.

— (2005) 'Understanding the alien in our midst: Using citizenship education to challenge popular discourses about refugees'. In Osler, A. (ed.) *Teachers, Human Rights and Diversity.* Stoke-on-Trent: Trentham.

— (2006) *Refugee Children in the UK.* Maidenhead: Open University Press.

Rutter, M. (1985) 'Resilience in the face of adversity: Protective factors and resistance to psychiatric disorder'. *British Journal of Psychiatry,* 147, 598–611.

Ruurs, M. (2016) *Stepping Stones: A refugee family's journey.* Victoria, BC, Canada: Orca Book Publishers.

Sales, R. (2002) 'The deserving and the undeserving? Refugees, asylum seekers and welfare in Britain'. *Critical Social Policy,* 22 (3), 456–78.

Salisbury, M. and Styles, M. (2012) *Children's Picturebooks: The art of visual storytelling.* London: Laurence King.

Sanna, F. (2016) *The Journey.* London: Flying Eye.

Sarland, C. (2005) 'Critical tradition and ideological positioning'. In Hunt, P. (ed.) *Understanding Children's Literature.* London: Routledge.

Save the Children (1997) *Let's Spell It Out: Peer research by the Horn of Africa Youth Scheme.* London: Save the Children.

Schlick Noe, K.L. and Johnson, N.J. (1999) *Getting Started with Literature Circles.* Norwood, MA: Christopher-Gordon.

Scholes, R. (1985) *Textual Power: Literary theory and the teaching of English.* New Haven, CT: Yale University Press.

Schwartz, E. (1995) *Crossing Borders/Shifting Paradigms.* Online. http://hepg. org/her-home/issues/harvard-educational-review-volume-65-issue-4/herarticle/ multiculturalism-and-children-s-literature_299 (accessed 22 October 2014).

Serafini, F. (2009) Understanding visual images in picturebooks. In Evans, J. (ed.) *Talking Beyond the Page: Reading and responding to picturebooks.* Abingdon: Routledge.

Serraillier, I. (1956) *The Silver Sword.* London: Jonathan Cape.

Shor, I. and Freire, P. (1987) *A Pedagogy for Liberation: Dialogues on transforming education.* Westport, CT: Bergin and Garvey.

Shrodes, C. (1950) *Bibliotherapy: A theoretical and clinical-experimental study.* Oakland, CA: University of California Press.

Sipe, L.R. (1998) 'How picture books work: A semiotically framed theory of text–picture relationships'. *Children's Literature in Education,* 29 (2), 97–108.

— (2008) *Storytime: Young children's literary understanding in the classroom.* New York: Teachers College.

Skidmore, D. (2000) 'From pedagogical dialogue to dialogical pedagogy'. *Language and Education,* 14 (4), 283–96.

Skidmore, D., Perez-Parent, M. and Arnfield, S. (2003) 'Teacher-pupil dialogue in the guided reading session'. *Reading*, 37, 47–53.

Smith, A. (2006) 'Paddington Bear: A case study of immigration and otherness'. *Children's Literature in Education*, 37 (1), 35–50.

Smith-D'Arezzo, W.M. and Thompson, S.C. (2006) 'Topics of stress and abuse in picture books for children'. *Children's Literature in Education*, 37 (4), 335–47.

Sokoloff, N.B. (2005) 'The Holocaust and literature for children'. *Prooftexts*, 25 (1 and 2), 174–94.

Spivak, G. (1988) 'Can the subaltern speak?' In Nelson, C. and Grossberg, L. (eds) *Marxism and the interpretation of Culture*. Chicago, IL: University of Illinois Press.

Stephens, J. (1992) *Language and Ideology in Children's Fiction*. Harlow: Longman.

Stewart, J. (2011) *Supporting Refugee Children: Strategies for educators*. Toronto, ON: University of Toronto Press.

Stewart, S.L. (2008) 'Beyond borders: Reading "other" places in children's literature'. *Children's Literature in Education*, 39 (2), 95–105.

Styles, M. and Nobel, K. (2009) 'Thinking in action: Analysing children's multimodal responses to multimodal picturebooks'. In Evans, J. (ed.) *Talking Beyond the Page: Reading and responding to picturebooks*. Abingdon: Routledge.

Sullivan, A.K. and Strang, H.R. (2002) 'Bibliotherapy in the classroom: Using literature to promote the development of emotional intelligence'. *Childhood Education*, 79 (2), 74–80.

Swindells, R. (2004) *Ruby Tanya*. London: Doubleday.

Tan, S. (2006) *The Arrival*. Melbourne: Lothian.

Thibault, M. (2004) *Children's Literature Promotes Understanding*. Online www.learnnc.org/lp/pages/635 (accessed 24 October 2014).

Tolfree, D. (1996) *Restoring Playfulness: Different approaches to assisting children who are psychologically affected by war or displacement*. Stockholm: Radda Barnen.

U.S. Government (1949) 'Trials of War Criminals before the Nuremberg Military Tribunals under Control Council Law No. 10', Vol. 2, pp. 181–2. Washington, DC: U.S. Government Printing Office. Online. http://history.nih.gov/research/downloads/nuremberg.pdf (accessed 20 October 2014).

UNHCR (1951) *Convention and Protocol Relating to the Status of Refugees*. Online. www.unhcr.org/3b66c2aa10.html (accessed 18 September 2014).

— (2016a) *Global Trends 2015*. Online. www.unhcr.org/uk/global-trends-2015. html (accessed 30 September 2016).

— (2016b) *Global Trends: Forced displacement in 2015*. Online. http://www.unhcr.org/uk/statistics/unhcrstats/576408cd7/unhcr-global-trends-2015.html (accessed 22 March 2017).

— (n.d.) *Internally Displaced Persons Figures*. Online. www.unhcr.org/pages/49c3646c23.html (accessed 22 October 2014).

Unicef (1989) *A Summary of the United Nations Convention on the Rights of the Child*. Online. www.unicef.org.uk/Documents/Publication-pdfs/UNCRC_summary.pdf (accessed 26 October 2014).

van der Kolk, B.A. (2005) 'Developmental trauma disorder: Toward a rational diagnosis for children with complex trauma histories'. *Psychiatric Annals,* 35 (5), 401–8.

van der Kolk, B.A., Weisaeth, L. and van der Hart, O. (1996) 'History of trauma in psychiatry'. In van der Kolk, B., McFarlane, A. and Weisaeth, L. (eds) *Traumatic Stress: The effects of overwhelming experience on mind, body and society.* New York: Guilford.

Vermeule, B. (2010) *Why Do We Care about Literary Characters?* Baltimore, MD: John Hopkins University Press.

Vygotsky, L. (1962) *Thought and Language.* Cambridge, MA: MIT.

Watters, C. (2008) *Refugee Children: Towards the next horizon.* Abingdon: Routledge.

Watts, M.F. (2004) 'Telling tales of torture: Repositioning young adults' views of asylum seekers'. *Cambridge Journal of Education,* 34 (3), 315–29.

Wells, G. (1992) 'The centrality of talk in education'. In Norman, K. (ed.) *Thinking Voices: The work of the National Oracy Project.* London: Hodder and Stoughton.

Williams, K. and M.K. (2007) *Four Feet, Two Sandals.* Grand Rapids, MI, and Cambridge: Eerdmans.

— (2009) *My Name is Sangoel.* Grand Rapids, MI, and Cambridge: Eerdmans.

Wollman-Bonilla, J.E. (1998) 'Outrageous viewpoints: Teachers' criteria for rejecting works of children's literature'. *Language Arts,* 75 (4), 287–95.

Woodcock, J. (2002) 'Practical approaches to work with refugee children'. In Dwivedi, K.N. (ed.) *Meeting the Needs of Ethnic Minority Children.* London: Jessica Kingsley.

Wooley, R. (2010) *Tackling Controversial Issues in the Primary School: Facing life's challenges with your learners.* Abingdon and New York: Routledge.

Yandell, J. (2008) 'Exploring multicultural literature: The text, the classroom and the world outside'. *Changing English,* 15 (1), 25–40.

— (2013) 'The social construction of meaning: Reading Animal Farm in the classroom'. *Literacy,* 47 (1), 50–5.

Yule, W. (1998) 'The psychological adaptation of refugee children'. In Rutter, J. and Jones, C. (eds) *Refugee Education: Mapping the field.* Stoke-on-Trent: Trentham.

Zephaniah, B. (2001) *Refugee Boy.* London: Bloomsbury.

Zetter, R. (1991) 'Labelling Refugees: Forming and transforming a bureaucratic identity'. *Journal of Refugee Studies,* 4 (1), 39–62.

— (2007) 'Celebrating the 25th anniversary of the Refugee Studies Centre and the 20th anniversary of the Journal of Refugee Studies'. *Journal of Refugee Studies,* 20 (2), 161–2.

Index

Index

Index